Team Leadership in High-Hazard Environments

To my family and friends (you know who you are), who have always been there for me. Without your support this book would not have been possible.

I thank God for all the blessings in my life and for lifting me up along this journey.

Prov. 3:5–6, Matt. 19:26.

Team Leadership in High-Hazard Environments

Performance, Safety and Risk Management Strategies for Operational Teams

RANDY E. CADIEUX

Routledge
Taylor & Francis Group

LONDON AND NEW YORK

First published in paperback 2024

First published 2014 by Gower Publishing

Published 2016 by Routledge
4 Park Square, Milton Park, Abingdon, Oxon OX14 4RN

and by Routledge
605 Third Avenue, New York, NY 10158

Routledge is an imprint of the Taylor & Francis Group, an informa business

Gower Applied Business Research
Our programme provides leaders, practitioners, scholars and researchers with thought provoking, cutting edge books that combine conceptual insights, interdisciplinary rigour and practical relevance in key areas of business and management.

British Library Cataloguing in Publication Data
A catalogue record for this book is available from the British Library.

Library of Congress Cataloging-in-Publication Data
Cadieux, Randy E.
  Team leadership in high-hazard environments : performance, safety and risk management strategies for operational teams / by Randy E. Cadieux.
    pages cm
  Includes bibliographical references and index.
  ISBN 978-1-4724-3353-4 (hardback : alk. paper)—ISBN 978-1-4724-3354-1 (ebook)—ISBN 978-1-4724-3355-8 (epub)
  1. Teams in the workplace. 2. Risk management. 3. Industrial safety. I. Title.

  HD66.C327 2015
  658.4'022—dc23

                                                                    2014021936

ISBN: 978-1-4724-3353-4 (hbk)
ISBN: 978-1-03-283717-8 (pbk)
ISBN: 978-1-315-61194-5 (ebk)

DOI: 10.4324/9781315611945

Contents

List of Figures   *vii*

List of Tables   *ix*

List of Abbreviations   *xi*

Reviews of Team Leadership in High-Hazard Environments   *xiii*

Introduction   1

1   What is Effective Teamwork?   17

2   Authority and Responsibility in Operational Teams   33

3   Leadership in Operational Teams   49

4   Team Communications   81

5   Focus on Operations and Safety   107

6   Job Planning and Execution Analysis   145

7   Resilience, Adaptability, and Adaptive Capacity   173

8   Decision-Making Techniques for Operational Teams   199

9   Mutual Support and Backup   219

10   Time-Sensitive Risk Management   231

Conclusion: Integrating Team Leadership and Performance into Daily Operations   251

Bibliography   *259*

Index   *263*

List of Figures

I.1   Team leadership—the safety and performance link   13

2.1   Network-based decentralized authority structure   41

3.1   The leader–manager in operational teams   55

3.2   Team leadership strategies—leading from the front and the back   56

3.3   The shifting emphasis of designated and functional leadership during operations   67

4.1   The basic communication cycle   85

5.1   Operational performance with Focus Aids and PTA activity   114

5.2   Production surge and safety levels   142

6.1   Sample abbreviated/pocket checklist template   161

6.2   Equipment setup checklist (for figurative system)   163

6.3   Expanded equipment setup checklist (for figurative system)   164

7.1   Resilient program structure for safety and operational performance   182

8.1   Decision-making situation assessment   202

List of Tables

2.1   Summary of organizational authority structures   40

4.1   Verbal and non-verbal communication advantages and disadvantages   93

7.1   Characteristics of resiliency levels   177

8.1   Loss–gain analysis   213

8.2   Loss–gain analysis in naval aviation training (notional)   215

8.3   Loss–gain analysis in combat aviation operations (notional)   216

10.1   Risk Assessment Matrix, adapted from Marine Corps Order 3500.27B, *Operational Risk Management*   236

10.2   Long-term versus time-sensitive risk management   243

List of Abbreviations

AT   Assistant Technician

COA   Course of Action

CRM   Crew Resource Management

DL   Designated Leader

EO   Equipment Operator

ET   Equipment Technician

FL   Functional Leader

FRC   Final Risk Code

IRC   Initial Risk Code

JHA   Job Hazard Analysis

JSA   Job Safety Analysis

KPI   Key Performance Indicators

PPE   Personal Protective Equipment

PTA   Pause-To-Assess

SOP   Standard Operating Procedure

SPF   Single Point of Failure

SWA   Stop Work Authority

Reviews of *Team Leadership in High-Hazard Environments*

Team Leadership in High-Hazard Environments *is unique in that its focus is on the management requirements to lead successfully and achieve stellar safety performance in high-risk industries. Adherence to the model presented in this book will transform traditional views on safety leadership. Hands-on tools to take team leadership to a higher level are provided.*

Fred A, Manuele, President, Hazards Limited, USA

Randy Cadieux has pushed the envelope in exploring and discussing the intersection of technology and human capability in safety performance and operational excellence. Team Leadership in High-Hazard Environments *can help any organization discover hidden potential in human capability impacting productivity and safety in its operations.*

H. Landis Floyd, Principal Consultant & Global Electrical Safety Leader, DuPont

Randy has the rare gift of being able to take the research literature and present it in a way that is interesting and relevant to operational personnel. As a veteran US Marine Corps aviator he knows how to lead in dangerous environments. This is a refreshing and useful text. A must have for team leaders working in high hazard domains.

Paul O'Connor, Lecturer in Primary Care, National University of Ireland, Galway, Ireland

I think Randy Cadieux's book is a must for any leader with high-velocity teams that respond to important conditions. The book reads like a carefully constructed cookbook that helps you prepare your response teams for amazing performance.

Todd Conklin, Los Alamos National Laboratory, USA

Randy Cadieux has written an important, grounded set of operations-based guidelines that reaffirm the basics that are often overlooked in current breathless treatments of teams and leadership. Cadieux's analysis, anchored in deep experience with Marine Corps aviation operations, tackles such knotty issues as time-sensitive risk management, assertiveness, working in high-hazard environments, and adaptability. Each issue is summarized in actionable next steps. These clarifications of the sharp end should be read by all managers whose blunt end simplifications complicate the situations their operators face.

Karl E. Weick, Stephen M. Ross School of Business at the University of Michigan, USA

Introduction

Many approaches to team performance and safety take two opposing views. One view proposes that humans are the weak link in the performance equation; the source of errors, problems, and accidents. By following this view, corrective measures implemented by management may attempt to fix safety problems by controlling the faulty human with technology and rules, and seek to reduce error potential and performance variability. Another view purports that humans are the victims of poor system and technology design, where the causes of performance deviations, errors, and accidents stem from a system design failure, or inactive hazards that remain dormant until actualized through some type of chain of events, ultimately resulting in human failure and injury. Solutions to these types of problems often attempt to control the potential for errors by designing technology and work systems from the ground up to eliminate or reduce hazards so that when humans actually conduct their work activities, there is a lower potential for them to be exposed to hazards and there are fewer opportunities to commit performance errors. Although these are different viewpoints relative to safety and operational performance deficiencies, they often recommend similar corrective actions. Recommendations for fixing safety and operational performance problems often include various forms of new technologies, or strategies for reducing error potential through hazard controls, such as interlocks or barriers to protect humans from hazardous equipment and from the consequences of their own errors.

While both of these approaches to the management of human performance and safety offer solutions to many problems encountered by employees and teams as they conduct their work, there are limitations with both strategies. These approaches may presume that system designers (who create technology and rules) have foreseen every possible risk scenario and performance requirement, and that reliance on technology and rules will keep people and equipment safe. The approaches also presume that human thought and action to create safety should be constrained within pre-defined boundaries. Even more comprehensive approaches that examine the work system and attempt to devise ways to address dormant hazards and reduce error-producing conditions may be helpful, but technological fixes that constrain human performance variability may forego the benefits of improvisation and creativity that so often exist in the space of normal work activities. With many design approaches, the ability of individuals and teams to actively contribute to safety through their everyday work often becomes an afterthought, emerging once the work system has been designed and hazard controls have been developed. These design activities often take place first, and then individual workers and teams are required to perform their jobs to fit within the hazard control framework. Rather than being a proactive part of safety creation, individual and team work activities at the operational level (where the production work is really done) are still seen as something that must stay within the safety constraints that have been designed by others. Additionally, leadership at the operational team level is often overlooked as a source of proactive safety development.

This book attempts to join multiple safety and performance viewpoints by taking a different perspective from the beginning. The conceptual roots of this book are grounded in a team operations and safety performance system used in United States Marine Corps aviation operations, known as Crew Resource Management (CRM). In Marine Corps aviation the human operator is considered the most important element of system performance, so systems must be optimized to place the operators in a position where they can perform at peak levels. However, for several reasons, including human performance variability, an approach that relies solely on human action will have limitations with its effectiveness. For that reason the concepts in this book have also been combined with aspects of system safety to form a more comprehensive approach to team operational and safety performance. The ideas described in this book include ways to optimize both individual human and team performance through behavioral approaches, while also explaining ways work systems may be designed to place the human in the optimal position to perform at peak levels. One of the overall goals is to describe a way to create integrated work, safety, and performance systems that enable people to make decisions in real-time for both safety and performance goals, that facilitate the capacity of human imagination and creativity, and which view the proficiency of a well-trained worker and excellent team leaders as a means to actively manage safety and work performance to meet the performance goals of the organization.

Team Performance and System Safety

As previously described, a great deal of the material in this book has been derived from US Marine Corps aviation CRM. While CRM is typically thought of as an aviation-specific program, this book breaks CRM down into manageable components so that readers in other industries may be able to apply elements in their workplace. CRM may be seen as a methodology for mobilizing human and technological resources for optimizing operational effectiveness, efficiency, and safety. The CRM-derived concepts in this book are largely based on my experience with CRM while serving as a US Marine Corps officer and aviator, where I worked with aircrew teams in numerous high-hazard environments. While CRM is not a remedy for all human performance deficiencies and hazard mitigation, it does offer a method for helping teams interact in a more cohesive fashion. Over the years, CRM has evolved in the Marine Corps and has helped to facilitate improved crew coordination and ways to reduce performance errors, as well as ways to detect and correct errors before they lead to catastrophic consequences, which makes it an interesting model to help other organizations improve team and crew performance.

You may wonder, though, with so many modern resources to improve system design, why is there an emphasis on team performance? Many of the aircraft in today's Marine Corps fleet are either new or upgraded designs, or they are older designs with upgraded technology. These systems are so robust that the likelihood of major mechanical failure is low, yet due to the complexities associated with technology improvements, there may be even more room for errors to occur at the point where crews interact with the technology and with each other. The same case may be made for many modern work environments where technology has been designed, purchased, and implemented in the effort to improve safety.

The same technology that has been designed to improve safety in some functional areas has the potential to cause unique challenges in other areas. So, the individual workers and teams using this technology face additional hazards that are often introduced as an unintended consequence of technology design. Although safety technology can be very helpful, any type of engineered system that does not address human and team interaction may be missing a critical element of performance and safety functionality. So, performance strategies that include ways to help teams interact effectively and efficiently, to adapt to the changing demands of the work environment, and to balance safety and performance may offer assistance in managing safety at the edge of technology. Using these team-oriented approaches may improve workers' ability to use equipment, software, and hardware to their advantage while continuing to employ the capacity of human initiative and skill to actively create safety while work is being performed.

It would be a mistake, however, to ignore the system as a whole in favor of focusing only on team performance strategies. A comprehensive methodology for managing safety and performance should not only emphasize human capability to manage safety through team interaction, but should also incorporate a system-oriented approach. System safety may be described as "the application of engineering and management principles, criteria, and techniques to achieve acceptable risk within the constraints of operational effectiveness and suitability, time, and cost throughout all phases of the system life-cycle" (*Department of Defense Standard Practice for System Safety* 8). The concepts described in this book include ways to manage the design of work systems to include practical ways of integrating technology, team performance strategies, planning, learning, and risk mitigation throughout the organizational system, so that a balance between risk management, safety, and performance may be achieved. From that standpoint, this book attempts to match human actions with system safety.

Constraints on Safety Interventions

When looking at any safety or performance intervention program, designers cannot simply look at the desired end-state. Resource constraints must be examined as part of the design strategy. Constraints come in many varieties, but one of the most influential constraints is funding. While system design or redesign efforts are noteworthy, in that they often attempt to make the operational work system easier for employees to use, oftentimes funding limitations make it unrealistic for managers to implement radical design changes in an effort to alter the operational environment for safe job performance. Decision constraints force leaders and managers to make the best decisions they can, but ultimately, force them to leave something on the table. These omitted mitigation strategies could be additional safety barriers, software, or other features to improve performance. The consequences of these constraints can be compounded as well, because employees themselves often have little influence over the design process, unless their organizational leadership makes it a priority to seek their input. Safety interventions, then, are often the result of a series of trade-offs, when what is viewed by decision makers as the best option among safety resources is selected. Ultimately, the employees and teams are left in a position to make do with the results of these decisions. The deficiencies that remain are often ameliorated to some extent with team actions, which can help to close the gap in remaining risk areas. Ameliorating deficiencies in this manner is not optimal, but it is the reality faced by many operational teams and is a reason why team performance is such an important part of work system design.

The Safety and Performance Link

Another challenge with safety and performance relates to the specific views people hold regarding these two organizational attributes. While performance may be measured in tangible metrics, such as numbers of items produced or time of product assembly/task accomplishment, safety is harder to measure. Safety is often measured by the mishaps that do not occur, which is intangible and extremely difficult to count. Even examining safety based on trends and accident rates is problematic and does not always accurately reflect how safe an organization really is. Historical data, such as injury and illness reports, may also be poor indicators of safety because they capture past data and do not necessarily point to future hazards. Historical comparisons may bring challenges, particularly when safety levels appear to be increasing. As accident rates decrease over time, there is often continued expectation by those inside and outside the organization that safety performance will get better and better, continually driving down mishap rates. The problem emerges when the safety rate plateaus; if an organization is not continuing to drive down these rates they must not be safe enough. Conversely, when the mishap rate is low, organizational leadership may feel that the organization is indeed safe enough, causing leaders to let their guard down, yet the factors that may blend together to create the next mishap may be lying dormant somewhere in the organization. Additional problems can emerge when production requirements are increased, and measurement becomes more problematic when safety and production goals conflict.

Safety and production/performance are often seen as competing goals. When production is increased, safety defenses and barriers frequently decrease, and when programs are developed in an effort to improve safety, employees may not be able to meet production goals within the safety constraints. These challenges show the complexity and difficulty linking safety and performance together. However, strategies that tie safety and performance programs into an integrated framework with linked goals may help to create a new definition of organizational performance. If safety is viewed as an integral component of operations, processes, and procedures, it becomes part of normal work, rather than simply a competing goal that must be considered after production numbers are achieved. In an effort to help readers develop this type of strategy in their organizations this book emphasizes work planning and execution using a synergistic approach, where safety and performance goals are inextricably linked, requiring a concerted effort on the part of organizational leadership to clearly define performance goals and reconcile them with acceptable levels of risk. Strategies and techniques presented will show readers how to make this link, and these strategies can help leaders at multiple organizational levels to understand ways to design team-oriented programs from the ground up to optimize these two goals.

Leadership as a Central Theme

Of course, since the title of this book includes the word "leadership" it is obvious that the process of creating safety and performance systems that integrate work system design and team-based approaches wouldn't be possible without strong leadership. When we think of leadership it is often tempting to think of executive-level employees, such as Chief Executive Officers, Chief Operations Officers, and other high-level employees who work in what is often referred to as the "C-Suite." However, this book takes a different approach to leadership, and focuses on leadership at the team or crew level, where the operational work (such as production, maintenance, and operations) is actually done and where employees are closest to the hazards. There is an additional emphasis as well, and that is the nature of the hazards themselves. Leaders who lead teams in high-hazard environments face unique challenges as they direct their teams every day to accomplish the performance goals of the organization and help their teams stay safe throughout the process. These high-hazard situations include environments where employees are routinely exposed to hazards that have the potential for catastrophic outcomes and/or where the costs of failure include disastrous consequences as a result of poor performance.

The concepts explained in this book are presented for all types of readers, regardless of your background or leadership experience. Even if you do not have leadership experience, as you read this book you will discover that there is a potential leader in all of us. Sometimes the right approach or training can help bring out the leader in us, and can help refine our leadership skills. So, while the material presented covers a range of safety and performance concepts, the presentation is often from a leadership standpoint, providing advice or coaching strategies that you may use to help your organizations design better ways to work and to help your teams work more safely and effectively.

Essential Components of Team Leadership in High-Hazard Environments

In order to design a safety and performance program that effectively combines teamwork-based methods and a comprehensive system approach there are certain essential attributes that must be adopted and integrated into normal operations.

As a team leader, understanding these fundamental concepts is critical for creating a team environment where employees can balance safety and performance, obedience to rules and the need for initiative and creativity, and the ability to work together to accomplish performance goals safely while under enormous pressure to get the job done on time and according to the performance standards set by the organization and/or the customer. For people who lead and manage, or work on teams in high-hazard environments, there are certain foundational components that must be well-understood and practiced on a regular basis.

While there is no magic formula for success, there are certain attributes that can help teams achieve high levels of performance while working within the acceptable risk boundaries as set forth by the organization. This book describes nine key areas, which are referred to as the Essential Components of team leadership and performance. The nine Essential Components are interrelated and are the focus of individual chapters within this book because they play a critical role in the design of team performance and safety training programs. By studying these areas and using the information in each chapter, organizational leaders, managers, and supervisors will gain an understanding of key factors that will help them design, develop, and implement team training programs that improve the way employees work together, the way they plan and execute their job functions, and the way they mitigate hazards. Additionally, since these planning and mitigation tasks must be accomplished using a system-oriented approach, this book describes how work systems and work environments may be designed or shaped so that teams are placed in a position to do their optimal work, maximizing the potential for human and team performance. The nine Essential Components are as follows:

1. **Authority and Responsibility in Operational Teams.** This component of team leadership includes ways that organizations prescribe leadership authority to certain employees and how oversight for team activities can be designed into leadership systems. This component also includes ways that organizations task teams with their specific work and how they provide operational control for safe job performance. The Authority and Responsibility in Operational Teams chapter is designed to show employees at multiple levels how operational control affects task execution and how team members can be part of the control loop to influence safety and performance-oriented outcomes.

2. **Leadership in Operational Teams.** While each of the Essential Components is necessary to form a complete team performance

program, this component is one of the foundational elements and underpins many of the other Essential Components of team leadership. Leadership in Operational Teams includes an explanation of leadership concepts to readers at multiple levels. The various roles of leaders and the types of leadership are explained, including Designated Leadership and Functional Leadership. Despite potential preconceived ideas about leadership (such as who can be a leader and who cannot), this chapter explains how every team member, regardless of leadership training or experience, can be a leader, particularly when safety and operational performance is concerned.

3.   **Team Communications.** Communications between leaders and employees within a team, as well as intra-team communications are a critical part of safe operational performance. Therefore, Team Communications includes a description of fundamental communications concepts, and then delves into greater detail, describing specific communications aspects related to teamwork in high-hazard environments. This material includes descriptions of how communication can significantly impact safety and mission outcomes. Examples of effective and ineffective communication are provided as well as recommendations for effective team communication techniques for improved safety and operational performance.

4.   **Focus on Operations and Safety.** How often have you heard someone say something like, "If you just pay more attention you won't make those mistakes?" It can be so easy to think that if we simply will ourselves to focus more on our tasks that we will be better and safer. While attitude and behavior may play a role in our ability to focus, there is much more to concentrating on work tasks than simply paying more attention. Many operational tasks are affected by the work environment and external factors that are often beyond employees' control. Focus on Operations and Safety helps explain the challenges associated with operational execution and maintaining a high level of concentration in high-hazard environments, and describes the impacts of unanticipated events and unrecognized hazards on job performance. Readers will also learn about the concept of situational awareness, which can be a highly nebulous and often misunderstood term, and how it can impact safety and task execution. This section also describes

techniques and strategies team leaders and workers can employ to help maintain higher levels of focus and minimize the impacts of error-inducing situations. These strategies include ways to design and use checklists in a methodical fashion to stay on task and to mitigate the effects of numerous internal and external distractions.

5. **Job Planning and Execution Analysis.** Purposeful job planning and analysis is often a major building block for successful mission execution. Like the foundation and frame for a building, planning and analysis before jobs begin provide a structure for identifying hazards and other factors that could degrade operational performance and safety during job execution. Additionally, planning is an iterative process, which does not end the moment work commences. Job Planning and Execution Analysis highlights the need for pre-job/pre-mission safety planning tools and the requirement for operational teams to constantly update their risk management plans as tasks unfold. This section provides leaders and team members at multiple levels with knowledge to help crews and teams plan jobs as safely as feasible and continue planning and reassessing hazards in a recurring fashion as tasks progress during operational execution.

6. **Resilience, Adaptability, and Adaptive Capacity.** These terms may seem like foreign concepts to some readers, particularly if you are used to highly prescriptive rule-based work systems, but this Essential Component of team leadership is necessary reading for anyone who works in high-hazard environments, because despite our best efforts to control the operational environment, jobs do not always unfold the way they were planned. The Resilience, Adaptability, and Adaptive Capacity chapter builds upon the lessons learned in the previous section (Job Planning and Execution Analysis). This chapter is designed to help employees understand the concept of resilience at varying levels, how resilience fits into operational execution and relates to levels of safety, and how a lack of deliberate planning for resilience can leave organizations and teams vulnerable to unanticipated threats or hazards. Additionally, this chapter explains the concept of adaptive capacity, which includes planning adequate safety resources and a "defense-in-depth" approach. Adaptability and high levels of adaptive capacity are often necessary in high-hazard environments when teams do not have the luxury of stopping work when unforeseen threats or hazards emerge during job execution.

7.   **Decision Making.** Decision making is a critical leadership skill and a key component to successful mission accomplishment, yet as a leadership skill, it is often taken for granted. Many organizations simply assume that leaders, managers, and supervisors area good decision makers by virtue of their position or job title, and therefore spend little time providing coaching on strategies for making sound decisions in the face of operational hazards. As an Essential Component of team leadership, the Decision-Making Techniques for Operational Teams chapter is designed to help leaders understand the responsibilities of decision makers in operational teams and how decision makers can arrive at their conclusions. Strategies and techniques for effective decision making are explained to help employees at multiple levels understand how safety and decision making are linked. This chapter provides a structured process, or a sort of roadmap, to help leaders assess the situation and use a system-oriented approach to identify potential solutions, strategies for action, and ways to handle the difficulties associated with making decisions during high-hazard operations.

8.   **Mutual Support and Backup.** While many organizations shun the concept of employees speaking up or asserting their position if they disagree with leaders or managers, the power of individual action can be a very influential force. Employee assertiveness can be a key component for maintaining reliable performance in the face of hazards or errors that could derail successful job accomplishment or result in serious injury or damage to equipment. The Mutual Support and Backup chapter is designed to help leaders and employees understand how they can support each other for safe mission accomplishment and how they can be empowered to speak up when unsafe events occur. Strategies are presented to help team members understand how to demonstrate assertiveness during unsafe and uncomfortable situations, even if barriers within the organization make this a difficult endeavor. Leaders will understand how enabling team members to become a proactive part of safety management by supporting each other and by voicing their concerns can directly contribute to successful job outcomes.

9.   **Time-Sensitive Risk Management.** No safety and performance-oriented team leadership system would be complete without a discussion of risk management. While risk management is often thought of as something that is done in a planning room on a large

table (which is true to some extent), this operational process is not complete once work commences. Along with the Resilience, Adaptability, and Adaptive Capacity chapter, which helps show teams how to adapt to changing work conditions, Time-Sensitive Risk Management explains how teams must reassess and manage risks in real-time after the job commences. This chapter shows leaders how to refine their job planning and risk management strategies that were developed prior to the commencement of work and adapt them to manage risks that unfold during job execution. Additionally, many traditional risk management activities take place when there is time to deliberately think through operational processes and make sound decisions by seeking input from numerous personnel, utilizing numerous resources, and developing quantitative and/or qualitative results to be recorded and used in planning systems. Time-Sensitive Risk Management takes a different approach and is designed to help leaders and employees understand methods for mitigating risks during job or mission execution when there is little time to conduct a comprehensive qualitative or quantitative risk assessment.

Assumptions

In order to effectively make the case for adopting the team leadership strategies and techniques in this book, several assumptions are made. As you read this book, it will be helpful to understand these assumptions because the material is written from a specific standpoint. The goal is not to convince you that these assumptions are correct necessarily (as that might need to be a separate book altogether), but to start the discussion of team leadership from a common perspective. The following points are assumed to be true (at least at the time of writing):

1.   Regardless of the ubiquity of automation technology and robotic processes, humans will be involved with work for the foreseeable future.

2.   Even with robust autonomous processes and safety technology, humans will not be completely removed from hazards in the foreseeable future.

3.   The need for human decision making will remain, even in environments with automated systems and autonomous processing and control.

4.   Strategies for improving safety and performance must be developed using a system-oriented approach where impacts are considered across the various elements, not in isolation.

5.   Regardless of the rigor applied to hazard analysis and risk assessment, there will always be some degree of uncertainty related to operations in complex systems because we can never know everything and as systems continue to grow and adapt new risks will emerge, which by their nature will involve uncertainty.

6.   Protecting human life and organizational resources, and striving for excellence in operations and safety is a worthy goal for organizational leadership.

Assumption 6 is somewhat easy to grasp or you probably would not have reached this point in the book. Assumptions 1–3 may be argued, particularly as new technologies move humans farther away from the sharp end where work is performed, where hands grasp tools, such as wrenches, aircraft controls, or scalpels, and where hazards often occur. While it is true to some extent that technology is being designed to protect employees from hazards and that processes are being designed to remove humans from exposure to numerous hazards, there are still many industries that rely heavily on the hands-on task accomplishment by operational teams. Even with outstanding technology and other hazard controls, the trade and craft of oil rig workers, engineering field crews, utility linemen, commercial aircraft pilots, surgeons, nurses, and other medical specialists, and many other hands-on occupations will continue to place humans at a point where hazard exposure may occur, where the consequences of failure are catastrophic, and where long-term and time-compressed decision making will be required. Even in highly automated production plants, human decision making is still required in many areas, and when humans interact with robotic technology, complexity is increased and errors may reveal themselves in new ways.

The intent of this book is not only to explain strategies for individual and team performance (including hazard mitigation) in general terms, but to offer a framework which leaders, managers, supervisors, and line employees can actually use to design, develop, and implement programs within the workplace to mitigate hazards and to ultimately improve organization performance (regardless of the sector or industry).

While many resources explain human performance and the interpersonal skills needed to effectively work as a team, this book provides actionable recommendations, which are designed to help you as the reader be better equipped to build leadership and team-based programs that integrate performance and safety concepts from multiple disciplines into a combined approach. By using a multi-faceted strategy for safety and operational performance management, including deliberate methods for team interaction, operational risk management, and work system design through team involvement, this book attempts to teach you how to create a more robust and integrated operations and safety program, where each part of the system is reinforced. While technology can be purchased and rules created to help manage a safety program, as shown in Figure I.1, team leadership strategies that facilitate sound work system design and the proactive management of safety and performance are the link which holds the other pieces together. By adopting the concepts in this book organizations may be able to develop a stronger framework rather than simply relying on rule-based or technology-based safety programs. While rules and technology can be important factors in safety design, team leadership and the proactive involvement of team members is a critical element of operations and safety success.

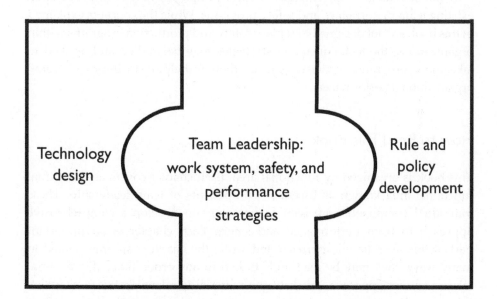

Figure I.1   Team leadership—the safety and performance link

The Bottom Line

If any of the information in this Introduction seems confusing, here is the bottom line that readers should care about. *Team Leadership in High-Hazard Environments: Performance, Safety and Risk Management Strategies for Operational Teams* is written to teach leaders, managers, supervisors, and employees at all levels how to effectively work as a team, particularly in high-hazard environments, where the consequences of failure are significant or where the very nature of the operating environment exposes teams to hazards on a routine basis. This book not only explains the concepts, but also offers practical techniques and ways to actually implement the information for results. The intent is for you to gain knowledge on how to improve individual and team performance and safety, which should ultimately affect your organization's bottom line.

By learning how to improve team coordination and authority, leadership, communications, operations and safety focus, job planning and analysis, resilience, adaptability, adaptive capacity, decision making, mutual support among team members, and time-sensitive risk management, as well learning the strategies for integrating these concepts into daily operations, readers will have a wealth of actionable information to build completely new or improve upon existing team performance and safety programs. While the concepts explained in this book are not designed to replace safety and production programs within organizations, the techniques and strategies may be studied and applied to take those programs to the next level, thereby helping to improve overall organizational performance.

How to Read This Book

This book is organized by functional area. Each chapter covers an individual functional area known as Essential Components of team leadership. These individual components are seen as necessary to develop a comprehensive approach to team performance and safety. Each chapter is an important part of this team-based approach and while the chapters are interrelated in many ways, they may be read and studied in any order. Since this material takes a system approach, much of the material is related between chapters. For example, effective leadership in operational teams requires excellent communication skills. As the reader progresses through the material it should become apparent how each functional area complements the others, ultimately forming an interlocking framework, where the total team performance and safety concept is enhanced by the application of every functional area and

Essential Component. So, it is important that you read this book in its entirety, even if you skip from chapter to chapter.

The ultimate goal for readers is to be able to take the theoretical concepts in this book and apply them in the field, in the medical treatment room, on the production floor or job site, or anywhere else your actual work environment exists. Whether you currently serve in a leadership role, are an aspiring leader looking for more information, or are an employee or team member seeking ways to improve the safety and operational performance of your teams, this book offers you a way to create change and a way to take your performance to the next level. Leadership, team performance, and operations and safety success do not exist in isolation. Each element is linked and is a key contributor to organizational achievements, and those who seek to improve these areas undertake a worthy endeavor. This endeavor is also a value to be upheld, a process to be followed, and a journey to undertake. The journey is where the learning occurs. Welcome to the team leadership journey!

Chapter 1

What is Effective Teamwork?

Leadership in high-hazard environments presents unique challenges to both the team leader and team members. Leadership alone is a challenging skill, but when combined with the difficulties of managing work and coordinating team actions amongst operational hazards, or while faced with high amounts of pressure to get the job done, team leadership takes on a new meaning. Coordinating the actions of individuals so that a common goal can be accomplished is often easy to describe, but hard to achieve. How often have you heard people make comments about effective teamwork? Statements like, "we need better teamwork" or "we need to work more effectively as a team" resonate within organizations, yet these statements are often met with blank stares and little to no action or follow-through. That might be because in many instances effective teamwork is not well-defined, and therefore, cannot be well understood. Maybe, first, it will help to describe what effective teamwork *is not*. Against the backdrop of high-hazard environments, ineffective teamwork begins to take on a unique meaning.

Ineffective teamwork has higher consequences in high-hazard environments, which are often unforgiving, when the results can be devastating. Consider the following examples of ineffective teamwork and the impacts:

- A crew is conducting a cutting procedure on an underwater gas pipeline, where a diver is required to cut a section of pipe with a hole saw in order to tap into the pipeline. The crew consists of a diver, who is underwater with a saw, and a crew above the surface of the water, including a supervisor. During the process of cutting into a section of the pipe, the diver realizes something is wrong. When he attempts to assert his position and tell the supervisor he believes there are problems with the job, the supervisor uses his authority and directs the diver to go back underwater and continue cutting. Subsequently the diver cuts into the gas line, releasing natural gas into the water (*Accident Investigation Report* 2–3).

- The crew of a four-engine military transport aircraft is conducting an approach to landing after one of the engines has been shut down as a precautionary measure. During the approach to landing, the crew inadvertently swaps power levers, attempting to add power to an engine that is already shut down, effectively rendering the aircraft with the power equivalent of two engines. This ultimately results in the aircraft crashing short of the runway, causing catastrophic damage and numerous injuries (Marciniak).

These are real-world examples of team-based situations that occurred where teamwork was not effectively used to accomplish the desired goals at the time of the operations and where safety was compromised, at least partially, as a result of breakdowns in teamwork. These cases are not meant to lay blame on any of the crews involved in the situations, and there are certainly more contributing factors than ineffective teamwork, but are used as examples to show how collapses in teamwork can negatively affect mission outcomes, potentially allowing the consequences of hazards to escalate. By identifying ineffective aspects of teamwork we can then turn to a productive discussion on the elements of teamwork that help team members to function more productively and accomplish the goals associated with their operations. Some general symptoms of ineffective teamwork may include:

- Poor communication: Team members do not effectively communicate essential job requirements, either through written, electronic, or verbal means.

- Uncoordinated actions: Team members work either in isolation or near each other, but their efforts do not appear to be in sync. This often results in task repetition, where two or more people perform the same task (leading to waste and lost productivity), tasks not being performed at all (when one team member thinks another team member is doing the work, leading to serious task omissions), and overall errors in task performance.

- Unfocused efforts: Much like uncoordinated actions, unfocused efforts disrupt the flow of team activities. This may mean that individual team members lack a clear understanding of what job aspects they should perform, or could be the result of a distracting and hazardous operational environment, resulting in confusion and tasks not being completed correctly or not being completed by a certain deadline.

- Internal conflict: A truly disruptive aspect of teamwork is unmitigated internal conflict. If team members are in intermittent or continuous conflict with each other or the team leaders, the result can be degraded productivity, efficiency, and focus.

- Improper staffing and training: When teams are not staffed with the correct number of qualified individuals, job accomplishment may be extremely difficult to achieve. Additionally, if employees are not properly trained to do their jobs, even the right number of employees for the work at hand can still result in a lack of adequate job quality and safety.

- Lack of shared objectives: This can often be one of the key indicators and causes of ineffective teamwork. When team members and leaders do not have a common understanding of what the job is and why they are performing the necessary tasks, it can be extremely difficult to harness the collective energy and commitment to perform the work correctly, to avoid discord within the team, and to commit to necessary levels of safety.

- Lack of continuous performance and risk assessment during high-hazard operations: Oftentimes, after a job commences, risks that were identified prior to work commencement are not reassessed, and when new risks emerge, they are not viewed with the same level of scrutiny, or, due to a lack of open and honest communications, the potential significance of the risks are not brought to light. Additionally, errors are not assessed in terms of their potential downstream impacts and potential cascading effects.

While we could continue to discuss these attributes in more detail, this list at least begins to help us understand some of the traits that degrade effective teamwork. Additionally, although these qualities tend to impede individual and team performance, they are not necessarily unusual or uncommon in many organizations. So, in many organizations trying to maintain high levels of productivity and safety, there are teams that lack the necessary communication skills, training, or tools, lack overall work system coordination, lack focus and are filled with unproductive internal conflict, that are not staffed with the right number of trained employees, and that lack shared objectives and a true understanding of the team goals. Yet, many of these teams are still able to function at passable levels. While this may be true, and even though jobs may be completed, teams that function in these ways are missing the opportunity to achieve exceptional performance, with less waste, and with increased levels of safety. In other cases, teams with these types of traits have consistent low levels of performance and struggle to keep up with basic processes. If they struggle to keep up with basic work accomplishment, how would they perform if the job requirements increased due to internal or external factors, such as shortened deadlines, decreased budgets, or staffing cuts? By building effective teamwork strategies from the beginning and integrating these strategies into organizations' teamwork requirements, teams should be better-suited to handle changing performance demands and may be more adaptable to internal or external change.

Now that we have looked at some of the characteristics of ineffective teamwork, we can turn to the task of creating a common framework or description of effective teamwork, and since our focus is on teamwork in high-hazard environments, any definition or description will necessarily include concepts related to hazardous work. For the purposes of our discussion, let's define effective teamwork as, "the coordinated and cooperative efforts of a team that are adequate to accomplish shared performance and safety goals." This definition highlights the need for cooperation, coordination, and a common shared objective, while meeting the safety goals of the team.

Effective teamwork, then, may be described as a state or mode of operating where individual actions are coordinated in such a manner that supports safe and successful mission outcomes. Notice that our definition describes teamwork as a state or mode, as opposed to a static property. This is because in order for teamwork to remain effective, team actions must be actively managed and coordinated, and teams must be overseen by competent leaders. Effective teamwork is a continuous process, not something that is simply achieved once and for all, like a qualification. Much like a sports team that may win championship titles in one season and must continue to work season after season to maintain that level of achievement, operations teams must continue to pursue actions that help maintain levels of effectiveness. Additionally, in order for teams to exist and operate in this condition of effectiveness, certain attributes must be driven by the team leader and adopted by each team member.

Elements of an Effective Team

While the topic of team effectiveness could be the focus of an entire book by itself, a short description of effective team attributes will help frame the discussion on teamwork as well as subsequent chapters on the Essential

Components of team leadership in high-hazard environments. This section of the chapter will identify and expand upon certain key attributes that may help teams operate more effectively and at optimal levels. This effectiveness may include several benefits, including increased coordination, fewer errors, earlier error identification (and perhaps correction), reduced rework and waste, and improved accuracy of results. Additionally, since this book is highly focused on teams that operate in high-hazard environments, safety should also be tied into the definition of effectiveness. Identifying and describing these key areas should help you understand some of the qualities teams need to operate effectively and understand how to integrate these concepts into employee and team-improvement programs. Many of the following attributes will also be covered in more detail throughout the book, including Chapters 2 through 10, which relate to the Essential Components of team leadership in high-hazard environments.

SAFETY FOCUS

One of the main characteristics of teams that operate effectively in high-hazard environments is a focus on safety. While some may argue that safety is simply an add-on attribute that teams look to develop after they build proficiency in their craft or trade, safety is actually an integral and necessary quality teams need so they can work at optimized levels for job accomplishment. This is because safety helps teams to limit or eliminate unnecessary risk, and to reduce waste through the preservation of human and material assets. When organizations fail to design safety into tasks, processes, and operations, the employees doing the work tend to be exposed to increased hazards on a regular basis and in some cases, the severity of hazard consequences may be misunderstood, or downplayed. Unmitigated hazards, when combined with human exposure, can often result in injuries or fatalities. Even a single lost-work day from a work-related accident can impact operational teams and their ability to conduct work effectively. Therefore, safety should be viewed as a critical element of effective work system design and an emphasis on safety is a key characteristic of effective teams. High-performing teams will place an emphasis on identifying risks, determining where and how things can go wrong, ways employees may be hurt, and strategies for mitigating these hazards. This process should be built into work planning strategies so teams view it as a "normal way of doing business" rather than an addendum after planning is complete.

TRAINING AND QUALIFICATION

One of the hallmarks of effective teams is an emphasis on ensuring employees receive adequate job training and evaluating employees for task/job proficiency and competency by a qualified evaluator. There is a distinct difference between training, proficiency/competency, and qualification. Training may be described as the process of learning a craft or skill, while proficiency or competency is a measurement of the ability of an employee to actually effectively apply that training in an operational context. Qualification is the final step after an employee is deemed proficient or competent after undergoing an assessment by an authorized evaluator. It is important for supervisors, team leaders, and managers to understand the difference. Effective teams are comprised of individuals who have achieved the required level of qualification for their position through a training and evaluation process. Additionally, training and qualification in effective teams typically falls into at least two categories: Initial and Refresher (also called Recurrent) Training and Qualification.

1. Initial Training is typically conducted when a team member is preparing to work in a new position. He or she must complete training and pass an evaluation before being allowed to work on a team without the supervision of a trainer.

2. Refresher Training is typically conducted at pre-defined intervals, and should be designed to help ensure that team members maintain the knowledge, skills, and abilities required to complete a task or job. When teams fail to utilize a refresher or recurrent training approach, team members may be operating with outdated knowledge and/or performance gaps may not be detected.

COMPETENCY AT ALL LEVELS OF THE TEAM

While it may be tempting to think that only certain members of the team need to be competent, effective teamwork really requires every team member to be qualified and competent at the job being performed. Some may think that only the employees at the sharp end (those doing the work and closest to the hazards) need to be qualified and proficient, but it is essential for supervisors and team leaders (even if they are removed from direct hazard exposure) to possess the appropriate level of proficiency and qualifications in order to properly supervise and manage the job or operation at hand and to be able to effectively lead the team during operational execution. Team leaders may not necessarily need to be qualified or competent at every job being performed by each team member, but they should at least have an understanding of the specific tasks that need to be completed during the process or operation. If supervisors and management/ leadership staff are not competent and qualified at their oversight duties, they may lack the ability to properly direct the actions of team members and they will often lose credibility in the eyes of their subordinates, which can make followership problematic. Consider a situation where a stand-in supervisor from another department is called in to oversee a team during an operation where he or she has little to no knowledge or experience. This supervisor is in a poor position to make decisions and team members may see this supervisor as incompetent (and perhaps rightly so). This perception can degrade team effectiveness and reduce the authority of the supervisor.

APPROPRIATE RANGE OF EXPERIENCE

Effective teams are not only made up of competent and qualified individuals, they also employ a variety of experience levels and expertise so that a balance is achieved between operational execution and ongoing training and learning. When organizations neglect to staff their teams and crews with this range of experience several problems can occur, ranging from a lack of knowledge (leading to poor task execution and a reduced ability to effectively solve complex or unexpected problems) to a lack of organizational knowledge transfer between experienced and novice team members. A well-balanced team includes the following qualities:

- Experienced employees who are willing to mentor and train new employees.

- Supervisors who take a hands-on approach and who help other team members solve problems and learn from their successes and errors.

- Experienced team members who are consistently focused on training their replacement(s), whomever they may be. These team members understand that continuity of skills and knowledge transfer is required for continued team and organizational effectiveness and learning, and therefore do not feel threatened by sharing this knowledge with others. Since they do not feel threatened by this knowledge transfer, they are not afraid to impart their experience to other team members.

- New-hires and lesser-experienced employees, who are willing to learn, are eager to contribute to the team's goals, and who are also willing to share their knowledge and ideas. Novice employees are just as important as experienced employees because they will provide the continuity when more experienced employees leave the team as a result of retirement, job transfer, or personal reasons. Novices can also present a fresh perspective to older/more experienced employees who may have become set in their ways, and this fresh perspective can often reveal opportunities for team improvement.

COLLABORATION

Effective teamwork includes a spirit of collaboration. While it may seem obvious that collaboration is a requirement for teams to accomplish their goals, it is quite easy to ignore the need for team members to cooperate with each other. By not deliberately focusing on the collaborative nature of effective teams, employees may get very comfortable working independently, apart from other members. This can even occur when employees are working in close proximity to each other. Collaboration in its simplest form means working together, which includes participating with each other when key decisions are made, such as during resource allocation. Effective collaboration includes an understanding of the personal and professional attributes every person brings to the team, from the technical knowledge, skills, and abilities required for the job, to the non-technical aspects of team interaction, including supportive and helpful attitudes, social interaction and motivational skills, and the ability to listen and facilitate team activities. Many of the requirements for developing a collaborative work environment are the responsibility of senior leaders and managers (above the team level, such as director-level positions), but collaborative facilitation flows down to the team leader and supervisor level. If organizational and local leaders do not facilitate a collaborative work environment many of the team activities will be disjointed, potentially resulting in waste, rework, and even in failure to complete job requirements.

SHARED MISSION OBJECTIVES OR ORGANIZATIONAL/TEAM GOALS

One critical element of team effectiveness is the requirement for shared objectives or goals among team members. This means that all team members have been briefed on the overall goal of the mission or job, as well as specific task completion requirements. It can also be helpful when team members are told how their specific tasks or job completion requirements fit into the overall process or operation, which helps them understand their contribution to the "the big picture," or other areas within the organization. This description could include how effective job accomplishment will enable meeting customer or stakeholder needs. While this explanation may not make team members better at their individual crew positions, it may help provide additional motivation to work together as a team, particularly when employees have a strong connection to the organization and its mission. Tying their individual/team actions to organizational and/or mission success may help shape positive team-oriented attitudes and may help link individual action to overall vision or goals.

LEADER'S INTENT

Leader's Intent is derived from a term known as "Commander's Intent," which is a concept that has been used in the military to help set the environment for effective and efficient teamwork. Leader's Intent is a guiding principle or set of principles that, in the absence of prescriptive orders, tasks, or job statements, allows team members and supervisors to make decisions during job planning and operational execution. Leader's Intent is helpful if it is in the form of a statement regarding the desired outcomes of the job or process (*Command and Control* 72). This deliberate statement may be known as a Leader's Intent Statement, which helps provide a vision of a desired end-state to team members, who can then wrap their minds around what their team leader wants accomplished. Since a well-defined Leader's Intent Statement explains what needs to be done, but not necessarily how to do the work, it allows employees a degree of freedom to use their knowledge, skills, abilities, and collaborative capacity to complete the job in the most effective and efficient manner feasible.

DISTRIBUTED LEADERSHIP AND DECISION MAKING

Effective teamwork requires team members who can make decisions that are in the best interest of both employee safety and job accomplishment. This type of decision making can often be most effective when those closest to the work being performed are allowed to provide leadership and either make decisions locally or participate in the decision-making process. Rigid hierarchical organizational structures often require team members to send information through a structured chain of command, ultimately waiting on someone at the top of the chain to make decisions. This rigid hierarchical structure frequently requires information to be transferred through a series of people or departments, a decision to be made, and an answer regarding the decision to be transmitted back through the organizational chain of command to those who will actually do the work. While this methodical process may be required in some cases, particularly when high risks are involved and there is plenty of time to wait for the decision, in many situations, streamlining the decision-making process and distributing leadership authority to lower levels, including the team leader or supervisor level, may help teams to work more efficiently.

Those at the point where the work is being performed often possess the most accurate and relevant information and are often in the optimal position to decide what needs to be done to mitigate risks and to effectively accomplish the tasks at hand. Allowing local experts to take part in the decision-making process also adds a degree of effectiveness because team members doing the work often understand the right solution to problems that may occur once a decision is made and work commences. At the highest level of distributed leadership, teams work in a networked fashion, where information is rapidly shared and decisions that fall within pre-defined boundaries are made without a need to elevate these decisions to higher levels. Chapter 2 will describe the concept of networked teams as well as distributed leadership and decision making, and Chapter 10 will describe the concept of elevating decisions based on risk ratings and making risk decisions at the appropriate leadership levels.

SHARED MENTAL MODEL

A shared mental model, in simple terms, may be explained as an individual understanding by each team member and a collective understanding (by the entire team) of job objectives and team member activities necessary to effectively accomplish these objectives. A shared mental model has two components:

1.   Individual understanding of tasks: Each team member understands his or her job responsibilities and roles, and understands how these responsibilities and roles relate to effective job accomplishment.

2.   Collective and integrated understanding of tasks: Each team member also understands the job responsibilities and roles of other team members and how every team member's responsibilities and roles fit together for effective accomplishment of a job.

A shared mental model helps team members work together effectively because it helps to shape the work environment for a high degree of coordination. In the absence of specific or prescriptive orders team members will often understand what needs to be done because they understand how activities fit together (particularly when combined with a strong Leader's Intent Statement). To illustrate the concept of a shared mental model, consider a group of people working together on a puzzle. The group is broken down into sub-groups, which are assigned a section of the puzzle. Each group member understands what the puzzle should look like when it is finished and understands the section(s) of the puzzle that he or she is working on, as well as the sections other sub-groups are working on. In a similar fashion, a shared mental model may be used to help team members understand their individual roles, the roles of other team members and sub-teams, and the desired end result.

EMPOWERMENT

Empowerment relates directly to the level of team effectiveness because the level of empowerment in a team will often determine the level of individual contribution to team actions as well as a team member's willingness to contribute to problem solving processes. High levels of empowerment are often visible when barriers to effective employee action are removed or reduced, such as communication barriers or layers of red-tape for resource requests, and when team members are encouraged to contribute to the decision-making process. Low levels of empowerment are often visible when employees are prohibited from voicing opinions and when team members' efforts at job performance are degraded through layers of bureaucracy and burdensome communication requirements. Empowerment requires leaders to support their team members during job execution and collaborative processes.

STANDARDIZATION

Standardization is one of the hallmarks of effective and well-disciplined teams. Standardization means that job planning and execution requirements are created so that work can be performed in the same way nearly every time a job is conducted. Highly standardized teams develop tasks, procedures, and processes that can be repeated on a consistent basis, helping team members to achieve reliable, consistent, and expected outcomes. A comprehensive standardization program includes a methodical process for designing training and procedures, for evaluating the effectiveness of these procedures, and for measuring the degree to which instructors, trainers, and evaluators adhere to standardized training and evaluation requirements. It also includes a process to measure the degree to which team members' activities match these standardized procedures. Rather than crews using ad hoc or locally-developed procedures, standardization puts this information into formal work systems and policies, and pushes the information out to leaders and other team members. This helps to build a shared mental model. While there may be some jobs that require variances from standardized procedures due to certain abnormal conditions, effective teams need a standardized work system to provide the basis for effective and safe procedures, and any adaptations required due to emergencies or abnormal conditions will typically use standardized procedures as a basic starting point prior to adaptation.

INITIATIVE

This may seem like a contradiction, since the previous section described the importance of standardization, but another characteristic of high-performing and effective teams is the ability to implement individual and team initiative to solve problems. While it may seem paradoxical to include the concept of initiative as part of effective teamwork, particularly when set against the backdrop of standardization, when viewed from a creativity and improvisational standpoint it can actually be a helpful addition to the standardization process if used correctly. As operations take place and teams learn from each job they complete, it may be apparent that the previously developed standardized procedures do not work as effectively as designed or planned. Initiative is a way of fostering creativity to identify gaps or improvement areas in procedures and processes, and ultimately to improve work systems overall. Team members who are encouraged to invent creative solutions to problems are often more productive team members. Initiative must be used with caution, however, particularly in high-hazard environments and when the effects of errors can include devastating consequences. Local initiative that requires deviation from standardized procedures should be balanced with proper supervision and input from all affected work areas or departments because in some cases locally-designed procedures can contain unidentified hazards and unintended consequences. When employees and teams use initiative to develop new procedures, there should be a process for rapid feedback from other team members or departments that could be affected by those new (often untested) procedures.

Additionally, when initiative is fostered to create new ways of carrying out tasks, lessons should be captured and fed forward into the planning system. In this fashion, initiative becomes part of the support structure to help ensure planning continues to evolve and that new ideas are examined in a fashion that allows them to be vetted, and then input into the work system design process. Ultimately, when initiative is used in this fashion it becomes part of the overall process for creating standardized procedures and, therefore, is a complement to the standardization process.

INNOVATION

Like initiative, innovation involves action on the part of individuals and/or groups within a team. While initiative often means acting without direction or orders, innovation refers more specifically to the act of creating something new or different. Innovation should become part of an explicit process to improve safe, effective, and efficient work systems. High-performing and highly effective organizations and teams understand that products, services, and processes must be continually updated to meet customer and/or stakeholder needs, and organizations that understand the need to create new procedures to meet these demands have the ability to pass concepts from innovation activities to operational teams.

Innovation at the operational team level becomes even more of an imperative in high-hazard environments when new operating processes or capabilities are introduced into an environment where operational procedures have become highly institutionalized. Oftentimes when new organizational capabilities are developed and introduced operational teams are expected to use older, more established procedures and work methods (including ways to manage risk) to accomplish the work and mitigate hazards, yet these older ways may not be compatible with the new processes. Innovation may help bridge the gap between old and new risk mitigation techniques and may help to improve operational effectiveness and efficiency in the process.

Although the human capacity for creativity can be quite amazing in many cases, formal innovative processes within operational teams may not always develop naturally, particularly if this is not part of an organizational culture. Therefore, organizations wishing to develop more effective teams should build a process to help operational teams participate in the creative process. This could include a formal or informal process where innovation groups are created and staffed by volunteers from operational teams and meet on a regular basis to determine what new processes or procedures should be created to improve the existing work systems. The results of this collaborative process could even help the organization as a whole develop products and/or services which could be developed and deployed internally to help improve their own operations, or externally as a new business capability. Additionally, by including input from members of operational teams (those employees who actually do the work) into the innovation process, organizations can help ensure that innovation plans will be executable in practice because those doing the work are typically in a better position to know what works and what doesn't compared to planners who are far-removed from the operational processes. Operational teams can also develop their own innovation groups or committees, which could work in parallel with the standardization process. Ultimately (like the concept of initiative), locally developed innovations should be vetted through an appropriate system-oriented group, including membership from key departments, including (but not limited to) safety, operations/production, logistics, human resources, and Information Systems.

SYNCHRONOUS EVOLUTION

Synchronous evolution means that as parts of an organization change, other parts of the organization are kept informed and necessary changes to related parts are made to ensure that the organization functions effectively and makes changes in tandem. In simple terms, this could mean that when a change in a procedure used by one part of a team is made, the rest of the team is kept informed, and, if necessary, changes to related procedures or processes used by other parts of the team are updated. Contrary to synchronous evolution, asynchronous evolution means that changes to one part of a system can occur while other inter-related parts of a system remain unchanged (Leveson, *Engineering a Safer World* 95). In organizational terms this could mean that changes to one section or division within the organization or team are made without necessary changes to interrelated or affected sections. Asynchronous evolution can have detrimental effects on team performance, and has the potential to introduce hazards in new ways that operational teams may not anticipate. Job procedure changes are an example. If a high-hazard piece of equipment is modified and all personnel who use or are affected by the equipment are not informed of the changes, the result could be disastrous. What seems wise to one part of the system or team may be highly damaging to another part of the system or team. Synchronous evolution requires leaders to view teams and the organization as a system with many interrelated parts. When changes to one part of the system occur, the other parts of the system (team) must be examined to determine the impacts. Changes to the affected/ related parts of the team should be made, as necessary, to help prevent gaps in safety and performance from developing.

ADAPTABILITY

In today's rapidly changing operational environment, employees and teams must be able to adjust their operating procedures and processes as customers, stakeholders, and the marketplace put new demands on organizations for improved products and services. As many organizations are customer or stakeholder-driven, they make changes to product and service offerings based on market changes, or modify processes or procedures to squeeze out more profits from each item produced or service delivered. Upstream demands can affect the downstream operational teams in unique and often unanticipated ways as they work to implement these process changes. Teams that are trained to be adaptable and that cultivate adaptability as a skillset may be in a position to adjust work intelligently and safely to match upstream organizational demands so that the downstream negative impacts on those doing the work are minimized. In high-hazard environments, adaptability presents a unique challenge and is a required skill, because the market pressure on the organizations is often unlikely to let up simply because those closest to the hazards are exposed to new or additional threats. Therefore, teams that embrace the understanding that change is inevitable may be in a better position to adapt to those changes by anticipating the need to mitigate new or additional hazards in different and potentially innovative ways and by devising ways to adjust operations ahead of time so that the risks have been thought through and ameliorated when the eventual changes do take place.

LESSONS-LEARNED PROCESSES

Truly effective teams seem to be able to maintain highly-reliable output over time. Their production and safety performance remains at high levels despite individual employee turnover and other changes in the organization. One way this effectiveness can be achieved is through learning systems, which include a process for transferring knowledge from one group to another and between individuals. High-performing organizations view learning as a critical component. Individual employee, team, and organizational learning should include a formalized lessons-learned process and system, so that teams can capture knowledge and experience from jobs or events, including positive and negative aspects of team performance, and methods for improving performance and safety in the future. An effective lessons-learned system will help employees capture knowledge that may not be written in a book and which can help stabilize knowledge gaps when experienced employees leave the organization and when younger or less experienced employees are hired.

WORK SYSTEM DESIGN

Work system design is the culmination of many other team elements and organizational programs, including innovation, lessons-learned, training, and standardization. It is the formal process of designing, developing, testing, implementing, maintaining, and improving the processes for how work is performed. The way work is performed should be considered (and examined as) a system because it includes inputs, transformational processes, outputs, and interaction with the operational environment. Rather than work procedures being designed in a vacuum (without input from multiple affected individuals and departments), work tasks, procedures, processes, and policies should be designed using a diverse team, so that multiple areas of expertise are considered, including (but not limited to) safety, operations/ production, logistics, human resources, and Information Systems.

Conclusions

This chapter has served as a primer for a description of effective teamwork, and has described certain overarching attributes of effective teams. While the list of effective team attributes is not meant to be exhaustive in nature, it serves to provide a common framework as we probe deeper into the key elements necessary to create teams that integrate operational safety, work system design, and performance into normal operational activities. The remaining chapters of the book will provide more detailed information on many key elements required for creating high-performing and effective teams. As you read through the chapters, consider how each Essential Component of team leadership and performance may be added to your existing training programs, and/or consider ways you and your teams might be able to design completely new training programs that incorporate this material in order to improve team effectiveness, performance, and safety.

Chapter 2
Authority and Responsibility in Operational Teams

Two foundational elements of team leadership, which directly impact operational performance and safety, are authority and responsibility. The ways organizations empower team leaders by affording them appropriate levels of authority (and the pathways to exercise that authority) and the ways leaders are held accountable through appropriate levels of responsibility directly influence operational team performance. Despite this relationship, the ultimate effects often remain unnoticed by those leaders and managers in the organization who are far-removed from the point where operational teams actually perform their work. The concepts of authority and responsibility are so important to the ways teams carry out their functions during routine/normal, abnormal, and emergency operations that they can immediately affect levels of initiative, efficiency of operations, and productivity. Additionally, high-level organizational leaders and managers may place teams and team leaders in positions where safety is either enhanced or compromised as a result of the organization's approach to these leadership components. By designing organizational leadership structures that enable team leaders to possess the appropriate balance of authority and responsibility, and training teams in methods to implement distributed (or decentralized) leadership, organizations will be in a much more advantageous position to capitalize on the amazing capacity of human creativity and performance compared to organizations that adopt a rigid hierarchical structure for operational control.

This chapter will describe how authority and responsibility relate to team performance, how team actions are coordinated and directed, and how actual job execution is controlled in operational teams. Additionally, since authority and responsibility at various levels impact safety and performance, this chapter is also designed to teach you ways to organize your teams for improved performance and safety-related decision making using the concept of distributed leadership. To further explain these concepts, it is necessary to describe team leadership methods, authority assignment, and the management of responsibility in order to take advantage of the strengths employees bring to the workplace. By decentralizing and distributing leadership authority across teams, organizations have the potential to realize gains in efficiency and productivity. This is often accomplished by placing leadership responsibilities (and operational control activities) in the hands of those closest to the point where the work is performed. To some this may be counterintuitive and to others it may seem obvious, but in any case, uncovering this aspect of team leadership will help build an understanding of ways leadership authority and responsibility philosophies can either enhance or degrade team effectiveness.

Team Leaders and Authority

When we think of authority, many ideas come to mind. We may see images of people in positions of power who give orders and preside over organized groups of employees, and these visualizations are largely accurate in many instances. In an operational context, authority really has to do with a leadership or management position and the power afforded to a person in that position. Through an organization's human resource decision-making processes certain employees are placed in positions of power and are granted various degrees of authority so they may create and/or enforce rules and determine what functions need to take place. This simplistic view is not necessarily that helpful, though, particularly when we are looking for ways team leaders can effectively lead their teams in high-hazard environments while accomplishing the performance goals of the organization. When taken to a more hands-on level, authority may be thought of as the right of a team leader to direct the actions of a team for successful mission accomplishment. So, we are looking at two levels of authority. At one level of authority, leaders determine *what* needs to be done and at the next level of authority, leaders actually control the actions of teams and determine *how* jobs are carried out to meet operational and safety goals. Both types of leadership are important for mission success, and the way these types of authority roles are distributed will be expanded upon in this chapter.

Responsibility and the Role of the Team Leader

How often is the word "responsibility" used without a great deal of consideration of its true meaning? For the purpose of our discussion on responsibility, let us consider the concept of duty and obligation. Team leaders, managers, and supervisors who are placed in positions of authority (whether they are at higher levels of authority, creating rules and determining what operations need to be performed, or at hands-on levels of authority, where they direct the actions of operational teams) have an obligation and a duty to ensure that authority is used appropriately. As they use their authority in the operational context, they should stand ready to take the necessary steps to ensure that rules, policies, and operational decisions as well as the activities related to the direction of specific team actions, are carried out in a professional manner and to accept the consequences of failure, should it occur. Responsibility is a commitment to doing what is required to help assure success and to answer for the team if, or when, failure occurs. The most effective leaders understand both authority and responsibility and feel a sense of commitment to both. Additionally, as we will discuss further, it is possible to distribute (or delegate) levels of authority, but not full responsibility. This is because regardless of the cause(s) of failure, ultimately those in positions of authority must answer the tough questions and stand in defense of the team, if necessary, when operations do not unfold as planned, when outcomes do not meet the organizational objectives, and when accidents occur. Responsibility ultimately rests with leaders who are placed in positions of authority. The following sections will describe ways leadership authority and responsibility may be used to increase levels of productivity, efficiency, and safety, and will describe the benefits of distributed leadership authority.

Organizing Authority and Responsibility Structures for Operational Effectiveness

There are several ways authority and responsibility can be exercised, and the levels of control exerted by centralized elements within the organization, such as executive-level staffs and business units high up the chain of command, have a direct effect on operational team effectiveness and the speed at which teams can plan, make decisions, and take action to support the performance and safety goals of the organization. Generally speaking, the more concentrated (or centralized) authority is within an organization, the longer it takes to plan, decide, act, react, and adapt when faced with conditions of uncertainty or when changes are needed. Uncertainty and change are realities in today's fast-paced, technology-driven economy, so teams that are constrained by centralized authority may be at a disadvantage when rapid action is needed. This not only affects organizational competitiveness, but may also impact safety, because centralized authority often places teams in a position where approval must be obtained prior to taking action, even if that action is necessary to effectively mitigate risks. Leadership and operational control authority structures may be broken down into three types: centralized, hybrid, and decentralized. Each type involves differing levels of authority centralization.

CENTRALIZED AUTHORITY

The degree to which authority is centralized or decentralized is often related to the overall organizational structure, leadership philosophy, the nature and type of work performed, the mission and/or safety criticality of the operations being conducted, and levels of trust. Organizations using a centralized approach to authority are frequently organized with a rigid top-down hierarchical structure, and oftentimes direct approval from the individual(s) in charge is required before employees are allowed to take action in order to perform a job. In the absence of direct orders or task approvals supervisors and employees must wait until direct authorization is given to perform work, which may include prescriptive requirements regarding how the job should be performed. While this type of structure may work in some high-risk organizations, it can also create an organizational climate where employees lack initiative and are fearful of making wrong decisions. Additionally, in certain high-hazard operations, this centralized pooling of authority may have the potential to increase risk. In many cases, when hazards occur during front-line operations the workers, supervisors, and team leaders at the point where the work is being performed often either have a sound understanding of what needs to be done to mitigate hazards directly or can provide input to the decision-making process. If they are kept out of the decision-making input and feedback loops, organizations may forego opportunities to benefit from their input.

HYBRID APPROACH TO DECENTRALIZED AUTHORITY

Organizations using a slightly more decentralized approach may realize gains in efficiency and knowledge transfer. A slightly less rigid structure exists where an individual or group is designated in writing with the authority to determine work that needs to be performed, but this organizational structure also allows the delegation of specific task direction to lower-level leaders or managers. This is where distributed/decentralized leadership begins. In these situations operational teams are given the work requirements by the individual or group authority, but the leader in the position of authority does not provide prescriptive instructions on how to perform the job. Rather, leaders at distributed levels who are closer to where the work is being performed (either physically and/or through operations expertise and knowledge) direct the actions of the team performing the tasks. With this slightly decentralized approach, authority exists at both a centralized level and is also distributed to other team leaders. It allows flexibility for decision making and action by operational leaders, managers, or supervisors, who are empowered to take action because the individual ultimately in charge has delegated the authority to carry out the specific job actions. Although team leaders at local levels share responsibility for successful outcomes and must answer for failure in their areas of expertise, the ultimate responsibility still rests with the centralized authority. Even though authority may be delegated and distributed to those with specific expertise, with this approach to leadership, the centralized authority still has an obligation to ensure that the job is completed satisfactorily or that failures are mitigated and corrected. Consider the following example: a Senior Vice President is responsible for field engineering services, is in charge of oversight for all policies and procedures, and is responsible for the success or failure of his teams. By empowering the team leaders or supervisors of operational teams to act, this Senior Vice President is still in charge, but ensures that subordinate leaders, who are often closest to the work being done, who understand the problems faced during operational execution, and who can determine effective solutions, are allowed to make decisions and carry out actions to complete the job.

This hybrid approach to authority structure has the potential to increase operational effectiveness and efficiency over more rigid organizational structures, but in order for decisions to be made at the lower levels, the organization must ensure that lower-level leaders are placed in a position to achieve success. This requires providing excellent training to employees, creating qualification and evaluation programs to verify that employees are technically competent and proficient, creating leadership development and mentoring programs, and building high levels of trust between senior managers, team leaders, and subordinate employees.

While this decentralized approach offers the potential for improved organizational efficiencies through team action and less hierarchical red tape for decision making, it may not be appropriate for every organization. Leaders should examine their work processes, operating procedures and rules, and the need for direct permission by teams to conduct certain types of work. For example, many jobs require safety planning tools and hazard analysis prior to work commencement, such as Job Safety Analysis (JSA) or Job Hazard Analysis (JHA) forms. These forms must typically be completed and approved through a signature process prior to commencing work. Some organizations may require a tight control structure where a central office or individual completes and/or provides signature approval, while others may train team supervisors to conduct hazard analysis and risk assessments and fill out the JSA/JHA form. If employees and team leaders are trained at conducting pre-job safety planning this is a way to further distribute job-critical tasks and to help decentralize this control away from higher levels of leadership, which increases efficiencies. Additionally, where feasible, if a front-line supervisor is delegated the ability to grant work approval and signature authority for the JHA, JSA, or other job planning hazard analysis tool, this could not only help streamline work processes, but may also help provide a more thorough degree of hazard analysis and operational awareness, particularly if this supervisor is highly familiar with the work to be performed and the hazards potentially encountered.

If a tighter degree of control is required, employees and team supervisors could conduct their pre-job safety planning and then a higher authority could review and approve the JSA or JHA prior to work commencing, which is an example of a hybrid approach. If one central office is required to sign a JHA or JSA this could impede operational efficiency, but for some high-risk operations this may be a wise choice. For lower-risk operations perhaps the JSA or JHA sign-off could be completed by team leaders. Another question that must be asked is whether or not a task can be safely delegated. Delegation of duties plays a large role when control is decentralized, which is why the need for excellent training and high levels of individual and team proficiency are required. Leaders in positions of authority cannot simply delegate jobs or tasks and the decision-making requirements that go along with them to incompetent or unqualified team leaders or employees.

NETWORK-BASED DECENTRALIZED AUTHORITY

The final level of decentralized authority is when teams are organized in a much more loosely-structured operational decision making fashion. This structure takes decentralization in the process even further than the hybrid approach. While every organization must have someone in charge, with the authority to make decisions on what types of activities and functions must take place, by distributing authority to other parts of the organization operational efficiencies may be increased. In this decentralized fashion, networks of teams who are close to the work being done identify what work functions need to be carried out and have the delegated authority to determine the ways those activities are conducted. This is the ultimate form of decentralizing and streamlining operations and decision making. With this concept organizations have one individual (or a group of individuals) with authority who delegate many aspects of this authority to lower-level business units or departments, and to certain leaders within these departments. The lower-level leaders may in turn distribute some of this authority to front-line supervisors who can make decisions on how work is to be performed.

This fully decentralized fashion creates a network of leaders who have both the authority to determine what jobs need to be performed and how the specific tasks should be carried out, as well as the responsibility for successful and safe outcomes. In this case, authority and responsibility rest with the leader who has been designated by the organization to provide leadership oversight in certain functional areas. Figure 2.1 shows a depiction of this type of organizational structure. It pushes the delegation of operational decisions and actions to lower levels because there is less control from higher elements within the organization. A great example of this networked structure can be seen in military aviation squadrons. The US Marine Corps KC-130 Hercules is a multi-engine transport and refueling aircraft. In each KC-130 squadron an Operations Officer (a director-level position) provides leadership and oversight to missions that have been assigned to the unit. Each mission is assigned to a Transport Plane Commander (or aircraft commander), who is both the leader in charge of the specific aircraft and its crew, and the specific mission itself. The aircraft commander has the delegated authority from the unit to operate the aircraft and lead the crew to accomplish the mission. If the mission is a failure, the aircraft commander will be held accountable for the results and must take responsibility for the actions of his or her crew, and if there is a mishap or accident, the aircraft commander's actions will be heavily scrutinized. So, in this case, authority and responsibility for the specific functional area rest with the aircraft commander, yet the Operations Officer must still provide oversight and tracking of the missions. This concept is even expanded if a particular mission requires more than one aircraft.

This example could be overlaid on multiple other industries as well. Think of this concept as an individual business unit or leader within the organization maintaining oversight of multiple autonomous or semi-autonomous teams. Each team has a leader who can make operational and safety decisions about what needs to be done and how the activities need to be performed to safely and successfully accomplish the objectives of the specific operation. This organizational structure facilitates a great deal of effectiveness and efficiency because those closest to the work are allowed to decide what needs to be done and how to do it, which can help capitalize on employee and team initiative for improved performance. Because there is less control from top-level leadership, this type of structure requires a high level of trust and employees must be well trained and proficient at their tasks. Team leaders must also be highly effective at motivating their teams and providing the necessary guidance and oversight to ensure mission success. Ultimately, in this type of organization some of the overall responsibility for job outcomes (particularly taking ownership of the consequences of accidents or major performance failures) may still fall on the shoulders of an individual or group with the ultimate authority because delegation does not absolve leaders for final outcomes, even if distributed leadership makes employees at lower levels responsible for success or failure in their functional areas. This helps explain why high levels of trust are required. It takes a great deal of trust for a high-level leader, such as an Operations Director, to be willing to say to a team leader or supervisor, "I know ultimately I am responsible for the operation's success or failure, but I am putting you in charge of this task. You will be held responsible for success or failure in your functional area, but I will also have to answer for the end result if you fail." This requires faith and confidence, which is why a network-based, decentralized approach to authority must be supported by programs and policies that nurture high-trust relationships.

Table 2.1   Summary of organizational authority structures

	Centralized Authority	Hybrid Approach to Decentralized Authority	Network-based Decentralized Authority
Characteristics	1. Authority to make decisions regarding what work to be done and how to do the work rests with a centralized authority. 2. Rigid hierarchy. May involve micro-management of tasks. 3. Team leaders may only communicate up and down vertical chain of command. 4. Biased toward seeking permission prior to taking action.	1. Centralized authority determines what needs to be done, but empowers leaders at team level to make decisions on how to do the work. 2. Somewhat looser hierarchical structure. Delegates authority for functional tasks. 3. Team leaders communicate with their team and local network, but central authority may be more involved in communication process than in completely decentralized structure. 4. Teams afforded a degree of freedom to act in specific functional area, but may need permission for certain tasks.	1. Authority to make decisions migrates to leaders in charge of teams doing the work. Centralized authority provides oversight and awareness, but does not dictate what work needs to be done or how to do it. 2. Network hierarchy. Loosely structured and agile. 3. Team leaders may communicate freely with adjacent, upper, and lower echelon teams. 4. Biased toward action and seeks information from the best sources in network. Keeps authority informed.

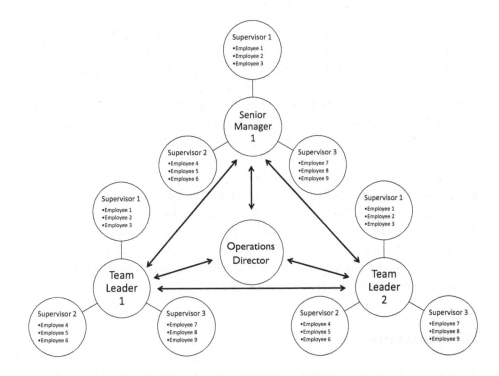

Figure 2.1   Network-based decentralized authority structure

A Final Word on Responsibility

As previously described, an overarching concept related to authority and responsibility should be noted; leaders may delegate authority, but may not delegate complete and ultimate responsibility. Leaders may delegate the authority to take action while still maintaining responsibility for the outcomes, including safety outcomes of the job. This may seem a bit contradictory, when compared to the way leadership is structured in network-based decentralized approaches, but it often has to do with levels of responsibility and specific functional areas. Even when authority is delegated in a decentralized fashion, this does not mean there is a lack of oversight. When delegation occurs, leaders must still provide some level of oversight for the processes to ensure employees are adequately trained and competent at their jobs, and that information is sent from the operational team level to those leaders with ultimate oversight. Oversight, which is different from micro-management, is a way for higher-level leaders to be kept apprised of operations and safety situations without dictating prescriptive requirements to those doing the work. Oversight could be thought of as a way of helping higher-level leaders avoid the "asleep at the wheel" situation, which is when top-level leaders seem to be unaware of the activities taking place in their business units, departments, or teams. Finally, leaders should not think they can be absolved from the consequences, even when responsibility for specific functional areas is decentralized and distributed to those leading the teams that conduct the work and are closest to the hazards. In today's competitive environment, when things go wrong and when accidents occur, investigations typically follow. Each layer within the organization is typically examined to determine what was done to help design and support operations so they could be performed as safely as feasible. Even when leadership is decentralized and line-level leaders are responsible for the work success or failure at the point of the operation, top-level leaders who feel they are completely freed from the oversight responsibility may be mistaken, so it benefits them to put management structures in place that help keep them informed of the operational and safety status of work as it unfolds, even if they are not controlling team actions directly.

Information Flow

Information is communicated differently in centralized and decentralized leadership authority structures. As previously described, in centralized authority environments, with tight control, information must often pass up and back down several layers within the hierarchy before decisions can be made and communicated to the operational team. This centralized information flow might be appropriate in some organizations, but there are drawbacks associated with this format, including time delays for responses. In high-hazard operating environments, time delays can sometimes mean the difference between success and failure and may create a situation where hazards and errors that could otherwise be controlled or trapped actually escalate into higher severity consequences or cascading failures. When operational teams must communicate requests through multiple layers within a chain of command this can result in delays in action as team members await a response from decision makers. This may certainly be appropriate in operations where time is not as much of a factor, and when risk-informed decisions that require a large degree of oversight and input from others must be made at higher levels of authority. On the other hand, for some operations (including time-critical hazardous situations) these time delays could negatively affect production and safety, particularly when teams already possess the knowledge and resources to make on-the-spot decisions to correct the situation. Additionally, when the time-space for action is limited due to potential cascading failures or escalating consequences, teams must be empowered to make decisions. Using centralized authority, leaders often want to delay action to obtain more information, but under time-sensitive hazardous circumstances, when teams are unnecessarily restrained from taking action, the consequences resulting from unwarranted delays or inaction could potentially be worse than the impacts from acting with limited information.

As an example, consider the following scenario: A field engineering team is nearly complete with a complex repair job on a large generator when they identify a previously unrecognized hazard. The team has been working for nearly ten hours and fatigue is setting in. The team assesses the risk, and based on the risk assessment procedures determines the risk to be low. The team also understands how to mitigate the hazard using proper procedures, but since this hazard was not previously recognized during the pre-job planning process, permission must be obtained to mitigate the hazard and continue with the job. Information is sent to a headquarters section, where an Operations Manager and Safety Manager discuss the situation. They are comfortable with the proposed solution, but company policy requires the Operations Director to make the decision before operations may continue. Since the Operations Director is in a staff meeting she is not available for another two hours. By the time she provides authorization and the message approving the continued operation is sent to the field engineering crew, the elapsed time from when the job commenced is now almost 13 hours. At this point fatigue could become a larger contributing factor to hazards than the original hazard and from a production standpoint, this job has been extended by at least three hours as a result of information flow constraints.

Contrast this format with the information flow utilized in a networked and decentralized authority structure. With a networked authority framework in place information flow can be much more rapid and decisions may often be made at lower levels within the organization. Value may be added through collaboration and decentralization may facilitate resilience and adaptability because streamlined information flow helps teams to learn, and to prepare for and react to unexpected events.

When examining the previous field engineering team example, information could have been shared much more rapidly and decisions made sooner, reducing fatigue levels, total job time, improving production, and enhancing safety. Rather than sending information through the chain of command and waiting on a decision from the Operations Director, the team could conduct a time-sensitive hazard analysis and risk assessment exercise, and when the risk was determined to be low the engineering team leader could make the decision regarding risk mitigation and control implementation. As this was happening the team leader could have informed the Operations Manager or Safety Manager so they would be kept apprised of the situation (thereby maintaining oversight and a degree of ultimate responsibility). It may help streamline information flow as well if the organization has some pre-defined rules for decision making. For example, if the organization had a policy which allowed team leaders to make risk decisions regarding control implementation for low risks, it would be understood that the engineering team leader could make this decision at his level. In this decentralized structure information flow does not constrain action, but enables it, provided the action fits within pre-defined boundaries.

An additional benefit of networked structures is the ability to distribute safety-related duties. While safety departments are an essential part of the organization, decentralized authority formats can distribute some of the safety functions to numerous team leaders and employees, which is like having an army of eyes and ears on the lookout for hazards. This, in turn, can increase the overall organization's capability to actively manage safety. Since Safety Professionals cannot be in all places at all times using networked and distributed decision-making approaches may help push safety to those at the sharp end closest to the hazards, who know what solutions will work.

Streamlining Action with Leader's Intent and Adaptable Rule Boundaries

This chapter has described some of the benefits organizations can realize if a decentralized and distributed authority structure is used to empower teams. In order for decentralized authority to be effective leaders must be clear with their intentions by describing the goals of the operation, process, or job to be performed. Leaders who understand what needs to be accomplished can set their teams up for success by issuing a clear description of the desired end-state. By doing this, leaders explain what they want done and the teams are then allowed to use their procedures, resources, skills, and intellect to conduct the work that will meet this goal. The Marine Corps refers to this as Commander's Intent. "A well-conceived concept of operations and commander's intent should convey a clear and powerful image of the action and the desired outcome" (*Command and Control* 72). So, when combined with a clear description of the operation or work to be accomplished and the desired goals, leaders can set teams up to accomplish their tasks using the most appropriate work methods, hazard controls, and human and material resources.

Rather than using the term "Commander's Intent," non-military organizations should consider describing this as Leader's Intent, which may be more understandable and more widely accepted by those without a military background. While the terminology may be different, the definition and meaning are the same. Leader's Intent may be applied in many organizations to provide vision and guidance regarding the intended outcome and to provide goal-based statements from which downstream actions may be developed. Leader's Intent may be particularly helpful when operations do not unfold exactly as intended. Operations rarely go as precisely as planned and no two operations are completely alike, and even if multiple jobs are similar in nature, seemingly minor differences can have a significant impact on risks and outcomes. Additionally, there is often a degree of uncertainty with many work activities. Some of the factors that cause variances from plans and induce uncertainty include unanticipated events, unrecognized hazards that are present after work commences, unsafe conditions, or emergency situations. When these conditions occur it can result in time-compression, where decisions must be made rapidly, and under these circumstances there may not be a great deal of time available for specific direction from higher levels of authority, and this may be partially mitigated if a networked/decentralized authority structure is used. In the face of uncertainty and time-compression, a well-defined Leader's Intent may help employees and teams gain a clearer understanding of what they should do in order to accomplish the end goals and the things they should avoid that could potentially undermine these goals.

A well-defined Leader's Intent is typically bounded by guidelines and can include explicit safety goals. These guidelines can be in the form of adaptive rule-based boundaries to provide a degree of safety for the team members and can include upper and lower limits if needed. By using this safety-boundary concept teams will have a safe space for action to perform their job requirements and as long as the teams stay within these boundaries, the Leader's Intent combined with these guidelines will facilitate effective job performance, even in the absence of prescriptive orders. Adaptive rule-based boundaries allow team leaders to determine the appropriate level of rule compliance to effectively accomplish the operations and safety goals, without violating the absolute rule requirements (such as upper or lower limits).

An example could be a Leader's Intent statement that includes a boundary to complete an operation in no more than 11 hours to avoid excessive fatigue. This means that if a job normally takes eight hours teams can finish sooner if they are ahead of schedule, but if conditions change and they need more time on the job, they can use up to 11 hours (the upper boundary limit) to complete the task. Another example of boundaries could include a situation where employees are allowed to determine the Personal Protective Equipment (PPE) requirements based on risk assessments, as opposed to following a blanket policy. In this case the team leader and employees work together to mitigate risks by determining the appropriate level of PPE for the conditions. For example if crews are conducting energized electrical work the job may include boundaries, with increasing levels of protective clothing and equipment required as team members move closer to the energized hazard source and/or as the hazard level associated with the work to be performed escalates. At no point in time would the team be allowed to wear less than a minimum required amount of PPE (lower boundary limit), but when exposed to the maximum hazard level they would be required to wear the maximum amount of PPE (upper boundary limit). With this approach, the team adapts based on the changing conditions to mitigate risks in real-time so that safety is maintained, while not negatively impacting the team's ability to do the work. Some organizations are comfortable assigning maximum mandatory rules in all cases because there is a perception that it makes teams safer, yet in some cases prescribing a maximum limit for all operations could actually impede operations if the equipment is not required for the given risk conditions. For example, if employees are removed from hazard exposure, yet are still required to wear the maximum amount of PPE simply because it is a prescriptive rule, and the PPE actually induces additional hazards (such as restricted visibility and movement), it could impede the employees' ability to perform their jobs in the less hazardous environments. In those cases, the overarching PPE rule could degrade operations and introduce additional hazards. Alternatively, an adaptive approach can enhance both operations and safety and at no time should boundary limits be violated. It may be helpful if these types of rule boundaries are pre-defined for certain scenarios and if risk assessments are conducted ahead of time to help ensure that acceptable risk levels are achieved and employees are safe enough if they remain within these rule boundaries.

When combined with a strong Leader's Intent, adaptive rule boundaries may add an additional level of flexibility to decentralized authority structures. Yet, while Leader's Intent offers operational efficiencies, it may not be appropriate with heavily prescriptive rule-based operations or in strict process-oriented environments. Additionally, Leader's Intent is not an excuse for deviating from standard procedures. Ultimately, leaders and managers must determine if the use of Leader's Intent and adaptable rule boundaries will fit within their organizations.

Applying Authority and Responsibility Concepts to Teams in Your Organization

It is one thing to read about authority, responsibility, and distributed leadership, but it is quite a different situation when you are faced with the question of how to apply these concepts within your organization. Before attempting to apply these concepts or trying to rapidly change your organization, you should first consider the current organizational structure and types of hierarchies. Consider the authoritative structure and hierarchy and determine if it resembles a centralized authority model. If so, identify opportunities for networked teams and decision-making processes. Additionally, you should determine if there are ways to streamline information flow so the information gets to those who need it in an efficient and effective manner. From a safety standpoint, determine if there is a way to distribute safety duties to a network of "safety agents" who are on the lookout for hazards and ways to mitigate those hazards. This is a way to put more power behind the safety program and in many cases this can be contagious. When other employees see team members engaging on safety issues, particularly if they are rewarded for their efforts, it may inspire others to follow.

Reshaping authority structures requires trust and collaboration. One reason is because sometimes lowering previous levels of control may be seen as a threat to job security for those in positions of power and control. This can be understandable and a degree of empathy on the part of those making the authority structure changes may go a long way in helping to smooth out a potentially turbulent transition. Reinforcing the overall goals of the organization may help justify a more network-oriented approach. Try to help leaders and managers understand that the changes are designed to improve organizational and team performance, which may include the additional benefits of freeing up their time to work on other critical tasks. These concerted efforts may help to ease the transition into decentralized authority structures.

While this chapter has focused largely on authority as it relates to team performance and safety, this network and distributed leadership concept can be applied to the business environment as well. In today's rapidly changing marketplace networked approaches are helping many businesses take advantage of emerging opportunities. As the speed of information flow around the world increases, businesses that use a network approach are often able to adapt faster and make decisions more rapidly, which in turn can help to create more competitive and innovative products and services. This same concept may be applied to team leadership for safety and operational improvement.

Finally, decentralized leadership authority can decrease the need for tight control structures through "…spontaneous, self-disciplined cooperation based on low-level initiative, a commonly understood commander's [leader's] intent, mutual trust, and implicit understanding and communications" (*Command and Control* 110). By creating a shared understanding among leaders and employees regarding the shift in authority structures, distributing leadership and decision-making processes, and implementing a streamlined and more effective and efficient flow of information, organizations can work toward building a much more capable operational structure. This new structure may help facilitate increased levels of innovation, decision making, performance and production, as well as higher levels of safety.

Conclusions

Moving from a centralized leadership authority structure to a decentralized and networked structure may be a new concept to some, but has the potential to add tremendous benefits. By decentralizing the points where decisions are made and how teams' actions are directed, organizations may realize the benefits of increased team efficiency, effectiveness, initiative, and innovation. Leaders attempting this type of transformation must remember that even when authority is delegated to lower levels, those lower echelon leaders are responsible for managing outcomes to the best of their ability in their functional leadership areas, but ultimately this does not absolve the higher levels of leadership from ultimate responsibility. So, in simple terms, remember that it is possible to delegate authority, but not complete responsibility. Lower-level leaders should be held accountable for their actions (and inactions), accepting responsibility for their team efforts, but oversight must be maintained at higher levels within the organization to some extent, which can serve as a balancing mechanism to help teams stay on track. Ultimately, leaders must choose an approach that will fit within the organizational and safety culture and which will not negatively affect operational or safety processes. With every decision to change an organizational structure, there are potential consequences elsewhere in the organization. If the mission-criticality and safety-criticality of tasks and processes will tolerate distributed leadership authority and decision making a network strategy may help teams achieve greater levels of performance and safety, which will ultimately improve the organization as a whole.

Chapter 3
Leadership in Operational Teams

Leadership is often a misunderstood and misused term. Understanding what leadership is, how it applies to operational teams, and how it can be used as a tool to infuse a team with confidence, motivation, and a drive to achieve superior production and safety performance is critical to building operational excellence. This chapter will discuss several areas of leadership, and particularly how it relates to teams that work in high-hazard and/or high-stress environments. As you read the chapter, try to put away any preconceived ideas about leadership and management, because as you will soon read, when dealing with teams in high-hazard environments, the lines between leadership and management may intersect and specific leadership and management duties may blend together. Additionally, this chapter will discuss ways that employees at multiple levels within an organization may become leaders, even if they are not performing specific leadership jobs.

Management versus Leadership

Before beginning a discussion on leadership development in operational teams it will be helpful to first discuss the differences between management and leadership. While the line between management and leadership can be somewhat blurry when oversight is required for operational team planning and the execution of work, there are some distinct differences. Describing these differences as well as some of the activities managers and leaders must perform will help frame the discussion before moving deeper into the actual methods for building individual and team leadership.

MANAGEMENT ACTIVITIES

Management activities are designed to exert a degree of supervision and control over people, processes, and systems in order to efficiently accomplish tasks. They are often related to meeting deadlines, planning and controlling costs, and achieving certain performance objectives. Some examples of management activities include:

- Material and resource planning: Determining team resource requirements, such as equipment and tools, information and communication systems, Personal Protective Equipment (PPE), and the right quantity and quality of employees to make up a specific team to perform a specific job.

- Financial planning and budgeting: A highly important management function involves setting budgets through a planning process and remaining within budget constraints as operations commence, as well as adjusting those budgets when it is recognized that additional resources are needed.

- Project control: A project is a way of performing an activity within a specified amount of time, with a specific goal or goals, and within a set budget. Project Managers are typically concerned with keeping the project within budget constraints, ensuring the project is completed within the required timeframe, and that the final products or services meet the planned and expected performance.

- Milestone achievement: Managers set interim goals and milestones along the path to long-term success. While some projects or programs may not be completed for months or years, managers typically set short-term targets to control the project schedule, thereby staying within planned cost, and meeting performance requirements. Project milestones are measureable and achievable short-term goals.

- Executing program plans: As previously stated, a large portion of a manager's duties include planning, but once planning reaches a certain stage, operational execution begins and managers become concerned with the execution phase of a project or program. Managers provide the right amount of oversight to help project or program execution stay on track so that milestones may be reached, changes may be identified, and adjustments implemented to help prevent projects or programs from getting derailed and to help prevent the creep of project scope, which can raise costs and delay development.

- Tactical communications: Tactical communication involves management and team member interaction at the project, program, or smaller team level and is related to shorter-term objectives, as opposed to long-term visions.

LEADERSHIP ACTIVITIES

Leadership activities are often designed to motivate employees and teams to accomplish a bigger, longer-term vision and strategy. Rather than focusing on exerting control over people, resources, and expenditures, leadership serves to remove obstacles and empower employees through support, nurturing, empathy, and providing a balance between guidance and control structures to allow teams to accomplish goals in the way they see fit. Leadership allows teams to do the work that needs to be accomplished through a supporting and motivational relationship, as opposed to a controlling and prescriptive approach. Some examples of leadership activities include:

- The Big Blue Arrow: This is often a term used in the military to describe overarching strategic visions and the macro-level details that are related to the big picture as opposed to micro-level details related to individual actions. Leadership in this sense includes a focus on what needs to happen, including interdependencies between different departments and multiple team interface requirements, as opposed to how to make those things happen. The how-to portion is often distributed to managers, supervisors, and line employees. As we will discuss later, though, these other managers and supervisors may also serve as leaders.

- Vision setting: A vision can be thought of as a conceptual description of a desired end-state, without going into too much detail. It is meant to provide a mental image of a desired goal, such as what the organization should look or feel like. Leaders set the vision and communicate it to team members so ideas may be stimulated, and momentum and motivation can be generated (Kotter, *Leading Change* 71).

- Strategic communications: As opposed to tactical communication, which relates to short-term, localized, or micro-level goals, strategic communication relates to the activities necessary to achieve the overarching vision. Typically it will involve larger portions of the organization and span multiple business units or departments in order to build a shared vision.

- Coalition building: A coalition is like an alliance comprised of multiple departments and/or individuals with a shared purpose. A coalition can be a powerful force in achieving a strategic vision and one of a leader's responsibilities is to help build these coalitions by gaining buy-in from other leaders in power positions who can assist with carrying out the activities necessary to achieve the common goal (Kotter, *Leading Change* 67–8).

- Interaction with external actors for stakeholder buy-in and confidence: Leaders often interact with and network with those outside of their local teams or departments. This can be through formal or informal networks, but a key leadership skill is the ability to make an impact on others outside of local circles of influence. The relationships effective leaders build can help to pay dividends in the form of support and buy-in when new programs or projects are introduced or when critical resources are needed. With small team leadership this can mean networking with peers or leaders in adjacent teams or departments.

- Shaping policy: Leaders use their confidence and interpersonal skills to help shape policies, procedures, or rules to steer them in the best interest of the organization, particularly when it comes to improving performance and safety.

- Shaping the development of overarching guidelines: Leaders understand that subordinate employees need guidelines to follow in order to do their jobs effectively. Ambiguous or contradictory rules or policies confuse employees and often lead to employees trying to choose the right rule to follow (until something goes wrong and they are blamed for not following a rule). Leaders can help shape and guide the development of guidelines, which help employees make decisions during planning and operational execution. An example of a guideline could be a leader's statement that "We will never accept the risk of a fatality, even if it means canceling an operation." Guiding statements can help influence policy and more prescriptive rule creation.

- Accountability and discipline: While these may be two uncomfortable words to discuss, they are a necessary part of leadership and teamwork. Regardless of their work position, employees, supervisors, managers, and leaders should be held accountable for willful violations of rules (which is different from a mistake or error). Sometimes accountability requires discipline as well, and while accountability and discipline are often viewed as management functions, leaders can set the organizational tone for accountability and discipline expectations. Additionally, willful violations require investigation, and if routine willful violations are discovered, this may indicate a system problem. In those cases, disciplining a single individual may have limited impact and system-level corrections may also be in order. Leadership is not for the faint of heart and it requires a willingness to make difficult decisions and put in the hard work to correct deficiencies at multiple levels.

When Leadership and Management Intersect

While leadership and management often include unique types of duties, when they are simply viewed as distinctly separate functions, opportunities for improvement at the organizational level and the operational team level may be missed. Although leadership and management are different, there are often times when the lines get blurred and leadership and management actions intersect and cross over. In some cases managers must pick up where leaders leave off, like in a relay race when the baton is handed from one runner to the next. During this process leaders must ensure a smooth transition, which may require a hands-on approach. Managers often refine and execute the strategy put in place by leaders. Additionally, when managers run into barriers as they try to do their work using their normal level of effort, formal and informal networks, and following their prescribed management processes, leadership qualities and subsequent activities may be necessary to push through these barriers. This is why, in reality, excellent managers are able to step up into the leadership role when necessary and excellent leaders are also competent managers, who can take a hands-on approach while directing team activities. When personnel reach this level of effectiveness and can work at these levels, organizations will be rewarded by their efficiency and ability to take action in multiple situations, as the line between management and leadership becomes less important.

When a leader has created an overarching vision and strategy and received buy-in from the organization, at some point the vision and strategy must be converted into actionable plans that include achievable and measurable milestones. Additionally, when these project or program goals are reached along the way, these achievements should be seen as short-term victories, and employees' efforts should be celebrated. This act builds confidence and cohesiveness among team members and helps to build the momentum for further gains.

Additionally, strategic communication, which is often seen as a leadership function and is based on overarching large-scale strategies, at some point must be converted into tactical communication (at the smaller team level). This type of communication is generally more narrowly focused, more specific in nature, and oriented towards shorter-term timelines and the executable tasks as the vision is put into motion through project or other operational activities. Another area where management and leadership intersect is when a manager realizes that teams are either demotivated or that team performance is slipping. Managers who are able to recognize these performance deficiencies before they become overly problematic, and are able to conduct team discussions, team-building exercises, workshops, or other team-improvement actions can be the critical link in helping to keep teams well balanced and performing at optimal levels.

While leadership interfacing with external stakeholders is often required for buy-in and confidence, the same type of activities are often required within the organization at the team level. Interfacing with employees to gain their buy-in and to build confidence is equally as important as interacting with external actors, because ultimately it is the employee support that is needed to carry out the work that has been designed and promulgated through programs or policies. So, some of the same skills that are needed by high-level leaders are needed by leaders and managers at lower levels of the organization.

So far we have described the differences between leadership and management activities, yet by more closely examining the requirements of both leaders and managers in the operational context we begin to see that drawing a specific distinction between the two duties is not necessarily as important as determining the overall skills that can help leaders, managers, and supervisors (regardless of their job title) become more effective at planning, coordinating, and executing operational tasks. As these personnel perform their required duties and implement the most effective skillsets, they actually serve in the capacity of a leader–manager. So, from this point forward the distinction between specific job titles and unique functions will not be discussed and it will be assumed that effective leaders of operational teams will possess a range of leadership and management skills and the ability to shift between each skill. It is, however, important to understand the shifting requirements and Figure 3.1 shows the line between leadership and management, and some of the associated activities required by leader–managers.

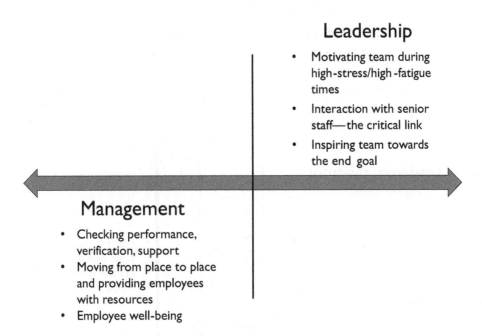

Leadership

- Motivating team during high-stress/high-fatigue times
- Interaction with senior staff—the critical link
- Inspiring team towards the end goal

Management

- Checking performance, verification, support
- Moving from place to place and providing employees with resources
- Employee well-being

Figure 3.1   The leader–manager in operational teams

At any given time, leaders may need to use their skills and abilities to control team activities, including verifying work performance, obtaining and allocating resources, and looking out for employee well-being and morale. These leaders may also need to motivate and inspire team members, particularly in high-stress work environments, and interact with senior staff members to provide status updates on work/project performance, which is a critical link in maintaining communications to help senior levels of authority maintain oversight for operations. Additionally, operational team leadership often requires team leaders to roll up their sleeves and do some of the dirty work with their teams. Even if, as a team leader, you are not necessarily competent at performing the specific operational tasks in a given functional area, there are often opportunities for you to locate yourself with your team in a supporting and guiding role, serving the dual roles of the leader–manager. This type of support can go a long way in helping to gain the support and respect of the team members, particularly when they see that you care about them as they work at the sharp end or "in the trenches."

Another helpful concept leaders of operational teams should understand is the different types of leadership styles. While every human being has certain natural tendencies, by describing and adopting specific leadership styles, team leaders can put themselves in a position to be as effective as possible when different skills are required. The two styles are leading from the front, and leading from the back. Figure 3.2 illustrates the two styles and provides guidance about when they may be needed.

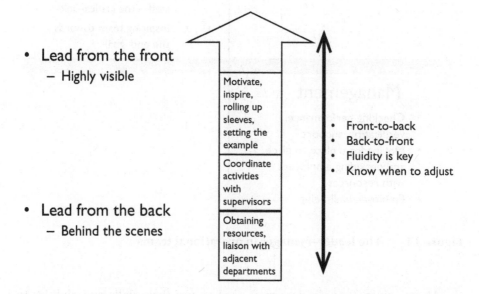

- **Lead from the front**
  - Highly visible

Motivate, inspire, rolling up sleeves, setting the example

Coordinate activities with supervisors

Obtaining resources, liaison with adjacent departments

- Front-to-back
- Back-to-front
- Fluidity is key
- Know when to adjust

- **Lead from the back**
  - Behind the scenes

Figure 3.2   Team leadership strategies—leading from the front and the back

When we think of leadership we often think about loud heroes who stand in front of crowds drumming up support. While this is often necessary, leading from the front does not always take the form of a stereotypical notion. While leading from the front includes the need for team leaders to be highly visible, it sometimes includes the softer skills of inspiring through setting the example and communicating directly with employees to let them know you care. Leading from the back is less visible, where team leaders work to obtain key resources and make critical liaison with senior levels of authority within the organization to keep them updated of operational progress for oversight purposes. Both styles of leadership are needed and one of the key skills required by team leaders is knowing when each style is required and at what times they should be used. By maintaining the capacity to adapt and adjust your style based on the needs of the team and the organization, you have the ability to be a more effective leader than those who simply maintain one leadership style, which may limit their productivity and may restrict the performance capabilities of the team.

The Two Types of Leadership

Some of the highest-performing teams have come to the realization that leaders come in many forms, and leadership capacity goes beyond job titles. By designing specific leadership authority structures and simultaneously empowering employees to take on short-term leadership roles, organizations may find that operational execution becomes smoother and safer, and performance goals are achieved more frequently. These lessons have been learned in US Marine Corps aviation operations, as well as other elements of the military, and through this process, two types of leadership have been discovered: Designated Leadership and Functional Leadership (*NATOPS General Flight and Operating Instructions* 3–17–18). Designated Leadership and Functional Leadership positions are quite different and, therefore, the characteristics associated with each type of leader are somewhat different. While there may be some common attributes between the two, it is important to highlight the differences because as you learn these concepts and potentially begin creating your leadership development programs, the characteristics described here should help you to identify individual and role-based attributes for each type of leader.

DESIGNATED LEADERSHIP

This type of leadership relates to Chapter 2's discussion on authority. Designated leaders are assigned in writing by the organization and are granted a degree of power to make decisions related to the type of work to be performed, resources, and operational execution performance and safety requirements. For the purposes of this description, we will also refer to an individual who is a Designated Leader as a DL. From a team leadership perspective the DL typically has the final responsibility for mission success or failure and safety outcomes in the operational context. The DL is often seen as "the one in charge." DLs often serve a more long-term role, such as on a program or a project, and are typically in place for the duration of the assignment. Alternatively, DLs may serve in routine daily roles, such as a shift supervisor overseeing daily production tasks. The DL is normally a decision maker (at least at his or her functional level), but may accept input from others and may delegate certain decisions to functional/technical experts in some cases.

FUNCTIONAL LEADERSHIP

Oftentimes due to specific project challenges, operational or functional information requirements, or safety-critical portions of operations, it becomes necessary for employees who are not necessarily serving in assigned leadership roles to step up and serve in a temporary leadership capacity. This is known as Functional Leadership. Functional Leaders (or FLs) are often needed in high-hazard environments when their expertise is required to provide input to the decision-making process. FLs typically serve a more short-term role, during a specific portion of a job. They could be sought out for their expertise in a specific functional area, or their knowledge could be required because they possess safety-critical information that could dramatically impact the way operations unfold, including the potential for mitigating injuries, equipment damage, process disruption, or environmental impact.

CHARACTERISTICS OF DESIGNATED LEADERS

While it is up to each organization to decide for itself which employees are placed into Designated Leadership positions, there are certain attributes required of DLs that may help those individuals become more successful in these leadership roles.

- High level of proficiency, skill, and procedural acumen: Although DLs may not necessarily be the members of an operational team doing the majority of the hands-on work, it is helpful for them to have a level of technical understanding of the operations they are overseeing. While DLs do not necessarily have to be functional experts in specific operational functions, they should understand the job requirements, understand the capabilities needed to build and lead a cross-functional team of experts, and should have enough technical knowledge to have intelligent and productive conversations with functional experts on the team and with senior leaders higher up the organizational chain of command.

- Willingness to accept responsibility for mission outcomes: As described previously, DLs are often the employees who must answer for mission success or failure. Regardless of functional responsibility which may be delegated to lower-level leaders, supervisors, or team members, ultimately, when operations go well, it is often the DL who is seen as the one who led the team to success, and conversely, when operations do not go as planned and when outcomes fail to meet the organizational expectations or objectives, the DL must stand in "the hot seat" and answer the tough questions. This requires a strong backbone, a courageous attitude, and a willingness to answer the barrage of questions when operations are seen as failures and when incidents or accidents occur.

- Decisive: DLs must be able to make decisions in a timely manner and should have a demonstrated ability to make sound decisions that meet the operations and safety objectives while abiding within the resource constraints surrounding the decision criteria. A successful decision-making quality is the ability to avoid knee-jerk reactions, and to balance the speed of decision requirements with available resources and personnel to help with the decision-making process. Successful DLs gather the appropriate information and know when to bring in functional experts (including FLs) to assist with the decision-making process.

- Thoroughness: When reviewing information and making decisions, DLs are thorough and do not overlook key details or take things for granted. If conditions are highly complex, the DL will not overly simplify the situation. Any assumptions are made explicit, which means that if there is any information lacking and there are specific areas of uncertainty the DL explains this to everyone who needs to know (team members, sub-team leaders or supervisors, those up the chain of command, and laterally to departments that could be affected).

- Supervisory approach to operations, without micro-managing: Even DLs must provide a level of oversight. This is particularly true because they are placed in a position of authority and will likely take the ultimate responsibility for the operational and safety outcomes. If operations are not successful (due to the failure to meet customer or organization requirements or if an injury or mishap occurs) the DL will be required to provide the relevant information in response to inquiries and/or investigations. Leaders should not fumble around after-the-fact searching for information that could be gained through ongoing professional oversight. Supervision is seen as a way of supporting the team, backing team members up when problems are identified, and providing help when needed. On the other hand, supervision at the DL level does not mean micro-management. DLs must know when to let subordinate leaders, functional experts, and line employees do their jobs.

- Coaching and assertive attitude: DLs understand that (regardless of their job title) part of the leader–manager role includes coaching and mentoring subordinate leaders and employees, and identifying ways that can help them improve their performance. In some cases this may mean coaching subordinate leaders about employee work deficiencies and allowing the subordinate leaders to make the corrections, rather than making the correction themselves (which helps to build leadership skills and confidence in subordinate leaders and supervisors). In other cases, this may mean taking a very assertive approach and making on-the-spot corrections themselves. In high-hazard environments team leaders understand that their role is not bound by traditional management or leadership types of activities and apply a range of coaching styles, depending on the situation and need at hand.

- Willingness to back up team members: As discussed, DLs are often the ultimate individuals to answer for mission failure, and if individual team members were deficient in their duties, then this should be brought to light, but a strong DL will know when to support the team and defend the team's actions when senior leaders in the chain of command try to point fingers and lay blame. For example, when operations do not go as planned, many times there are factors that are simply beyond the control of the team and which could not have been foreseen by the team prior to job execution. In these cases, some organizations use a procedure that attempts to rectify these problems by identifying someone to blame, retraining the employee, and creating new rules or policies. DLs must be highly competent at investigating problems, knowing when mission failure is a result of employee shortcomings versus factors that were beyond the team's control, and understanding when to defend the team as the chain of command comes looking to place blame on a team or employee. This is situational-dependent and DLs should know how to handle each type of case.

- Willingness to defer decision input to a FL when the situation requires it: It can take a great deal of humility to admit when you don't know the answer, particularly if you are in a high-visibility job position and when you are typically required to make high-stakes decisions, but one of the leadership traits DLs need to possess is the ability to defer decisions to (or at least seek input from) FLs or others with expertise in key areas. For many leaders admitting when you do not know the answer to a question or the correct decision criterion may be embarrassing, but it is a sign of professional maturity when a leader is willing to bring in functional experts to help make decisions in complex situations, particularly if the situation is outside your normal range of expertise. As a DL you are still responsible for the ultimate decision, whether it is right or wrong (or perhaps it is more apt to say if it is effective or ineffective), but by seeking input from others (as the time and criticality of the decision permits), you may be setting yourself up for a higher degree of success than if you go it alone and make decisions by yourself.

- Adopts a system-oriented approach to decision making: Similar to seeking input from others, DLs understand that decisions are not made in a vacuum and, therefore, understand that the impacts of decisions often affect more than one area of operations or business unit. By not only seeking input from others, but by also considering the range of outcomes from a decision, the impacts, and the potential unintended consequences, you may be in a better position to make smarter decisions that are effective on micro and macro levels.

- Proven record of success: Organizations should take a methodical approach to the assignment of DLs. The DL is in a position of power and authority and, therefore, should have a demonstrated track record of success. This record should include proficiency in jobs with progressively increasing levels of authority and responsibility. It is understandable that DLs need their first shot at a big role but, prior to being assigned to a critical leadership position, DLs should have demonstrated at least some of the other characteristics listed in this section, and organizations should take a cautious approach and provide mentoring to newly appointed DLs.

- The Three Cs and an L: Competence, Confidence, Credibility, and Likeability are very important attributes for DLs. DLs must be competent at their job and their ability to lead teams. Essentially, they must possess all of the previously described characteristics. Confidence is an intangible characteristic and is sometimes hard to get others to see, but it is an essential trait for leaders to possess. When leaders are confident in their abilities and decisions, others can sense that confidence and are often more willing to follow and lend support. Confidence is often based on underlying training and accomplishments, and is closely tied with competence. The more confident you are in your leadership abilities, the more likely team members will be to support your efforts (and as a leader, you need your team members' support). DLs must also possess a high level of credibility with their peers, seniors, and subordinates. Credibility is often earned and may be based on reputation and track record, and the higher your level of credibility, the more willing employees will typically be to follow your lead, and the more supportive peers and senior leadership authorities will be of your team's efforts. Lastly, likeability, although not absolutely essential, is a helpful characteristic. Remember this, though. No matter how well you try to please others, not everyone is going to like you. Some will like you a great deal and others will not, but leadership is not about being liked, it is about earning the respect of others. However, those leaders who are able to make a connection on some level with subordinates, peers, and seniors in the organization often have the almost imperceptible ability to influence others and gain support. Oftentimes this influence is based on the fact that people like them and tips the scales in their favor. If you can't have the L (Likeability), at least make sure you have the Three Cs (Competence, Confidence, and Credibility).

CHARACTERISTICS OF FUNCTIONAL LEADERS

Unlike Designated Leadership, which is more long term, either in the form of a permanent position or a temporary project-oriented position, as its name suggests, Functional Leadership involves leadership in key functional areas during job performance or related to specific situations, and is much shorter term in duration. Like DLs, there are certain characteristics that help employees to become effective FLs.

- High level of proficiency, skill, and procedural acumen: Like DLs, FLs also require a set of performance skills and a high level of proficiency, but at the FL level the skillset is often more technical in nature. The DL often relies on the FL for feedback and input in specific technical functional areas. This technical expertise often surrounds key operations functions and knowledge of hands-on work the DL does not possess. So, while the proficiency, knowledge, and skills requirements also remain for the FL, the nature of the skills are more localized to precise areas and functions. If you are serving in the capacity of a DL there will be times when you will need to tap into the fine-tuned knowledge of your FLs to help you make decisions on areas that could impact operations and safety. If you are serving in the capacity of a FL you may be required to provide expert opinions to your DLs to help shape decisions and outcomes.

- Willingness to make decisions when requested by the DL and/ or to provide specific recommendations and input into the decision-making process to assist the DL with his or her decision requirements: As functional (and often technical) experts, FLs will be sought out for their skillset and if they are timid or unwilling to make decisions or provide input (even if not specifically asked) operational team performance may be degraded. Therefore, a strong FL will be willing to speak up and provide information and decision support when needed, and a keen understanding of when to interject this input into the decision-making process will help.

- Willingness to speak up when an unsafe situation is observed: For many people it may seem like a natural reaction to speak up in the face of hazards or unsafe conditions, but for others this may be a strange concept to comprehend and even more difficult to put into practice. The ability and willingness to speak up is highly important for FLs, particularly when safety is concerned because it could mean the difference between an accident or injury compared to a near-miss. Organizations should work to create an environment where all employees feel like it is not only okay for them to speak up when unsafe situations or conditions are encountered, but also where they actually feel encouraged and empowered to do so. By creating this type of work environment, organizations have the ability to create a team of FLs who are willing to support the team and even potentially challenge authority if they feel it is in the interest of keeping the operational team safe. This highlights the temporary, yet important nature of Functional Leadership; a FL can be anyone who sees something of concern and raises that concern to the team and/or to the DLs.

- Works well and collaborates effectively with other team members: Since FLs are often technical/functional experts on the team they must be able to get along with others and provide constructive and helpful feedback during operations and when uncertainties arise. Rather than being divisive and disruptive when discussions are needed, a strong FL will be able to identify areas of conflict, provide input, help other team members understand each others' viewpoints, and help the team members work together to understand the shared objectives of the team and how they relate to the overall well-being of the organization. FLs build teams up rather than tear them down through their positive attitudes and actions. Additionally, since FLs are not DLs and do not possess authority over the team, they must be good followers as well as effective leaders. This means that when it is time to follow the DL, they step back into their functional role and carry out the direction or instructions as given by the DL. This continuum of leadership capacity (moving from leadership to followership, sometimes within a short timeframe) can be very challenging and can increase levels of stress, but an excellent FL will be able to transition from follower to leader to follower again fairly effortlessly. They are often so skilled at the art of working as an FL that others may not perceive the shift in behavioral styles, and to others they may just appear as extremely skilled workers who work well with other team members.

- Willingness to allow the DL to make the final decision: While this characteristic may seem identical to the previous point, there is a subtle difference. This is a choice and an act of humbling oneself and allowing the DL to make a final decision even if the FL disagrees with it. If team leaders lack the discipline to staff their teams with FLs who know how to step back and allow the DL to make the final decision when necessary, utter chaos may result, with nobody in charge. In any operating environment this is a poor operational state, but particularly in high-hazard environments excessive internal team conflict and leadership "head-butting" between the DL and FL can have more serious impacts on safety. Just because a FL makes a recommendation does not mean the DL must abide by it. As a DL there may be many times when FLs disagree with your decision, but as part of their training and mentoring, FLs must understand that unless it is a safety-critical issue where a wrong decision could lead to catastrophe, the final decision rests with the DL and this final decision may or may not include acceptance of the FL's recommendations.

- Proven record of success, or if a new-hire, a willingness to learn: As with the requirement for DLs to have a demonstrated track record of proficiency and success, FLs must also possess a demonstrated history of proficiency and success. This track record relates more to their functional area(s) of expertise and their ability to use their technical knowledge to support the DL with his or her decisions. There will be times when team leaders are selecting team members and the potential roster may include new employees. That is understandable, and, as described in Chapter 1, staffing teams with a quality spread of senior employees and less-experienced crewmembers is essential for building organizational knowledge, because this is how new employees learn in the operational environment. As a DL, when you staff your team with specific employees and when new employees may be on the selection roster, choose employees who have a demonstrated willingness to learn and be mentored, and who are open to coaching (including receiving constructive criticism) in ways to become a leader.

- Three Cs and an L: Like the DL, FLs should also demonstrate competence at their technical or functional job position, confidence in their ability to perform their job, and credibility in the eyes of their peers, subordinates (if applicable), and supervisors. If possible, they should be well-liked by their peers and senior personnel, which is often related to the Three Cs, but likeability is not as important as the Three Cs.

As an additional note on confidence and leadership, it may be helpful to explain the difference between artificial confidence and real confidence that can exist even under conditions of uncertainty. In some cases, particularly when leaders must make decisions under conditions of uncertainty, they will have to estimate risks and help develop strategies for risk mitigation. In these cases, admitting to a level of uncertainty in information and risk assessments should not be seen as a sign of weakness if the information is not available. After all, how can leaders predict what they can't even imagine? Being able to admit to uncertainty may be a sign of a strong leader. It is better to admit the lack of certainty about information than to pretend you have all the information and answers, yet some organizations may push team leaders to do just that. Employees may be able to see through an inflated sense of artificial confidence, which may actually degrade followership. It can be very difficult to accurately predict all risks, so uncertainty associated with a lack of information should not necessarily equate to a lack of confidence in team leadership. This is an important point to be remembered by senior managers, particularly if they pressure lower-level leaders to act as if they have all the information, even when they do not. It is possible to be a confident team leader even under conditions of uncertainty, and part of developing this confidence stems from acknowledging areas of uncertainty and developing strategies to deal with them.

Relationship between Designated and Functional Leaders

Now that we have described the differences (and similarities) between Designated Leadership and Functional Leadership, it is necessary to move towards a description of the relationships and the processes involved to effectively employee the types of leadership. There are certain times and situations when DLs need to rely on their FLs and unless they understand how this relationship functions and when to employ the strategies to effectively manage the relationship, team performance may be degraded, and hazards may not be mitigated effectively. From an overall process standpoint, the DL leads the team and directs the team actions necessary to achieve the final outcome or objectives of the operation or process. In some cases, if decentralized authority is used, the DL also empowers lower-level leaders and supervisors to lead and direct the actions of their sub-teams, and this distribution/decentralization often depends on the size and complexity of the operations. At various phases FLs may be required to step up and make decisions or at least inform the DL about critical and/or functional areas so the DL can make the final decisions. After the FL has completed the process of informing the DL about decision options and has made recommendations (or if the DL has delegated the functional decision to the FL and the FL has actually made the specific decision), the FL then steps back out of the leadership role and performs his or her normal job functions on the team. The FL stands at the ready to step up into the leadership role at any time, however, even after he or she has returned to regular work activities.

Why, you may ask, is it necessary to have this shift in leadership roles and responsibilities? There are generally two reasons. The first reason could be based on safety-critical situations. The FL could be someone who speaks up to bring up a serious safety concern and to explain how a hazard could potentially have serious or catastrophic consequences to team members (or other people nearby), to equipment, to operational processes (such as downtime), or to the environment. In this case the FL is someone who notices a serious situation and boldly calls the attention of other team members, including the DL, so that the problem can be rectified. This process often includes exercising a Stop Work Authority (SWA), which is often a procedure to be utilized when a dangerous situation is noticed. The second reason it may be necessary to shift leadership roles is when the DL needs specific technical advice or recommendations in order to proceed with the job safely. It will be helpful if we consider an example to further explain the relationship and shifting leadership roles.

Let's consider a notional high-hazard operation or project. Suppose that you are a team leader assigned by your organization to lead a team on a project to install a high-power generator system in an outdoor area that will supply power to a nearby facility. The climate is harsh in both the summer and the winter months, and the job will include numerous functional areas, including excavation, lifting equipment with cranes, electrical contracting work, and many other technical specialties. As the DL you are charged with the overall responsibility for successfully completing the project and mitigating hazards so risk is kept within acceptable limits. You must execute the vision given to you by leaders higher up in the organization and motivate your team to get the job done safely, so you will need to utilize your leader–manager skills.

During the course of the project some of the equipment is being placed in location by a crane. You are neither a crane operator, nor do you have direct experience operating cranes, but the team has a crane foreman, who is qualified and competent at crane operations and understands the job requirements. During the equipment installation, a problem with the crane load is noticed. As a DL you need to make a decision about changes in the plan for crane operations. At this point, you bring in the crane foreman (the FL) to advise you on the hazards and issues related to the problem with the crane loading. She advises you on the problems and the two of you work together to identify solutions. The foreman gives you her final recommendation, and you make the decision to implement that decision. If for some reason you disagree with that recommendation you seek more input from other FLs and functional experts until you make the final decision. Unless you have explicitly told the FL that the decision is hers, then you must make the final decision, take ownership for it, and take responsibility for the outcomes. This process is illustrated in Figure 3.3.

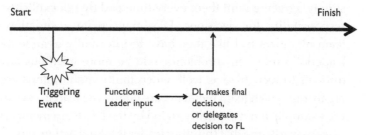

Figure 3.3   **The shifting emphasis of designated and functional leadership during operations**

While this hypothetical description involved an engineering project, the DL–FL relationship description and how to apply it may be overlaid on multiple industries, including medicine, where the doctor is the DL and a nurse is a FL, oil and gas, where a foreman/toolpusher is the DL and a motorman is a FL, and underground mining, where the shift supervisor is the DL and a driller is a FL. Choose your industry and you will likely find opportunities to apply this leadership concept. Implementation styles and trust levels in the organizations may be different, but this type of distributed leadership can be applied in most high-hazard industries.

Two Situations to Avoid

While empowering team members to become FLs and supporting them in the process, it is easy to assume that this process will become self-sustaining and self-managing, with no further input required to manage these types of leadership programs, but this would be a faulty assumption. If these types of leadership development strategies are not proactively managed and maintained there are certain situations that could creep into operations, derail the benefits of distributed leadership, and potentially cause organizations to revert back to their old centralized approaches. These two situations may be described as "Nobody's in Charge" and "Everybody's in Charge":

- Nobody's in Charge: This situation could result when DLs "check out" and assume that all FLs within a team have a handle on the required activities. They are, in essence, abdicating their authority, even if they have not expressly stepped out of their roles. By giving tacit approval to their team members' leadership efforts by simply agreeing with them every time and by not explicitly taking responsibility for decisions, DLs may create a situation where team members feel like they have to informally assume the team leadership role. This problem could be more insidious and more difficult to recognize as well, when faulty assumptions are made regarding which team members are taking the lead in certain areas. For example, if not explicitly stated by the DL, team members on all sides may assume that the other leader is taking action, when in fact, he or she may not be. Have you ever been in a situation when you assumed an employee would take care of an operational task, yet at the same time that employee assumed you were working on it? The end result is often inaction, where a specific task is not performed. To avoid this situation, DLs must use the leader–manager skill of team coordination, to ensure the team understands which job requirements are to be accomplished by specific crewmembers. Even if leadership is decentralized, there must be clear lines of communications, explaining who is expected to carry out specific tasks, functions, and decision-making requirements for certain functional or technical areas.

- Everybody's in Charge: This situation may result in power struggles if the organization does not set clear policies and guidelines describing the DL and FL relationship and who is ultimately the final authority for team activities. Additionally, if DLs do not create an atmosphere which helps everyone understand they are the ones in charge, team members with strong personalities may try to informally step up into the authority role, even if they are not designated as a leader for the operation. This can create serious breakdowns in teamwork and performance, and can degrade safety. Power struggles due to blurred lines of authority can cause confusion and chaos, and may result in a lack of clarity and focus, and repetition of tasks. If two people think they are in charge they may both direct teams to do the same thing at different times, and in different ways. This can also create confusion among employees who may not know who they should follow or turn to for help with their jobs. While DLs must empower team members and build trust among their subordinates in order to create effective FLs, they must temper this empowerment with the appropriate level of control, and may even need to remind employees that they are ultimately the one in charge. Team leaders (particularly those who operate in high-hazard environments) must maintain effective control over the team, and using the skills associated with the leader–manager is extremely important. As a team leader you may remind employees in subtle ways that you are the one in charge, by taking specific actions, but in many cases it is important to make this explicitly clear, particularly when subordinate employees have extremely strong personalities and attempt to take control of the team simply because they think they can do a better job.

Improving Decisions through Diversity

While there are challenges associated with developing and implementing programs and policies that encourage distributed leadership, there are numerous benefits to be gained in multiple organizational performance areas, including production and safety. Since distributed and decentralized leadership strategies push decision-making activities further away from the center of the organization and relocates these actions to those at (or closest to) the sharp end where the work is actually being performed, the leaders who really understand the true nature of the problem and who are often in the best position to make decisions are allowed to take action and solve problems. By moving decision making to those doing the work (or at least by seeking their input), authorities higher up in the organization may gain multiple benefits, including more effective decisions that solve problems with less waste or rework.

By decentralizing leadership, organizations can take advantage of the numerous backgrounds, skillsets, expertise, and experience of other employees, rather than requiring a select few individuals to make decisions either on their own or with little input from others. Centralized approaches may introduce potentially narrow frames of reference, but by distributing leadership and allowing others in this network to provide information and feedback, organizations may be able to create an atmosphere where diversity strengthens the organization. Diversity of thought can help leaders avoid "safety myopia," which can occur when leaders have a narrow focus on problems and solutions, and their range of responses becomes limited. They may have experienced so many similar problems in the past and seen so many similar solutions, that they cannot imagine problems outside of their experience and, therefore, may not consider alternative solutions. This bias can create a precarious situation, particularly when new risks emerge or when uncertainties exist.

By distributing leadership activities, authorities may seek opinions and feedback from leaders closest to where the work is performed, and even if an ultimate decision is made higher up the chain of command, this diversity of thought, experience, and expertise may be pulled from the network of leaders (who may in turn pull information from their teams) to help provide alternative viewpoints, which may help uncover new and more appropriate solutions. Diverse and alternative viewpoints are so important to the US Marine Corps that, in 2009, the organization began the process of creating a group of red teams that work with other Marine Corps units to challenge organizational thinking and offer additional viewpoints, which sometimes oppose the unit commanders' beliefs. These red teams are designed to strengthen and improve Marine Corps units by offering differing viewpoints and perspectives (Mulvaney 64–6).

Diversity can also bring in dissent and disagreement, which is often necessary to challenge deeply held beliefs about risk. By pulling input from networked leaders, and fostering an environment where dissenting opinions are encouraged, organizations can enrich the problem solving process by bringing in new ideas and a range of expertise and experience. While managing dissenting opinions requires time and thought, it can help organizations avoid a myopic focus on a simple set of solutions, which may not work in highly complex environments where hazards are not well-understood, or during non-routine operations. A distributed input approach, where nonconforming opinions are actually encouraged, may facilitate more advanced problem solving, risk identification and mitigation, and more effective safety and performance management.

This type of leadership requires trust, and if this is a new concept there may be resistance on the part of established, tenured leaders and managers. Decentralizing leadership, bringing in FLs to either make decisions or to help with the decision-making process, and requesting diverse and dissenting opinions can cause entrenched personnel to feel threatened. If you attempt to introduce this process into your organization it will take dedicated effort and reassurance to those already in power positions, and it may take a deliberate approach to help them understand these methods are designed to help and support, not to tear down their positions.

Operational and Safety Feedback Loops

While networked leadership strategies have the potential to offer tremendous benefits, we must apply caution to this leadership approach or we may fall into the trap that can result from a failure to exercise vigilance at the appropriate levels in the organization. Just because organizations advocate distributed leadership and decision making does not mean that higher levels within the organization can ignore what goes on when lower-level leaders are controlling team actions and making decisions at the line-operational level, where the work is being done. This may be a particularly risky approach when the high-hazard work has the potential for catastrophic consequences, and it puts the lower-level team leaders in an extremely difficult situation.

It is not fair for organizations to reap the benefits of distributed leadership, while failing to support the team leader who is working with crews in high-hazard environments. If team leaders are left alone to supervise the work and direct team actions, as well as make operational decisions, but are not provided with a support structure and a mechanism to send feedback laterally and vertically up the chain of command (however streamlined it may be), incorrect decisions could lead to disastrous results. This is why authorities higher up the operational chain of command do not abdicate ultimate responsibility, and part of an organizational leadership activity must include designing communication feedback mechanisms so that senior personnel may be kept informed of work progress and provide valuable resources to help operational teams mitigate risks. High-level leaders in the organization do not want to be "asleep at the wheel," assuming they do not need to be kept informed, therefore, communication feedback loops are necessary to help ensure hazardous conditions and situations are elevated to the right level in the organization so that appropriate action can be taken. If used properly, this feedback process will help build control loops so the organization can assist the operational team leaders, who will be empowered to make decisions, but will also be provided with the mutual support and backup (which will be discussed more in Chapter 9) to help them when needed.

Safety Leadership

From a safety standpoint, leadership offers organizations opportunities to bring performance to new levels. Safety activities should be an integral part of all operations, and organizations have the potential to take some of the safety management functions outside of the traditional safety department and distribute them to operational team leaders. Safety departments in many organizations are understaffed and typically have a high workload. Ultimately one of the goals in many organizations is to obtain safety buy-in from line operational personnel and to obtain compliance with safety regulations. These requirements and the associated enforcement of safety rules are often seen as a centralized responsibility of the safety department, which deploys "safety police" to observe and correct deviant behavior. By reshaping this viewpoint and distributing some safety responsibilities to team leaders, organizations can take further advantage of the distributed leadership concept by integrating safety activities directly into team performance processes. Additionally, by creating opportunities for operational team leaders to provide honest feedback to the actual performance of the safety programs, organizations may gain fresh insights on how work is actually being performed and ways to make it safer.

An additional function of safety leadership includes creating an environment where incident and accident investigation teams seek input from operational team leaders and team members, and that seek to identify problems from a system standpoint rather than blaming the individuals who were performing the work at the time of the incident or accident. While there are certainly times when human error is a causal factor to accidents, human error is often a symptom of underlying problems and system deficiencies. By creating an environment where organizations attempt to fix the system rather than "fix" the delinquent individuals, leaders may be able to elicit some extremely helpful ideas from employees. When operational team leaders feel trusted by the organization they may be more likely to seek feedback from their team members, which may be used to improve safety programs and help the safety staff align programs and performance to obtain greater employee buy-in. This feedback could be in the form of near-miss reporting, when employees come close to getting hurt, but manage to avoid injury. Near-miss reporting is a key aspect of safety management and leadership, which can help organizations understand the potential ways accidents can happen. Understanding how accidents might occur can help organizations mitigate future hazards and using leadership to encourage employee reporting of near-misses can yield potentially large payoffs. Additional employee feedback could even be in the form of participation on work system design teams, which can help safety staff members understand the impacts of safety program requirements on task performance, to understand the way operations are really performed in practice (as opposed to how they are designed), and to help close the safety gap between work design and actual job performance. By using safety leadership to build trust in the organization, leaders can bridge the gap between operations performance and safety, and design ways to integrate the two functions together, so that safety is seen as an essential aspect of professional work execution.

As a team leader, to truly obtain the necessary feedback needed from your teams it is essential that you work to understand their perspectives. This sometimes means rolling up your sleeves and working alongside employees. Even if you do not do their job or do the work with them, simply being with them and observing them in a non-threatening manner can show that you care about them. Asking employees what resources they need may also go a long way to help build trust at the team level, and as a team leader you should work to help your teams obtain the resources they need to effectively do their jobs. When this trust is built, team members may often be more likely to accept and comply with safety requirements even if they are not popular. Understand, though, that this interaction with employees does not necessarily mean being excessively nice or overly kind to employees all the time. Leaders can enforce rules and gain compliance while showing compassion and understanding, but being overly nice will not work with some employees. As a team leader you must understand the range of approaches that your team members need at certain times, and adjust your tactics based on the situation.

Leadership in High-Hazard Environments

While leadership activities can be exhausting on all leaders in multiple industries, team leaders that work with employees in high-hazard operations face unique stresses that can impact performance. In these operating environments team leaders and members must often contend with the stress of job performance, where catastrophic consequences could result in serious operational failures if the job is not performed correctly (such as with medical teams in an operating room where patient safety is essential), or where exposure to high-consequence hazards could result in team member injury or fatalities if hazards are not properly controlled (such as with mining or oil and gas crews). Both types of high-hazard environments (impact to performance or impact to personnel) affect team leaders and employees in unique ways. Since these types of jobs often require high levels of alertness, they can induce significant stress and fatigue. Additionally, when teams operate in these environments for extended periods of time without seeing the impact or consequences of these hazards occur, this could facilitate complacency, causing employees to let their guard down.

As a team leader, one of the key requirements for helping to mitigate hazards in these environments is to understand your teams. Empathy goes a long way, and understanding what your teams are going through as they perform their work, talking to them, and supporting them may help them to know you care. While compassion and empathy do not directly mitigate hazards, leaders who show they care may be in a better position to develop followers who are willing to follow orders, who comply with safety requirements, and who provide critical feedback to team leaders for improving safety and performance processes. Compassion and caring can go a long way in earning the team's respect.

Team Operator Safety Leadership Traits

A central theme in this book so far has been distributing and decentralizing leadership throughout the organization, so that both performance and safety gains may be realized. In order to accomplish this decentralization, leadership staff members must always be on the lookout for potential up-and-coming junior leaders or employees who demonstrate leadership potential. Organizations that truly seek excellence should not simply focus on operational performance traits, but should also seek to develop leaders who embrace safety as a critical component of performance. Some traits to look for in potential leaders include:

- Standing up for what is right: Employees who are willing to speak up and stand up for what they know is right often show a high level of integrity, which is required by strong leaders.

- Willingness to stop work when the environment is too hazardous or when there is an immediate danger to personnel: While many organizations have SWA policies, which provide employees guidance for when they are allowed to halt work activities, employees may be reluctant to actually enforce this right. This reluctance to use the SWA is often directly related to the organizational safety and production culture, but those employees who have demonstrated their willingness to exercise this authority may show a propensity for increased leadership potential. This is particularly the case when employees exercise this right even when there is overt pressure to suppress their dissent from peers or senior employees.

- Standing up to the pressure of supervisors when they know policies are being violated: It can be extremely difficult to stand up to the pressures placed on employees by supervisors, but when policies are violated team members who are willing to stand up to supervisors in the face of this pressure may be demonstrating a type of leadership trait which could help them in future leadership roles and responsibilities.

- Integrity: Honesty is a central requirement for effective team leadership. Organizations that strive for excellence in performance and safety should seek to promote and develop the leadership capabilities of employees who have demonstrated consistent integrity by doing the right thing and by maintaining honesty, even if it has the potential to bring difficult consequences.

- Willingness to interject their opinion even when nobody else is speaking up: In the face of organizational pressure it can be easy to succumb to groupthink, where everyone on the team is overtly in agreement, even if some team members truly feel disagreement on the inside. Employees who demonstrate a willingness and ability to interject their opinion when they are the only ones speaking up (similar to exercising the SWA and standing up to pressure) demonstrate the strong backbone required on the part of team leaders.

Leadership Development Strategies

The benefits of effective leadership can include significant performance and safety improvements, but many organizations struggle with how to develop leaders within their ranks. There are certain strategies that can be employed by organizations to help develop personnel into leaders and to foster an environment where leaders can thrive. The process of developing leaders has to start somewhere, and while leadership development can start at any level of the organization and flow in different directions (bottom-up or top-down), top executive-level support is essential for any type of leadership development program to survive. Once this support is gained, there are some strategies that can facilitate the development of leaders from within the organization:

- Start the conversation: By starting a conversation about the benefits of leadership and the potential ways performance and safety may be improved, you may be able to build enthusiasm and momentum for change. Additionally, when successes are realized (even small successes count) organizations can capitalize on this momentum. Leadership can be contagious and by spreading the word about the successes, this could encourage other motivated employees to seek out leadership opportunities. Additionally, when employees are given the opportunity to become FLs during operational planning and execution, they may be able to demonstrate some of the key leadership requirements for becoming future DLs.

- Design leadership training and facilitation councils: While many people feel that leadership is either a skill that you are born with or not, experience has shown that leadership can be taught. The US Marine Corps is continuously on the forefront of leadership training and development and has shown that numerous people can develop and refine their leadership skills. While it is true that some people have more of a propensity for leadership, even those who may not feel as though they are natural leaders may be able to build some level of leadership capability. This is why organizations seeking to empower employees to become leaders should design leadership training and facilitation councils, which should be staffed by a range of employee skill levels and experience, including those who are recognized leaders and mentors in the organization. By recruiting younger and lesser-experienced employees, mid-level employees, and more senior leaders, these councils have the ability to develop training programs that encourage employees to learn how to become better leaders in a safe learning environment. Additionally, by using a peer-to-peer learning environment, these training and facilitation councils can provide a means for employees to practice leadership tasks, critique each other on performance, design targeted training and improvement programs, and provide feedback to the organization as to how the leadership training may be improved.

- Allow employees who show the right potential to participate in leadership opportunities: When employees demonstrate the types of leadership traits described in this chapter, they should be afforded the opportunity to work in leadership positions. By giving these employees opportunities for leadership you are demonstrating that you care about their professional development, that you desire to reward them for successful achievements and professional skills, and that you trust them to perform jobs with increasing levels of responsibility. When other employees see their peers earn their way into leadership opportunities it could potentially influence them to seek out similar types of leadership roles. In this fashion, leadership becomes contagious and the overall organizational leadership capacity may grow.

Like a well-coached sports team, which has a depth of talent at each player position, organizations can build a depth of leadership capacities in multiple team member positions, so that regardless of the situation, employees are ready and able to step into a Functional Leadership role when needed. However, the implementation process will require the proper amount of oversight if it is to be effective. For example, even if employees show high amounts of leadership potential, they should not simply be thrust into a leadership role and left on their own to sink or swim. This "trial-by-fire" approach may work okay in low-hazard environments, where the consequences of failure have minimal impact on performance results. However, in high-hazard environments, where the stakes are high, leadership development should include a cautious approach.

Just as team leaders use risk management strategies to reduce the probability of hazard occurrence, and often the severity of consequences through the use of hazard controls, leadership development should follow a comparable risk management strategy, which prepares the leaders-in-training for success, reduces the probability of failure, and allows the effects of failures to be minimized. This process should include a mentor, who is an experienced and proficient leader and who has a proven track record in either DL or FL roles (or both). Initial opportunities should also allow trainees to fail gracefully, so that there is little impact to the organization. Potential leaders could be given controlled opportunities, where they serve as "pseudo-leaders" under the observation, instruction, and coaching of a mentor, which may minimize negative consequences. We often learn a great deal from our failures and shortcomings, so by allowing trainees to fail in a way that allows for learning, the potential blows to their confidence will be minimized and their future leadership abilities may be improved.

In order for this learning to be effective, organizations should also develop lessons-learned systems, which can help the individual leader-in-training and provide feedback to others who may also desire to become better leaders. Entire teams may also use this feedback as team members learn from leadership training successes and shortcomings. By learning as a team about what went right, what went wrong, and what can be improved, the team may discover ways employees can work together more effectively and the team members might understand the importance of becoming supportive followers of leaders-in-training. Lessons-learned may be a new concept to some organizations, and may require some instruction and coaching to help employees understand how the process is used. One strategy is to conduct a debriefing session after training. In this fashion, after leadership activities, which might include an operation where the leader-in-training functions as the pseudo-leader for a specified time, the team gets together to discuss the job, including what went well, what did not go well, and what could be improved. This debrief process is captured and recorded in a lessons-learned system which can be referenced by others from time to time. By creating a debriefing culture, where teams seek to learn more about performance and safety by discussing operations in an open and honest format, organizations may create an environment where continuous learning takes place. This learning can improve individual, team, and organizational performance. When potential leaders undergo this type of training, a truthful debrief between the mentor, the leader-in-training, and the team can provide outstanding feedback, and when this information is captured and shared using the lessons-learned format, the organization as a whole stands to gain as it becomes a learning organization.

Implementation Strategies

Organizations that are unfamiliar with leadership development should adopt a deliberate approach to the way these programs are introduced. If decentralized leadership is a new concept this process will likely include significant challenges and hurdles that must be overcome. One way to manage this process is to use a phasing approach, where distributed leadership programs are introduced little-by-little. This strategy may allow ongoing learning and improvement as the organization identifies better ways to use their team leaders. Another approach that could be used, which may be helpful when organizations want to take a trial run at distributed leadership, is to use A–B testing. This is where two divisions are set up with different leadership structures (one with decentralized leadership and one with a more traditional leadership hierarchical structure). They can perform identical or highly similar duties and the results (in terms of production, safety, quality, and other performance metrics you wish to capture and use in your organization) can be compared to determine if the distributed leadership approach proves to be more effective. This approach may take time, and organizations need to understand that this A–B testing cannot simply be tried one time and a decision made. It should include a phased-in approach with consistent feedback from employees and team leaders to determine what they like and what they don't like.

Additionally, leaders who are attempting to gain support and buy-in from the organization can consider using examples from similar industries where this leadership approach has been adopted. Even by examining completely different industries, the ways organizations within those industries have implemented decentralized leadership, and how they have succeeded in using the DL/FL relationships leaders can find new ways to adopt and implement new leadership methods. Self-organization can also play a significant role in leadership development. Employees with similar interests often band together and peer influence can be a powerful force in motivating employees. When groups of employees recognize the need for improved leadership and when they see the organization support leadership development programs they may be likely to join together and encourage each other to become better leaders by creating their own informal networks and programs. While self-organization can be highly influential on its own, organizations should seek to encourage and reward these types of leadership initiatives, but also provide coaching and guidance to help direct the efforts of self-organized groups. As previously stated, regardless of where leadership development begins (top-down, bottom-up, or through self-organized peer-to-peer initiatives), these programs must have top-level support because without the buy-in of top-level leadership at the executive level, leadership programs will be more likely to fail.

Organizations should also take care to ensure that employees at all levels have a shared understanding of the expectations associated with leadership development programs. The shared expectation is necessary to help teams avoid unnecessary conflict when FLs engage in problem solving and decision-making processes during operations. Without this shared understanding organizations risk operational team breakdown in the face of high-hazard environments because employees may view Functional Leadership simply as conflict. By helping team members understand how decentralized leadership and the relationship between DLs and FLs can support and improve production and safety performance, organizations may experience a smoother implementation process.

Conclusions

This chapter has focused largely on leadership, but it is important to remember that both management and leadership are critical to success at the operational team level. Leadership and management are both important skills, and they are not mutually exclusive. These skills may be used together, and the role of the leader–manager is a key element of team performance. The ability of leaders to utilize both leadership and management skills as needed, and knowing when to shift from one skill to the next is a key team leader attribute. Developing subordinate leaders and distributing leadership activities throughout the organization and down to the operational team level may help organizations open up new pathways to success. While this approach may introduce new challenges it has the potential to offer tremendous benefits in terms of production effectiveness and efficiency, and safety performance.

Despite these benefits, it may not be easy. Leadership is not for the faint of heart. It requires dedication, commitment, and resolve, and leadership development programs should teach both the concept of authority and responsibility. By taking a cautious and deliberate approach to leadership development, organizations may smartly introduce decentralized leadership within the organization so teams can operate efficiently in a networked fashion with appropriate feedback loops to keep critical elements in the organization informed. In this fashion, leadership authority may be delegated to those doing the work at the sharp end while ultimate responsibility is still retained at higher levels in the organization. Embracing these concepts may help propel organizations to new levels of safety and performance.

Chapter 4

Team Communications

Although communication is a fundamental aspect of our daily lives it is often used ineffectively at the operational team level. There are numerous reasons for this, including incorrect assumptions and expectations, and a lack of understanding regarding effective communication techniques. Communication is so important to team effectiveness that it can be a causal factor in operational team success or failure. In high-hazard environments it is essential for team members to communicate effectively with each other, that communication is properly executed between teams, and for operational team leaders to be competent at communicating meaningful information to higher levels of authority within the organization. By reviewing the fundamental aspects of communications and relating them to team performance, leaders can gain a deeper understanding of the need for quality communications at the team level and may begin designing deliberate communication techniques and protocols to be used with operational teams and within the larger organization.

Communications Overview

What does communication mean to you? We often talk about communication and take the definition for granted, assuming we understand what it means. At its basic level communication means the transmission and reception of information. This can occur in verbal and non-verbal formats. This basic description, however, does little to help us understand the meaning of effective communications or how communications may be used to facilitate safe mission outcomes and consistent performance.

Even in the most reliable, high-performing, and safest organizations poor communications can exist and can impede responsible action, degrade safety performance, and reduce operational effectiveness. This often occurs because the need for communication quality is either overlooked or understated. Organizations and operational teams often assume that quality communications exist in their teams and therefore may not understand the impact on operations.

However, in the often fast-paced operational environment that exists in high-hazard industries, production pressure, speed, haste, and a focus on getting the job done may overtake the focus on effective communications. Therefore, it is necessary for you as a team leader to understand the importance of deliberate communications and how to design effective communication strategies into your operational procedures and processes so that communication, just like vehicles, tools, machinery, and PPE becomes a critical component of safety and operations, and is viewed as a central factor in successful performance.

Before discussing various types of communication, let's take a step back and look at the most basic elements of communication. This will help provide a general reference point and a common framework for understanding how effective communication takes place. By studying the constituent parts of the communication cycle team leaders can then begin to understand how communication strategies can directly influence (and be influenced by) operations.

- The message sender: This is often the person who develops the message that is going to be delivered to the team. In some cases the message can be developed by one person or a group of people and delivered by someone else, but ultimately, the sender is typically the last one to have some type of ownership of the message before it is delivered or transmitted. The sender is typically the person who needs to convey information, such as an action that must be taken during operations. The sender does not have to be a certain rank or maintain any type of experience level, and can be anyone at any level in the organization who delivers a message. In some cases, leaders may develop a message and have someone else deliver it, and in these cases, there are responsibilities on the part of both the message developer (the root sender) and the transmitter (the immediate sender). The responsibilities on the part of the senders/ developers include proper message design and format selection, and ensuring the clarity of content and transmission. This means that the sender sets up the receivers for success, minimizes the amount of guesswork on the receivers' part, and helps create a message that is easy to understand, yet still includes the right content and amount of information. As a message development technique, if you are the developer/sender of a message, put yourself in the receiver's shoes, and ask yourself if the message makes sense. The sender must also determine the need for confirmation of message receipt and feedback. In some circumstances communication is one-way with no feedback requirements, but in high-hazard environments with numerous safety-critical tasks, the need for feedback in some form is often essential for mission success. The sender must also convey to the receiver what the feedback requirements are. Additionally, the sender needs to understand the most effective methods for information flow and formats. So, as you can see, the majority of the responsibility for effective communications in high-hazard environments (and even in low-hazard environments) falls on the shoulders of the message sender.

- The message receiver: This is the person or group to whom the message is directed, intended, and sent. Ostensibly it may seem like the receiver plays a very passive role in communications, but passive message receivers in high-hazard environments may inject confusion, possibly leading to operational errors if they do not understand and comply with some basic responsibilities. The receiver must actively listen and pay attention during message delivery. This means clearing his mind of extraneous thoughts during the delivery of a message and truly thinking through the content and meaning of the message. Additionally, if message confirmation and feedback is required, it is the responsibility of the receiver to provide feedback, just like it is the responsibility of the message sender to request feedback. The receiver must also ask for clarification if the message is not clear or if she is confused by the message content. As a general rule, message receivers should try to place themselves in the sender's shoes, and consider what the sender may need to hear or receive in terms of feedback. In many high-hazard operations a lack of feedback can induce stress or anxiety on the part of the sender. As a simple example, have you ever called someone on the phone and left your phone number with someone taking a message for you, yet this person did not read back your phone number to you for confirmation? Did that leave you with any level of uneasiness as you wondered if the person heard you correctly or if your phone number was transcribed correctly? Now imagine how stress inducing a lack of feedback may be in high-risk environments. A lack of feedback may leave the sender wondering if the receiver understood the message or if he will comply with the requirements in the message if a task is assigned.

- The message: This is often the central focal point and is at the heart of effective communications. In its simplest terms, the message is what the sender is actually trying to say or convey. This is the main point for the communication requirement. Verbal and non-verbal communications include messages, and regardless of the type of communication format, it is essential that the message be created with a high degree of clarity to help avoid confusion among receivers. Depending on the operating environment and the sense of urgency for message delivery, messages may be more or less concise. When speed of delivery is essential, concise messages may be more appropriate, but when there is more time available, the sender may be more deliberate in writing or speaking a highly detailed message. In either case, the message format should be appropriate for the operation or task, and the environment. When communicating with team members using operational terms it often helps to use a standardized lexicon that all team members are familiar with. Unfamiliar jargon or terms from a different industry may be inappropriate and cause confusion, so the sender, receiver, team leader, and team members must understand the need for common terms and how terminology can impact message clarity.

- Feedback: A critical and often overlooked component of communication is confirmation and feedback. Feedback can occur in numerous forms, such as visual signals (head nods, thumbs-up), verbal confirmation, such as when a receiver simply states, "I understand," or written responses to emails, text messages, or other written message formats. For some safety-critical tasks it may be necessary for the receiver to actually repeat the task instructions to the sender in order to provide the detailed feedback required to ensure proper message conveyance. Feedback requirements must be clearly understood by the sender and receiver and should not be taken for granted. For example, when a receiver simply replies, "okay," the response feedback may not be detailed enough for extremely prescriptive instructions. In a high-hazard operational environment, feedback completes the communication cycle by providing the sender with a confirmation that the message was received and understood by the receiver. Without feedback communication should be considered one-way, and if there is a requirement for feedback and that feedback is not received, the sender may often consider the message to be undelivered. This is another reason why it is incumbent upon the sender to determine feedback requirements and on the receiver to provide the desired feedback.

The basic communication cycle is detailed in Figure 4.1:

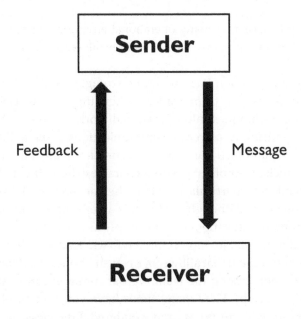

Figure 4.1   The basic communication cycle

Communication takes many forms, from the spoken word, to the written word, to digital communications on multiple electronic devices. Each format has its own unique characteristics, strengths, and drawbacks. By understanding the different types and forms of communication, and how they may be used among operational team members, team leaders will be equipped with an array of strategies and techniques to help develop more effective communication approaches to be used in high-hazard operations.

Verbal Communication

Verbal communication, including the spoken word, can be one of the most effective ways to share information between team members. It can take multiple forms, including face-to-face, which allows visual interpretation of facial expressions and body language. Other forms of spoken word communications include radio and telephone transmissions, which can be effective, but the clarity depends on signal quality, and prerecorded information such as digital messages, which may also be effective, but are limited in the amount of information that may be conveyed. Many forms of verbal communication, such as the spoken word, allow for the rapid delivery and adjustment of information in real-time, and may be fairly easy to change, and clarifying message content on-the-fly may be easier. In many operational environments teams rely a great deal on verbal communications, which typically allow for real-time feedback.

Verbal communication has numerous strengths and weaknesses, which must be understood by team leaders when they are working to design communication techniques into operational work processes. As stated, one of the positive attributes of verbal communications is the ability to develop messages rapidly and then clarify any inaccuracies or any part of the message that may be unclear. Another positive characteristic is the ability to obtain immediate feedback, particularly when the message is delivered in real-time with little delay. Although feedback is a key component with nearly all communications, organizations cannot simply assume that effective feedback exists. In order to obtain important feedback leaders need to create an operational environment that allows for open and honest feedback, even when it generates tension among the team. Verbal communication also facilitates confirmation of receipt. How many times have you sent an electronic mail message, not received a response, and wondered if the message was received, opened, or read by the recipient? With verbal communications, team members can often verify the message was received through the real-time feedback previously described.

One of the drawbacks of verbal communications is the inability to truly edit a message. With written communication, whether through electronic or paper transmission methods, the person who generates the message often has the ability to edit the content to achieve the desired effect. Unlike the written format, when a speaker opens his mouth and utters his words, the message cannot be deleted, and any potential damage from a poorly crafted verbal message may be difficult to undo. While in low-hazard environments a poorly stated comment could result in embarrassment, loss of credibility, and potentially poor work performance, in high-hazard environments, where teamwork and trust are essential for safe performance and hazard mitigation, a poorly crafted message by a team leader that results in mistrust and a loss of leadership credibility could ultimately affect safety. Once the message is said, it is said. Yes, leaders may backpedal and attempt to make corrections, but messages often stick in the minds of the audience, so the rapid delivery potential associated with verbal communications may also be a drawback as well as a strength.

An additional shortcoming of verbal communications, particularly in high-hazard environments where the potential impact can have drastic consequences, is the possibility of confusion if the message is not developed clearly prior to speaking. As team leaders in high-hazard environments it is important for you to think through your message, consider what you want to say before you speak, and then attempt to convey the message as clearly as possible to minimize confusion and misunderstanding on the part of your team members. Another drawback is the potential for misunderstanding and message reception challenges in high-noise environments. In many high-hazard operations noise is a common factor, whether it be exterior noise from mechanical equipment or vehicles, indoor noise in the form of alarms, signals, and technology hardware, or noise from team members and other personnel who are speaking at the same time. Excessive noise in the operating environment adds additional challenges for speakers trying to effectively convey a verbal message. While the spoken word provides many opportunities to effectively manage team activities, these drawbacks should be considered by team leaders when they devise their communication strategies and plans.

Non-Verbal Communication

Non-verbal communication can be conducted using numerous methods, including written instructions in a number of formats, signs, and symbols. Considering the challenges associated with verbal communications in high-hazard environments, a diverse approach to message development and delivery often makes sense, particularly when crews and teams are dispersed and may be unable to hear verbal announcements and messages. In many operational environments, particularly where jobs are conducted outside and span a great distance, teams may not be in verbal communications range. Even if they have radios or telephones, there may be instances where non-verbal communication techniques are more appropriate. Additionally, in high-noise environments verbal communications may be easily misunderstood, so written communication formats may assist team leaders and organizations with conveying the proper information to operational teams.

Non-verbal communication in the form of written messages can be conducted using many different formats, including memorandums, electronic mail, electronic information distribution systems (such as Intranets), and various social media applications. Each type has its own strengths and weaknesses, and different formats may be more appropriate at certain times, depending on multiple factors, including urgency, number of recipients, and feedback requirements.

- Memorandums and letters: With the advent of electronic communication mediums the art of writing quality letters or memorandums may be a diminishing skill, but its importance cannot be overlooked. While the speed and efficiency of electronic methods of communications can be extremely helpful, operational team leaders may often need to write and sign documents that must be staffed throughout the organization. Additionally, as a team leader who may write local team or crew policies, you should be adept at professional writing because the documents you create may be incorporated into overarching policy documents, which may be read by a number of people. Team leaders who are proficient at professional writing may earn credibility from those who read their work. There may also be an expectation among senior organizational leaders that operational team leaders are able to write effectively. An added benefit, and probably the most important aspect, is that well-written, clear, and unambiguous letters or memorandums can be very helpful when conveying operationally-critical or safety-critical information.

- Electronic mail: Email is a common form of business communication and can be used quite effectively by team leaders, even in high-hazard environments. Email offers many of the same benefits of more traditional forms of written communication, such as letters and memos, but also affords team leaders the ability to rapidly distribute messages to multiple recipients. Email can be especially effective when team members have electronic handheld communications devices, such as smartphones, that allow email delivery. For team leaders who must rapidly share information to teams prior to job commencement or during job execution, email can be a very effective tool. There are some drawbacks to email, and some industries may not permit email transmission of certain types of sensitive information. While email often makes crafting and delivering messages easier than with traditional letter or memo formats, email writing should include the same level of diligence when the sender crafts the message that would be used with those other methods, particularly if critical information is going to be conveyed to a group of recipients.

- Instant messaging: Instant messaging has become a common form of communication and allows team leaders the ability to develop short messages that can reach numerous people. Younger employees who may have grown up using instant messaging (such as text messaging on cell phones) as a common form of communication may be very comfortable with this form of communication, while older generations of workers may not be as familiar. So, team leaders should use a bit of caution when communicating through text messaging, and should use it sparingly. Additionally, since the character length of many text message systems is generally short (approximately 160 characters), it may not be appropriate for longer messages.

- Social media: Like text messaging, many younger employees are very familiar with social media, and are adept at using this technology on smartphones. Additionally, since social media has become a means for sharing information among families, even older generations of workers may be familiar with social media platforms. Social media provides a means for sharing multiple forms of non-verbal information, including documents, photos, videos, and short messages. Social media is becoming a highly ubiquitous form of communication, and in some cases it may be appropriate to share operational information on social media platforms, particularly if the organization uses a secure login with limited access. However, for some organizations the use of this technology, particularly with operationally-sensitive information, may not be appropriate as a means of communication.

- Standard Operating Procedures (SOPs): SOPs can be a tremendously effective way of communicating information to team members. SOPs often provide standardized lists of information about operational tasks with descriptive content for the various jobs teams must perform. SOPs may provide written instructions and guidelines, safety requirements, information related to hazard controls for risk mitigation, communication techniques, equipment lists, and other information teams may use to plan and execute operational tasks. SOPs can help streamline communications by specifying certain task requirements in advance, and actions that must be performed at certain times during an operation. By pre-defining those tasks in a SOP and by requiring crews to either memorize the SOP contents or refer to it during operational execution, organizations and team leaders may be able to reduce communication requirements during job performance. SOPs must be well-written and well-understood by team members or they may cause confusion and actually increase communication requirements while jobs are underway as team members try to clarify information in real time.

- Signage: Signage can be a very important and effective tool for informing team members of critical safety requirements. Signs in the forms of warnings and cautions can alert teams of hazardous conditions and, if well-understood, can help team leaders convey information about job status when they are not present and without the need for verbal communications. Since team leaders cannot be in all places at all times, signage may be very effective for conveying important information. In order for signs to be useful, they should be easily visible (in multiple light and weather conditions), standardized so all team members can readily understand them, and their meaning learned by team members before task execution commences.

- Signals: Signals can take many forms, including signage, hand movements, arm movements, light or aural signals (such as flashlights, vehicle lights, or horns/sirens), or equipment positioning. In high-noise and/or distracting environments that often go hand-in-hand with high-hazard operations, signals can be an effective primary or backup communications method. For example, in crane operations where employees are moving a load, hand and arm signals may be critical. In some industries and operations radio communications may be the primary means of communication, but if radios fail, then it may be possible to revert to hand signals between crewmembers. Additionally, in aviation, ground crews often communicate with pilots through the use of standard signals with arm movements and while holding wands in their hands, and visual light signals may be used by air traffic control towers to communicate with pilots when radio failure occurs. In military air-to-air refueling operations light signals may be used to guide receiver aircraft into position to receive fuel while airborne. Team leaders must use caution, however, when considering specific signaling to use. Signals should be standardized so all team members understand their meaning. Otherwise, a signal that may be intended to have a certain message may be misinterpreted by team members, and in high-hazard operational environments, which often have thin margins for error, misinterpretation of signals could result in serious errors, injury to personnel, catastrophic failure of equipment, or mission degradation or failure. SOPs may be an effective way to standardize signals and provide a document that team members can study to ensure signal comprehension.

Non-verbal communication techniques have the capacity to enhance mission effectiveness and efficiency, and while there are some potential drawbacks, these strategies have numerous positive attributes as well. One of the major strengths associated with non-verbal communications is the capability to design the message ahead of time so that message clarity can be checked and verified. The multiple formats available for non-verbal communication make it a highly versatile form to convey messages. Additionally, it allows for a degree of operational efficiency, particularly when signals are taught to personnel and well-understood prior to implementation. Non-verbal communications can also be highly effective in low signal-to-noise environments, when it is difficult for team members to hear and understand verbal messages.

Despite these numerous strengths, there are several drawbacks to non-verbal communication techniques. While it may be true that non-verbal messages can be quite clear, the time requirements to develop written messages, ensure clarity, and distribute them can be a weakness, particularly if there is a great deal of urgency, such as a hazardous situation which must be handled immediately to mitigate the risk. Additionally, during abnormal operations or non-routine situations where uncertainties exist, a standardized signal may not exist to convey an appropriate message. In those cases, team leaders and team members may attempt to create their own signals, which could add confusion to the situation.

Another challenge with non-verbal communications is the level of team member attention. Some team members may not be willing to read long messages and, in many cases, signals require receivers to physically view the sender of the message, such as with hand signals. Non-verbal messages may not afford team leaders, or others who are developing and sending the messages, immediate feedback. Unlike verbal communication techniques, where the message sender may receive feedback in the form of questions, facial expressions, body language, or voice inflection, these responses are often unfeasible with non-verbal strategies. While it is possible to develop response signals to be used by team members to confirm their understanding, in some cases, such as with signs, it is not feasible to expect immediate feedback and confirmation of understanding.

In order to be effective, non-verbal communication techniques must be standardized and understanding on the part of team members should be verified. In some cases, such as with signals during high-hazard operations, rehearsal of signals may be required prior to actual implementation in the real-world operating environment. Finally, if team leaders are trying to develop and implement non-verbal communication techniques, it is essential to ensure that team members do not simply make up their own signals or gestures, which is why standardization is such an important part of communication strategy and technique development. This standardization will take consistent leadership and management, with the team leader acting in the leader–manager role to consistently maintain and enforce the standardized communication requirements.

So, with all these various types of communication strategies, which one is best? It really depends on the specific situation and the needs of the team. Many factors can affect communications and oftentimes the nature of the operational environment itself, the time available to develop and transmit a message, feedback requirements, and the level of team member skill and understanding of the job requirements will drive the specific type of communication strategies and techniques. To be thorough, team leaders should consider a range of communication approaches, which can be implemented by using a layered approach or a defense-in-depth approach. For example, requirements for the composition of a qualified crew, required equipment, and operational process flow may be included in a SOP book, with a standardized briefing guide to help team leaders ensure that all required pre-job activities have been completed prior to job execution. However, these written instructions may need to be verbalized with feedback from the team during a pre-mission or pre-operations briefing. This verbal delivery in a group setting may allow for immediate confirmation and feedback of the pre-defined written procedures or requirements. As an alternative example, in some operations, the team may rely on verbal communication techniques for the primary transmission of information, but use pre-defined signals in case escalating noise levels distort verbal messages. Table 4.1 summarizes the advantages and disadvantages of verbal and non-verbal communication.

Table 4.1   Verbal and non-verbal communication advantages and
             disadvantages

Types of Communication	Advantages	Disadvantages
Verbal	• Rapid message development • Can clarify on-the-fly • Allows for immediate feedback • Confirmation of message receipt	• Inability to truly edit, (once said it's said) • May cause confusion if message is not developed prior to the verbal communication • Potentially less effective in high-noise environments
Non-Verbal	• Message clarity if message crafted properly • Multiple forums and formats • Operational efficiency (speed of signals and gestures if rehearsed and understood) • Potentially more effective in high-noise environments (hand signals may be effective when the ability to hear is degraded)	• Length of time to develop a clear message • Receiver attention (receiver may not be willing to read long messages and may require receiver to see sender in some cases) • Lack of feedback • May require standardization, pre-job confirmation of understanding, rehearsal, and validation

Effective Communication Techniques

The unique characteristics associated with high-hazard environments place various communication responsibilities on both team leaders and team members. In this operational context, many tasks are deemed safety-critical and if not performed correctly, mission or task failure could result (Ericson 478). In many industries mission failure can result in catastrophic consequences to both the customer and the operator organization. Therefore, by understanding some techniques for communicating effectively, team leaders and team members alike may be equipped with methods to help increase the probability of mission success and the ability to properly convey mission-critical information during high-stress, high-hazard environments, even under conditions of uncertainty.

- Verbal communication techniques: Message clarity is essential, so when the sender is developing the message it helps to think through the intent of the message. When the sender is developing a verbal message it is imperative that he thinks before speaking.

While this sounds extremely simple it is often more complicated in practice, particularly when the message delivery is critical and time-sensitive in nature. By thinking through the message rapidly, including what the sender wants to convey and the feedback requirements, it may help increase the probability of proper understanding, reduce confusion, and decrease the need for repetition. In some dangerous situations there may not be much time to think through the message, particularly if personnel injury is imminent, and in those cases, sometimes basic language may be effective. Stop Work Authority (SWA) policies, which allow any employee witnessing an unsafe act to halt operations may help in these types of situations. However, in less hazardous situations, where danger is not imminent, taking a few extra seconds to think before speaking could make the difference between confusion and associated time delays, and understanding followed by efficient action. Additionally, it is helpful if the sender understands the signal-to-noise ratio, and adjusts the message based on the receivers' ability to hear and understand. If face-to-face communication is taking place, the sender may also look for facial expressions and body language to either confirm or refute understanding. Additionally, it will help all team members if backup communication techniques and methods are considered, and it should be the responsibility of team leaders to help identify these communication requirements and resources. For example, in high-noise environments team leaders can consider the use of headset communications systems that also reduce outside noises, and they should also consider the impacts of equipment breakdown, such as battery failure or complete radio failure. In these instances it may be necessary to have replacement batteries on hand and have a range of visual signals prepared for use (such as hand signals or light signals).

- Written communication techniques: While written communication techniques can be highly effective, there are certain attributes associated with some forms of written communications that may help them to be more effective at properly conveying important information.
    - SOPs can be an excellent method for standardizing and organizing operational and job-related safety information, but the content in SOPs and their development should not be taken for granted. As a team leader preparing for high-hazard operations you should consider the information required in

an SOP and work with any appropriate operations and safety staff members to help design an SOP that is comprehensive enough to include the required information to help teams perform their jobs safely and effectively, yet not so exhaustive in nature that it includes non-value-added information. As you design SOPs you should also seek ways to combine operations and safety requirements that are pertinent to the job(s) that will be performed, which may help centralize the key information in one place, without extraneous information cluttering the SOP document. If additional information is required, such as reference material, this information could be included as an appendix to the main SOP document. In this fashion, crews have quick access to critical information when immediately needed, but non-essential information or supporting resources are still accessible while not getting in the way of the most important information. SOPs can often include pre-job briefing templates, minimum crew requirements and qualifications, equipment and machinery requirements, safety requirements (such as PPE), other hazard controls (such as physical barriers or the use of machine guards), safety rules or boundaries, communication requirements, maximum crew day/work day limitations, emergency procedures, contact phone numbers, and other information related to how operations should be conducted. While this list is not all-inclusive it may provide some guidelines to help you, as an operational team leader, develop a SOP document. It should also be emphasized that SOPs should be reviewed and updated regularly to reflect the most up-to-date information.

– Emails can also be an effective means for written communication, but care should be taken before hitting the "send" button on the keyboard, tablet, or smartphone. As a team leader, when you write emails think through the message you wish to convey, write the message, then read through it. Afterwards, make any necessary edits, and then re-read the message before sending. If time permits and the information is not operationally-restricted, you may even consider having someone else read the message for clarity and understanding. That person could provide feedback to help ensure the message states what you intend to convey. This may be especially helpful before you send the "angry email." It is easy to hastily type an email message when angry, but once you send it, it is gone, and you cannot take it back. Even with the technology in some email programs that allows you to delete unread messages, there may still be a chance for the message to reach some people. A better strategy is to ensure you follow these guidelines before sending the message, time permitting.

– Policy letters and guidelines can be a helpful way to convey information to operational teams. These types of letters are often used to explain or clarify rules, which may be misunderstood or which have existed informally, but have not been explicitly stated for all team members and employees. Policy letters or guidelines that include information about job performance should be easy to understand and should serve to clarify any ambiguous information.

– Signage effectiveness can be improved if deliberate steps are taken to ensure the message is clear, easily understood by readers, and is conveyed to personnel throughout the organization. By following guidelines in signage standards, such as the American National Standards Institute Z535 *Safety Alerting Standards*, organizations may be able to standardize signage and improve the message delivery, and become more efficient by harmonizing signs and symbols across the organization.

– Checklists can be an extremely effective form of written communication and can be a simple way to operationalize safety into everyday activities. Checklists can be one of the simplest tools to use, yet they can be highly valuable for making operations more efficient, for detecting and reducing operational errors, and for improving operational safety. In high-hazard environments where operations are team-centric, checklists can be a powerful instrument for infusing safety into normal tasks and for helping team members handle abnormal situations and emergencies. Several methods may be used for designing and using checklists. One approach is to use checklists as an overall guide, where task items are reviewed after task completion to ensure tasks were not skipped. The operator may go back over the list of items to verify that each item was performed. In this fashion, the operator may perform tasks from memory, as opposed to following scripted procedures and if items were skipped, the team member may go back and complete them. A slightly more prescriptive approach includes using checklists as "do-lists," where each item on the list is reviewed, the task is then performed, and finally the checklist item is marked off or mentally accounted for. Another strategy is the Challenge-Action-Reply approach, which is when two team members work together on a checklist, where one crewmember calls out a checklist item, the other team member performs the task step (or action step) and then replies to the challenge step to confirm completion. A third approach is to use the Action-Challenge-Reply method, which is when team members perform their tasks or procedural steps, then once the tasks are complete one team member reads the checklist item and then the appropriate team members who performed the tasks reply to confirm task completion. The Action-Challenge-Reply method requires a high degree of training, proficiency, and standardization, particularly because it may involve performing several steps from memory. Checklists may be used during normal, abnormal, and emergency operations and should have clear, unambiguous language and steps. Additionally, team members should be trained on the use of checklists and how they relate to task performance, because the underlying operational tasks often require technical understanding. Checklists cannot simply be used as a crutch for poor performance, and as a team leader, if you desire to use checklists, you must ensure that team members are properly trained and evaluated on checklist usage.

- Signal techniques: Whether signaling is accomplished using hand, arm, light, or sound signals, or some other method, team leaders should ensure the meaning of each signal is understood by all team members involved in the operation. A lack of standardization and understanding may cause confusion and add chaos to high-hazard operations, where tasks are challenging enough on their own, yet are made much more difficult when this additional disorder is introduced. Signal reception and feedback by the receiver are also important factors, particularly in low signal-to-noise ratio environments, where hearing is difficult and where hearing protection is often used to reduce the effects of noise. Team leaders must ensure that both the sender and the receiver understand the requirements for feedback, and that signaling procedures include a way for team members to provide clear, unambiguous feedback and confirmation to each other.

- Feedback techniques: Team leaders can help increase the probability of successful communications, and subsequent mission success, by developing communications procedures that require the message sender to clearly state feedback requirements. This does not necessarily have to be done every time a message is developed, though. In many cases, when communication protocols are standardized and written (such as in SOP documents, rulebooks, or procedure/guideline documents), the feedback requirements may be explicitly stated in writing. In this case, each team member simply memorizes and understands the requirements for feedback (which should include training and evaluation to ensure comprehension of the applicable SOP or other documents). As team members become more proficient at communicating and realizing the importance of proper feedback, senders may realize that in some cases it is more effective to specifically state the feedback requirements or expectations in the message itself. For example, in an email the sender could include some closing language, such as, "Please respond to this email and confirm that you understand the tasks." Alternatively, during verbal communications, the sender can ask a simple question to verify comprehension, such as, "Do you understand?" While this may seem very elementary, confirmation and feedback are often taken for granted, and this is one reason why communications can be so abysmal in many organizations and can sometimes be a contributing factor in accidents and incidents. Team leaders can also create policies that require receivers to provide confirmation of message receipt and understanding even if the sender does not explicitly request it. For example, suppose one team member is reading a radio frequency channel to another team member, who will be required to tune to that frequency at a specific time during a high-hazard operation or critical task. If the receiver reads back the frequency to the sender, even without being asked, this is a way to confirm message receipt and proper comprehension.

Barriers to Effective Communications

While there are numerous strategies, techniques, and procedures for improving the effectiveness and the efficiency of communications, which teams then infuse into their operations through proper understanding of these approaches, there are a number of barriers that can negatively impact communications. In some cases these barriers are highly overt and other times they are latent within the organization and do not seem so obvious. As an operational team leader, you should take it upon yourself to remove or reduce these barriers as much as feasible.

One of the barriers to effective communications is a lack of requisite technical knowledge required for the specific work situation or operational environment. This knowledge may be required of employees and senior leaders alike, and without a basic level of understanding regarding the operational tasks and factors affecting execution it may be difficult for team leaders to properly communicate requirements and updated information to team members and senior personnel. Team members must be qualified, competent, and proficient at their jobs and have enough training to understand instructions related to job requirements. Senior organizational employees who may not be required to perform the operational tasks, but who are required to provide oversight checks on job status must have a basic understanding of the overall job requirements. It is also incumbent upon team leaders to possess the technical knowledge and communication skill level to be able to convey key information to personnel who do not possess a high-degree of technical knowledge, particularly if those personnel are providing oversight checks on job performance. This may involve translational skills where key information is communicated in easy-to-understand non-technical terms to those unfamiliar with the technical aspects of the job.

An additional barrier to effective communications is a boss or supervisor that is overly aggressive. Similarly, if the overall organizational culture supports leaders and managers that are overly aggressive, this can create a climate that blocks effective communication, particularly when it comes to sending and receiving effective feedback. When those in power positions exert their authority in ways that suppress feedback, particularly when that feedback opposes their views or formal policies, team members and other employees may become less likely to provide truthful and open feedback. A lack of honest responses can place team leaders in a very precarious position. It is highly unlikely that team leaders will be correct every time they make a decision, so truthful feedback is essential for effective communication and teamwork. Groupthink can also be an insidious barrier to effective communication and in many cases team members may not even know it exists. It can cause team members to view problems from one standpoint, and reduce the level of diversity needed for a comprehensive approach to problem solving. Even when others have opposing viewpoints to the group, they may be reluctant to communicate their differing views because of a fear of reprisal.

The operational environment itself can also create barriers that reduce the effectiveness of verbal and non-verbal communications. As previously described, high-noise environments can place employees in a position that makes it difficult to hear, and in these situations, when team leaders provide instructions or when team members attempt to coordinate tasks verbally, high-noise levels may block proper message reception. While noise is a recognizable distraction, there are other less-obvious distractions in the operational environment that may reduce the level of communication effectiveness. Heat, cold, and precipitation may make it harder for employees to concentrate during discussions and when they cannot concentrate they may miss important instructions. In high-hazard environments this could result in serious consequences. Many outdoor operations span large distances and include multiple worksites. These dispersed sites often result in increased travel time, and when personnel must be in the physical presence of each other to communicate effectively, this can degrade communications. In time-sensitive situations where risks must be handled immediately this distance and travel time could adversely impact risk mitigation and operational decision making. Similarly, the location of a plant or business unit in relation to sub-units or divisions can create barriers to communication and feedback. If a main office is centrally located in one area, but sub-units where operations take place are dispersed across hundreds or thousands of miles, unless an effective communication and feedback structure is designed in multiple written and verbal formats, significant breakdowns in communication can occur. This may be especially true in organizations that have centralized authority structures and require each business unit to report information up the chain of command, which can overwhelm communication structures and delay needed feedback.

Just as the physical location of plants or business headquarters and business units can complicate communications, team structure and design may cause similar problems. Team structure can impact effective communications and if the physical and mental demands placed on team leaders exceed their capabilities, breakdowns in communication and team control can result. For example, if the span of control is so large that team leaders are required to constantly move from place to place to supervise multiple team members, they may miss critical messages, particularly if radio, telephone, or other remote verbal communication systems are not used. This is why it is important to manage team structures and to develop FLs who can assist when problems arise. Additionally, by empowering team members using decentralized leadership, such as through the creation of sub-team leaders, the span of control requirements and the demands on the team leader may be decreased.

If teams are broken down into numerous groups, yet these groups are frequently isolated from each other (either through distance or job function) this could lead to communication barriers as a result of group competition or the "us versus them" mentality. One of the best examples is the classic "maintenance versus operations" struggle. In these situations, the maintenance group often perceives the operations group to be comprised of employees who don't care if they damage equipment. When the damaged equipment arrives in their maintenance bays to be repaired, they may feel insulted because the "careless operators" broke the equipment they work so hard to keep in proper operating condition. Conversely, the operations personnel may feel that the maintainers do not understand what it is like to work under the demanding schedules and production pressure to get the job done and when equipment is not available due to parts order backlogs or other maintenance delays line operators may simply think maintenance personnel are inept at repair work. As a team leader, if you oversee multiple functional units within your team, you must strive to keep your teams cohesive. One strategy to build cohesiveness is to frequently gather all personnel together for group discussions, which may help build a shared understanding, or through cross-functional job sharing where employees from one group work with another group for short periods of time.

Formal rules and local management policies related to communication and information transmission may also cause barriers to effective communication. Organizations may specify ways information can be transmitted to and from certain departments, and this is often necessary to avoid information overload and to provide for a degree of order and structure. However, if information transmission policies are overly restrictive this could result in the inability of team members to send information or receive feedback in a timely manner. For example, let's suppose a purchasing or supply order department has a policy stating that supply requests must be faxed to a certain fax number, and in this case on Thursday afternoon a time-sensitive job is scheduled for the weekend. The operational team logistics specialist who will be working on the weekend job faxes the request for supplies and calls to confirm receipt. Since it is late in the afternoon the supply associate has left for the day and happens to have the next day off. At this point there is no way of obtaining the required feedback to determine if the request was received and processed. As a team leader you can see how this type of overly bureaucratic communication policy can impede operations and cause confusion. If organization or department rules are overly bureaucratic, they can impede effective operations and in this example, if there were alternative (or additional) ordering methods, such as voice or Internet-ordering procedures, this problem may have been alleviated.

The previous example emphasizes the need for multiple communication formats and also highlights the need for jobs and operations to be planned using a system approach. When organizations are not treated as systems, local policies can impact other departments and teams, even if they do not ostensibly appear to be immediately connected. When organizations fail to function as systems, where each department is interconnected with the others, isolation can occur. When departments or business units are either formally or informally isolated they may begin to take on a life of their own, and in some cases the personnel in the departments end up spending time defending their departments and fighting organizational "turf wars." Ultimately, if this type of isolation occurs it can take a great deal of strong leadership to break down the walls and to help department leaders and staff members understand the need for effective communication between departments and units. As a team leader you should guard against this type of isolation and take action to avoid it before it happens, or to remedy the situation if this isolation has already begun to take hold.

Removing communication barriers, or at least reducing the frequency of occurrence and the ways they can occur can help operational teams become much more effective at their jobs, thereby improving team and organizational performance in production, quality, safety, and reliability. Operational team leaders may have limited amounts of control and influence on organizational communication barriers, but at a minimum they can limit these barriers within their teams. By taking these actions at the operational team level team leaders can improve operational efficiency, and other leaders in the organization may witness their example and model their behavior.

Information Flow in Operational Teams

Even if leaders at the operational team level or the organization as a whole implement strategies to improve specific communication elements, the way information flows can still impact the results. Even if the level of clarity with the message is high, without a proper structure and framework for information flow, operations and safety performance may be impeded. For example, the developer or sender of the message must understand the target receiver audience. If the receiver audience is actually a group of people, the sender should understand which person or group the feedback needs to originate from. The sender needs to understand the process flow or path the message will follow once he or she transmits the message. This is particularly true for written messages, such as through email communication. If there is a way the message may be impeded, delayed, or distorted along the way this could cause serious problems for the sender. As an example, consider an operational team leader who is developing a pre-operations briefing the afternoon before a high-hazard job is to be conducted by an on-call field engineering crew.

The crew is geographically dispersed and will be flying into the job location that evening. The team leader wants the crew to be prepared when they arrive on the job site the next day so he sends the briefing information to each team member through email. However, he realizes that he is missing the email address for three personnel. So, he asks several other team members (who apparently know the email addresses) to forward the briefing information to those three employees. He finishes the briefing document and sends out the message before driving to the airport to travel to the job location. He has no way of knowing if the team members will receive the information, nor did he specify feedback requirements. Also, he did not confirm that each team member had the required document viewing software to read the document. Is this effective communication? Even if the team leader wrote the most amazing, detailed, and informative crew briefing, if the message does not make it to the appropriate receivers then the answer is probably "no."

While you may not work in a field engineering environment, you may be able to come up with your own examples. This theoretical case highlights the necessity of proper information channels and message flow. Organizations that truly want to develop consistent effective communications should consider designing systems to help ensure message flow and delivery channels and that messages are readable by all required receivers. Using the field engineering example, the organization could design web-connected Information Systems for distributing the job briefing information. If the team member information (including email addresses) was preloaded into the Information Systems, the team leader could upload the briefing, and the system could automatically distribute the information to the team members. The Information System could even include simple instructions telling employees how to provide feedback and confirm they have read and understood the crew briefing information, as well as how to ask questions or to seek clarification on ambiguous information. This is just one example, and as operational team leaders seeking to improve information accuracy and transmission in your organizations, you may consider additional or different methods, and work with your organizations to design new communication methodologies that help assure proper information flow.

Abbreviating and Streamlining Communications

One of the potential drawbacks, or unintended consequences, of strategies that attempt to improve communication effectiveness may be the overdevelopment of information requirements. As organizations examine ways to improve message development and delivery they may begin introducing more and more information requirements in an effort to further improve communications. This is understandable. After all, if a little bit of quality information is good, then a lot of quality information must be great, right? This is not always the case, though. In many cases layering unnecessary information on top of verbal or written messages can actually degrade effective communication. One of the challenges faced by operational team leaders is understanding the proper balance between effective message development, including the necessary information requirements, and the efficiency of message delivery and usage. If the information is too detailed or cumbersome crews or teams may not pay attention to or use the information, yet if adequate detail and information is lacking, it could place team members in jeopardy if critical safety-related information is omitted. The potential impacts could be exacerbated in high-hazard environments, where information related to hazards and mitigation strategies is essential for safe operational performance.

So, what is a team leader to do when faced with the need to meet operational efficiency targets, which result from the daily production pressure, while trying to maintain adequate information distribution? Streamlining message length while requiring crews to be familiar with information ahead of time is one strategy, and SOPs offer potential solutions. As previously stated, SOPs can be highly effective at including the right kind and amount of information. SOPs may also be used to streamline information by including administrative hazard controls in the form of standardized phraseology and pre-defined checklist confirmation/feedback requirements. For example, while a two-person crew, which is part of the operational team, performs a job, standardized checklists may be used to ensure the job is completed accurately and within safety parameters. The SOP could require one crewmember to make certain statements when work is conducted and the other crewmember to state specific feedback to confirm the status of certain tasks and safety requirements, such as verifying equipment is set up in proper, safe modes or conditions, and that each task step is verified to be completed safely and correctly. This way, the pre-defined checklist challenge and reply statements that have been designed into the SOP help teams to maintain positive control over the operation, to verify jobs are performed safely, accurately, and according to procedures, and to provide appropriate feedback between team members in real-time. Using this concept these types of activities may be incorporated into SOPs. Teams should be required to read and understand the SOP items, and then should be evaluated in the operational environment using these SOP items in practice. If the procedures are well-defined, and practiced/rehearsed by employees, and the employees are evaluated in practice to ensure understanding, SOPs may be used as a reference point to reduce the need for information requirements prior to jobs commencing. In some cases, extraneous communications during job execution can result in distractions and breakdowns in concentration, focus, and attention, and by using SOPs in this manner they can help streamline information and reduce this need for superfluous communications during job execution. When using this approach, organizations should conduct periodic reevaluations to ensure team members do not deviate from or forget SOP requirements over time.

While this list is not exhaustive, it provides some examples of how communications may be streamlined while still maintaining appropriate levels of safety. SOPs can be used to help teams understand operational and safety-critical information. Team leaders and the operations and safety departments should understand and continuously improve communications requirements and procedures so that essential information is transmitted effectively, yet is balanced to help teams achieve their safety and work objectives within the existing operational constraints. A well-developed team briefing and effective communication and information sharing is a key component to safe operations. Accurate information sharing prior to operations can help set the stage for successful work performance and hazard awareness. By taking a bit more time developing a proper message and ensuring accurate delivery and feedback prior to job commencement, operational team leaders may be able to save themselves, and the organization as a whole, a great deal of time by reducing the likelihood of accident occurrence and/or limiting the consequences of an accident if one does occur through the effective use of communications.

Conclusions

Communication is an integral component of everyday life, but effective communication is not easy. The need for effective communication is often understated, and oftentimes team leaders and employees simply assume that effective communication exists. While there are many types of verbal and non-verbal communication strategies and techniques, the specific level of effectiveness and appropriateness depends on the operational environment and the unique situation. It is essential to understand that all elements of the communication cycle (the sender, receiver, message, and feedback) are critical components required for proper information transmission. Organizational barriers and human barriers can both impede communications and leaders must work to break down, reduce, and remove these barriers or information transmission will be highly inconsistent.

One of the critical activities operational team leaders must perform is a consistent reevaluation of communications requirements as a whole and the changing dynamics of the operational environment to help ensure communication is continuous and that its effectiveness is constantly maintained. The need for effective communication should not be understated, as it directly impacts operations and safety. Team leaders that deliberately emphasize communication quality at all levels of the information creation and distribution cycle will be in a better position to proactively manage safety than those who simply view communication as an after-thought that occurs once operations commence.

Chapter 5
Focus on Operations and Safety

When teams perform operational tasks in high-hazard environments they are often exposed to such high levels of stress, fatigue, and distractions that maintaining a constant focus on task performance becomes extremely challenging. Additionally, as the time required to complete a job expands and as teams work relentlessly to accomplish their mission, the attention to safety can sometimes take a back seat to getting the job done. While teams may not intentionally deemphasize safety, mental and physical fatigue and the "tunnel vision" focus on job completion can reduce their ability to adequately recognize and control risks.

The high-hazard nature of many operational environments can include error-inducing factors, and placing crews in a position to anticipate and prevent errors before they happen, or, if unable to prevent them, to detect and correct errors before they cascade into deeper consequences is necessary for safe and effective operations performance. To prevent and manage errors, and maintain appropriate levels of safety, teams must be able to establish an initial focus on operational task and hazard control requirements and must maintain this focus from the beginning to the end of the job. By designing strategies to help teams focus on safe task execution, and by designing work systems to reduce the likelihood of error, team leaders and organizations can improve their potential for safe and successful mission outcomes.

Human Error in High-Hazard Environments

In many modern industries, particularly those that use ultra-safe systems for their operational processes, the level of quality and safety of equipment and tools may be so high that the statistical probability of an accident resulting from equipment failure may be less than an accident resulting from human error. However, although human error is often referred to as the cause of accidents and failures, in many cases human error is actually the result of other systemic factors. Fatigue, inadequate task design, poor communication, environmental factors (such as heat, cold, humidity, and precipitation), and inadequate team coordination, employee qualification, and task proficiency can each contribute to errors during job execution. These errors can then lead to incidents and accidents.

While organizations and team leaders often attempt to reduce human error potential by reminding team members to pay more attention and keep their minds on their tasks, these recommendations are often easier said than done. Additionally, employees may perceive those kinds of statements as empty words from bureaucrats who do not understand what it is like to perform dangerous or high-stress work on the front lines and at the sharp end. A more comprehensive strategy that attempts to reduce error potential by designing work systems that minimize hazards and enhance the ability of employees to succeed at task performance may place team members in a better position to mitigate errors.

Due to the nature of the work that takes place in numerous high-hazard environments, team members are exposed to a variety of factors that make them more disposed to error-inducing conditions. One of the influencers of error-shaping conditions is the amount of manual work required by team members (*Keeping Patients Safe* 62). When humans are involved in task performance and are required to manipulate tools, instruments, or equipment to accomplish a job, there is a potential for error. This isn't to say that automated systems aren't prone to error, and in some cases humans may actually be more capable than automated systems of adapting and handling abnormal conditions. However, as a general rule, when team members must perform manual work, the potential for numerous types of error exists. An additional factor that may influence the possibility of error is the level of consequence associated with poor performance (*Keeping Patients Safe* 62). When team members understand that poor performance can have serious consequences, this can create extremely challenging and stressful situations. Environmental and physiological factors, such as heat, cold, and fatigue can also increase error potential. Additionally, extremely difficult tasks, particularly those that require skills beyond the level of the team members, can introduce error potential into the operational environment (Chapanis 119). Another factor is the job design itself and how employees are required to work around hazards. When employees are required to perform their tasks while exposed to hazards, and must create their own procedures to avoid those hazards (such as manipulating their bodies to avoid sharp objects), this can lead to distractions during operations and increase error potential. Also, the nature of the work environment itself often requires employees to perform tasks in awkward and uncomfortable positions, creating additional error-inducing conditions.

There are also factors associated with the level of task loading and time available to perform those tasks that can influence error potential. When operators are required to accomplish procedures with high task loading in limited amounts of time it places unique pressures on them to fit the tasks into the time available. This increases the potential for mistakes in task execution or for steps to be unintentionally omitted. Alternatively, while it may not seem as obvious, low task loading can potentially induce errors. When team members are required to perform only a few minor steps over the course of a long job, it can result in unintentional complacency.

As a team leader reading this information what you may realize is that these are situations you and your teams face on a regular basis. This is often the nature of everyday work in high-hazard environments. Despite the high-hazard nature of the work, teams are faced with these circumstances every day and are placed in a position where they must adapt to their environments. While the optimal way of reducing this error potential may be to design the work system, tools, and equipment so that hazards are engineered out of the system, operators do not normally have that option, particularly in "legacy" systems that have been in operation for many years. Additionally, in many operations, the environment itself cannot be changed, so the human must adapt. Failure to adapt to the environmental and work conditions and to perform at peak levels may result in errors that cascade and grow, eventually leading to mission failure, and in many operations this is simply not an option.

Situational Awareness

One of the ways job designers and team leaders often try to reduce human error is by teaching the errant operators about the need for better situational awareness. Situational awareness can be a very difficult concept to understand and leaders often do not really know what they mean when they tell employees to have better situational awareness. It seems to have become an overused term and is often misused by those who lack understanding of its meaning and the follow-on implications on work systems. In simple terms situational awareness is "the degree of accuracy by which one's perception of the current environment mirrors reality" (NATOPS *General Flight and Operating Instructions* 3–18). Using this definition, when team members are told to improve their situational awareness, they are basically left trying to figure out how to increase the accuracy of their perception of the world and their operational environment. Does this sound like an easy task? Many leaders do think it is easy, and tell their team members to pay more attention and stay focused, expecting situational awareness to improve. While improved attention and focus are noteworthy goals, because of the aforementioned factors that shape error-producing conditions, they are not simple to achieve, and simply being told to pay more attention will not likely result in dramatic improvements in team performance. High levels of situational awareness require the team to understand the individual operational elements and tasks that take place during job execution, comprehend how those individual elements relate to team performance and objectives, and anticipate what will happen in the near future. Essentially team members must understand what is going on in the immediate operational environment and mentally project how their tasks will unfold over time, what the impacts will be in the near future, and how those impacts will affect them individually and how they will affect the extended team.

Task overloading, task underloading, poor task design, task demands that exceed team members' capabilities, complex technology, and unmitigated hazards can all work against the team and can reduce team members' abilities to understand the status of their work and the impact their work will have on future tasks. Additionally, when team members become extremely busy and succumb to the distractions inherent in high-hazard environments it can become harder to stay focused on the specific task at hand and to consider the impacts on future performance. It can also be extremely difficult for team members to maintain proper job focus while handling the distractions of the operational environment, including the pain and fatigue associated with awkward body positioning as they attempt to avoid hazards, and the demands made by other team members who may need help with their tasks. All of these distractions can reduce team members' abilities to maintain high levels of awareness.

While we often like to think we are great at multi-tasking, in reality task performance may be degraded when team members must divide their attention during the course of normal work. In many high-hazard operations it may be uncommon for employees to be able to conduct work without some form of distraction that requires them to shift from task to task. Additionally, when faced with unexpected or abnormal situations that may not have been anticipated, this can cause a great deal of confusion. However, "maintaining a high level of situational awareness will better prepare crews to respond to unexpected situations" (*NATOPS General Flight and Operating Instructions* 3–18). So, when teams understand their actions, and how their actions impact the overall job, they may be in a better position to adapt when job conditions change. But how are team members supposed to accomplish this? The answer may have a lot to do with work system and procedure design, training, and proficiency.

One way teams may be able improve their ability to focus on tasks while contending with the challenges, distractions, and error-inducing conditions present in the operational environment is through the use of standardized procedures and by ensuring team members have a high level of proficiency at their specific tasks. By using well-trained and proficient team members who execute well-defined and standardized procedures operational team leaders may be able to achieve more consistent performance because these crews will be in a better position to maintain focus despite the distractions. When team members are competent at their jobs and follow standardized procedures, the collective understanding of the overall team may be raised, which can help to improve focus on the tasks at hand, as well as overall attention and awareness. Unexpected conditions emerge quite regularly during high-hazard operations, requiring teams to deal with threats to safety and performance, and when they are highly proficient at their tasks and procedures, they may be in a better position to adapt and maintain focus on task execution while anticipating the effects on the overall team. Also, by designing the work system to include detailed planning, communication, and information sharing, team leaders may begin to create a shared understanding between team members, which may help to reduce errors and confusion, and which may also help to reduce the need for extraneous communication (which can be a distraction by itself).

An additional strategy to improve the design of work systems is to help team members cope with distractions, provide ways to help them deal with the stress of production pressure and high task loading, and give them a means of relief when the distractions, stresses, and operational hazards exceed their ability to handle these issues. This is a key requirement for team leaders in high-hazard environments. They must understand that not all crewmembers will handle these challenges in the same way and some may need more help than others. By designing and integrating tools and strategies into the actual work system, team leaders may be able to help teams maintain consistent and stable functioning through small adaptations and changes during job execution, which is preferable to complete breakdowns in performance. This process includes two strategies: Focus Aids, and Pause-To-Assess (PTA) activities.

- Focus Aids: Team members can become distracted and lose focus due to a number of factors. In some cases, distractions may be in the form of other team members requesting information or assistance. In other cases the distractions could be due to conditions associated with the operational environment itself, such as temperature extremes, low light conditions, changing work conditions, or unrecognized hazards. Regardless of the nature of the distraction, the ultimate effect is often the same; team members may forget what they were doing, commit errors (such as performing task steps incorrectly), or omit task steps. The end result could include safety incidents, accidents, or mission failure. Focus Aids may help crewmembers to handle distractions and refocus on their tasks, perhaps minimizing variances between their perception of the environment compared to what is actually happening, thereby helping teams to maintain higher levels of situational awareness. Focus Aids can come in many forms and although the type may be limited by the safety rules set forth by the organization, imagination and creativity can go a long way in helping team leaders and work system designers develop these tools to help improve situational awareness. Some examples of Focus Aids include timers and alarms (such as on digital watches) to help alert teams when a certain amount of time has elapsed, checklists, which may help teams stay cognizant of the steps that were completed (and those which remain), engineering controls that attempt to mitigate hazards and protect team members through various methods, such as temporary barriers or guards, and even verbal backup strategies, which may include assigning one or more team members the duty of reminding the team when to get back on task, the steps that had been performed, and the steps that remain.

- Load-Shedding: While this may be seen as a strategy of its own, load-shedding is related to Focus Aids. While this strategy is often used to describe reducing an electrical load, the concept of load-shedding may be used in a team-performance context. During high-stress work, team members can reach a point where they are doing so much that they can't keep up with all their tasks. Simply put, they "have too much on their plate," which can lead to lapses in performance, and in high-hazard operations this can lead to extremely negative consequences. When certain team members become so overwhelmed with task performance requirements, particularly during abnormal or emergency situations, they may assign some of their duties to other team members, thereby reducing their cognitive and physical load, which may help them refocus on their specific activities.

- PTA Activity: During the course of operational execution, abnormal and unexpected events can occur which place unique stresses on team members and although these situations may require immediate attention, the normal tasks may still need to be performed or at least monitored. Teams do not always have the ability to stop work and leave the job area when unexpected events occur. Whether a medical team is working on a patient, an electrical utility line crew is working to restore electrical power during a storm, or an oil rig crew is drilling for oil, when unexpected or abnormal situations occur, the teams must often remain on-site, dealing with the potential crisis while also tending to the normal tasks, or at least monitoring the normal tasks to ensure they do not exacerbate the abnormal situation. In some cases, it may not even be an abnormal situation that causes teams to be distracted. It could be the cumulative effect of fatigue, routine minor hazards, environmental conditions (such as heat, cold, precipitation, or humidity), noise, or the increasing demands of the work tasks themselves that place team members in a position where they are stretched to their mental and physical limits. In these situations it may be feasible for crews to conduct a PTA activity where they pause momentarily to assess the situation, regroup, conduct load-shedding and task distribution if able, handle the abnormal situation, and then recommence normal work at the appropriate time. The PTA activity gives them a short reprieve so they can gain some "breathing room" and temporarily cope with the situation, make immediate, time-sensitive decisions regarding how to handle the uncertain or abnormal event as well as decisions about normal task activities, and proceed with the newly adapted plans. In some cases, the PTA activity may not be appropriate, such as when extremely dangerous situations occur and work must be completely stopped. To help crews handle those types of situations organizations should consider implementing a Stop Work Authority (SWA) policy, which provides employees with the ability to call a halt to work during dangerous conditions.

Figure 5.1 shows an example of how Focus Aids and the PTA activity process could be used during operations. These lines demonstrate conceptually the difference in performance with and without Focus Aids, and while this diagram is notional and not based on actual performance data, it serves to illustrate how Focus Aids and PTA activities may be used to maintain consistent performance.

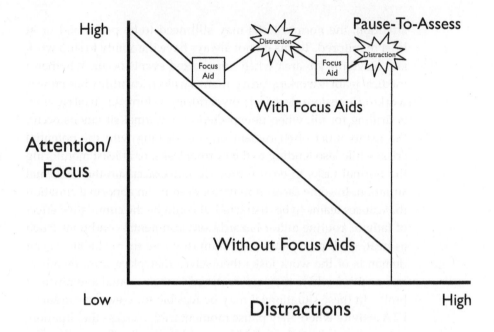

Figure 5.1   Operational performance with Focus Aids and PTA activity
Note: This figure is illustrative only and does not reflect actual reference data.

In Figure 5.1, let's suppose a cell tower maintenance crew is conducting maintenance work on a tower during an extremely hot day. Despite their detailed planning, some aspects of the job do not go as planned. After one of the technicians has climbed the tower and commenced work he realizes that he needs additional tools and supplies or, perhaps due to the pressure to get the job started, some tools were simply forgotten. He must stop work and coordinate with team members to retrieve the supplies. He is also fatigued from the climb and the heat, and perspiration is a further distraction. After beginning work these distractions are compounded when he realizes that he needs additional equipment and supplies. In this case, Focus Aids, such as a checklist or working with another team member who can help him remember where he left off in the task steps, may help him regain focus and attention, thereby increasing his level (and the team's level) of situational awareness. If the distractions were to continue to the point where he lost the ability to maintain focus on basic tasks the team could conduct the PTA activity to regroup. As a team leader you may consider your own examples of situations similar to this, and ways to use Focus Aids and PTA activities.

Team leaders must also ensure that any strategies and administrative tools they design to help maintain focus are in line with the operational and safety goals of the organization and that they do not violate any safety protocols or rules. Techniques for maintaining focus and situational awareness should be developed as part of the work system and should include input from team members and representatives from multiple departments in the organization (including safety and operations) to help verify they are designed properly and that unintended consequences that may be introduced into the operating environment are minimized. Teams should avoid creating a greater hazard than already exists through the introduction of non-validated techniques and procedures, which can further decrease focus and reduce situational awareness. This would defeat the purpose of the Focus Aids, so these tools should be vetted through appropriate processes.

In order to effectively use some of these strategies, particularly the PTA activity, team leaders and members must be able to recognize when situational awareness has degraded to the point where intervention is required. If these concepts are used regularly and integrated into normal activities, it may be feasible to reduce the likelihood of serious situational awareness degradation, but teams must still be prepared to face those types of encounters in case they do occur. Recognizing when situational awareness has diminished is an extremely difficult skill to develop, yet it is an essential trait team leaders must possess if they are to effectively deal with degraded focus during task execution. If teams fail to recognize when situational awareness has slipped to the point where they can no longer focus on the basic tasks necessary to maintain safe operational control, there is little chance they will be able to recover from these conditions without some type of mission loss, whether it be in the form of personnel injury or accidents, equipment damage, or the failure to accomplish the job requirements.

One strategy teams can adopt is to develop and use a mnemonic or acronym to help them know what to do when they encounter circumstances that begin to reduce the level of team or individual focus. Mnemonics are a form of memory aid that can help team leaders and employees rapidly recall the steps of a procedure. One key to correcting lapses in attention and focus is to detect attention drift early and to use strategies and techniques to bring team members' focus back to the task at hand, to help them understand what is happening in the current state, and to help them anticipate how their actions will impact the team in the near future. One mnemonic is the R–A–R acronym, which stands for Recognize–Admit–Request. The R–A–R strategy may be used individually and as part of a team-based approach where team members look for signs of confusion or reduced awareness in their coworkers.

- Recognize: If team members do not recognize when situational awareness has slipped, how can they adjust their activities and actions to improve it? Team members must recognize in themselves when the operational environment is placing excessive demands on their ability to perform their work. They should also be adept at recognizing this process in their coworkers, particularly if their tasks are tightly integrated or if they work in close proximity to each other. Having a team with a balanced level of experience and expertise may help facilitate the process of recognizing loss of focus and attention by other team members. An additional strategy to help teams recognize when attention has slipped is to compare what is actually happening in the operational environment with what was expected, planned, and/or briefed. Then, teams can determine the variances and examine potential causes of the differences. This can help teams make sense of the situation, and oftentimes it can require a group effort to put the pieces of the mental puzzle together to determine what is different, why it is different, what can be done to proceed safely with the operation, and who needs to be notified about the situation. An additional strategy teams can use to help recognize when awareness may be degraded is to identify areas where task saturation or other factors may be causing a loss of focus. By knowing oneself, knowing each other, and looking out for each other team members can take on a shared approach to keeping situational awareness levels high.

- Admit: In order to correct degraded focus and to raise levels of situational awareness, team members must admit to themselves and/ or to other team members that their attention is lapsing, their focus on the task at hand has slipped, and they are not sure exactly what they should be doing at that moment. Team members should avoid being dismissive if they feel like they are losing focus and that their awareness of their surroundings has slipped. They should also avoid being dismissive if their fellow coworkers attempt to explain this. From a personal standpoint, admitting to oneself that attention has been lowered to the point where help is needed may not be easy, and challenging other team members and confronting them about degraded attention and focus can be extremely difficult, particularly when more senior and experienced employees are confronted by junior employees. In order for team members to admit to themselves or to call each other out when focus and awareness has declined organizations must build a trusting and nurturing environment.

If trust is low, or if admitting that situational awareness has been reduced is viewed as a sign of weakness by the team or organization, team members may be less willing to acknowledge this and declare it to others. In high-hazard operations it is essential that the organizational safety culture be shaped in a way that builds trust and camaraderie between team members.

- Request: Team members should ask for assistance from other team members or team leaders to help rebuild their levels of situational awareness. This could mean calling in a FL for advice or assistance, such as a technical supervisor to check the quality and status of a job, or requesting resources, such as supplies, tools, reference manuals, radios, or any other equipment that may help teams make sense of the situation and determine what needs to happen next. Additionally, since confusion often results when focus has been degraded, when team members request resources from others, they should attempt to explain what they do not understand about the situation and request specific assistance if able. Conversely, in many situations, individuals may not recognize when they have lost focus and may not even understand when task performance is taking a turn for the worse. This is why effective teamwork is so important and why it is critical for team members to back each other up and call each other out when they witness attention slipping and errors being committed. Just like admitting that focus has been degraded, requesting help should be seen as a sign of strength, and leaders from the operational team leader level all the way to the top of the organization should help employees understand that they are expected to ask for help if needed. In some organizations asking for help may be seen by employees as a sign of weakness, so team leaders and the organization as a whole need to be sensitive to this and develop policies that encourage team members to ask for help when focus has been degraded.

Initial and Ongoing Focus

Up to this point, the discussion surrounding situational awareness, focus, and attention has largely been oriented on the execution phase of operations. This is largely because when situational awareness starts to slip it is often noticed during task execution, even if the decline has started earlier. Focusing and maintaining attention on operations and safety actually begins during the job planning phase and continues throughout the operation until the job is completed. Using a thorough and effective plan prior to the operational briefing and prior to job commencement often develops the initial focus. The plan sets the framework for follow-on operational execution and provides structure around the operations requirements to help ensure proper resources are identified, sourced, and allocated.

A thorough and well-developed plan helps set teams up for success. A comprehensive plan should not only include human and material resources, but should also include detailed hazard identification, assessment, and mitigation strategies (in the form of hazard controls). In this fashion, plans help team leaders cover both operations and safety requirements, which are integral to mission success. This overarching plan for operational and safety performance helps to build situational awareness and shared expectations before the job commences, thereby helping team members focus on their jobs when work begins. The pre-operations plan (or pre-job plan) should also be used as input to the pre-operations team brief, which is typically a presentation conducted by either the team leader or a senior team member that describes each critical aspect of the work to be performed, safety requirements, and an overall timeline and description of the operation. After the team is briefed, each team member should have a very clear understanding of their role in the operation, what is expected of them, how they should interact with other team members, communications requirements, hazard controls and other safety requirements, and what to do in the event certain emergencies occur. This pre-operations brief helps teams to set their initial focus and begins the process of developing situational awareness.

Part of the team briefing should include a description of the procedures or tasks to be accomplished during each phase of work, as well as the hazards associated with those tasks. By describing the hazards in this fashion, team members can begin to develop a mental picture of what the job will be like and the work conditions they should expect to see. Hazard identification is a critical component of pre-operational planning and briefing because, without proper assessment of risks, mitigation techniques may fall short of actual safety requirements, exposing employees to unacceptable levels of risk. This lack of proper safety oversight may also contribute to overall loss because unmitigated hazards can reduce team member focus or attention, increase distractions, and reduce situational awareness. Lower levels of focus can exacerbate the hazardous situations and without the proper hazard controls in place may lead to injury, equipment damage, or fatal accidents. On the other hand, when a rigorous hazard analysis and risk assessment process is conducted, where risks are identified by their constituent hazard components (probability of occurrence and consequence), team members are often in a much better position to maintain a higher level of focus. When proper hazard controls have been implemented, team members often have at least one fewer distraction, allowing them to place more of their attention on completing their assigned work rather than trying to figure out how to maintain their own safety while simultaneously performing their jobs. While safety is an ongoing individual and team responsibility and team members should always look out for their personal safety and each others' safety, a rigorous safety approach to operational planning should include ways to reduce risks by implementing various levels of hazard controls so that the individual team members are not solely responsible for mitigating operational risks.

After the initial focus on operations and safety has been establish and work commences, situation updates should be shared across the team to those members who may be affected by others' work. In many complex, high-hazard operations, the work done by one team member can directly impact the work performed by another team member, particularly when there is a high-degree of interdependency between tasks and when tasks are conducted in stages. For example, if Task 2 cannot be started until Task 1 has been completed, variances in Task 1 can directly impact Task 2 and the team member performing Task 2. The situation can be further compounded if Task 2 is commenced in parallel with Task 1, particularly if changes are not briefed in real time. Generally speaking, the higher the complexity of tasks and task interdependence, the greater the impacts changes may have on the overall operation. Using the situation update model, changes that are made in real-time should be considered critical pieces of information, which may create a need to re-brief the team with the changes and status updates. Unbriefed changes may inhibit ongoing focus and overall awareness about what needs to happen and may reduce shared awareness across the team. Additionally, as new hazards occur, or as previously-identified hazards change, real-time awareness, assessment, and mitigation will be required to protect the team and equipment. Individual team members and the team as a whole should conduct self and team assessments and use the R–A–R process as a guiding refrain to help them determine their level of focus, maintain awareness of changes, inform team members of changes or confusion in task execution, and request additional resources. As a team leader supervising operational activities you must maintain an ongoing awareness of task status and hazards, changes to the plan based on the actual operating environment, and an anticipation of how your team's activities will impact the overall job and potentially other related jobs being performed by other teams. Particularly, if your span of control is large, utilizing sub-team leaders (such as lower echelon supervisors) and proactive team members who recognize the need for deliberate individual and team-based focus and awareness strategies may help reduce some of the oversight burden, thereby improving your ability to coordinate team actions.

Anticipation of Outcomes and Projecting Task Impacts into the Future

One of the more challenging, but essential requirements for team members and team leaders is to understand current and ongoing activities and actions, and then anticipate how those actions will impact the specific task at hand, the work other team members are performing, and the operation as a whole. So far we have described how numerous types of conditions can result in attention lapses and the importance of focusing on the work being performed, but when team members mindfully work to concentrate, focus, and pay attention to their specific ongoing tasks, they may lose sight of the downstream impacts of their work. If it can be that difficult to maintain focus on the activities at hand, how can team members possibly be expected to expand their overall awareness of the current and future situations to ensure that operations continue to be conducted safely and that the end-state at job completion will be what they imagined and intended when the job was planned? As a team leader, aren't you already asking enough of your teams by requiring them to maintain focus and attention on their ongoing work? Although this overall awareness and anticipation of the future activities and end-states may seem like a daunting task, it is essential that teams and team leaders understand this skill and work to develop it as an individual and team-based performance characteristic, particularly in high-hazard environments. In those unforgiving settings small changes, unmitigated hazards, and errors that are allowed to cascade can have significant downstream impacts and may lead to many forms of loss.

While team members may not always understand the ultimate effects that occur during their task execution, a deliberate questioning and information-sharing strategy may help alleviate some of this burden of understanding. By asking a few simple questions, team members may start a crucial chain of information-sharing, where questions are asked and answered, or at least asked and passed through an information distribution network to those who ultimately need the information. When small changes occur, team members can note the information, ask themselves who needs to be informed, and who may be affected by the changes. This is another reason why a shared awareness of the team's tasks is an important element of effective teamwork. In some cases, team members may simply tell their team leader who will take action to distribute the information to those who need to know.

Using a simple example, suppose a crew is preparing to install a section of a tower at a job site using a crane to perform the operation. Simultaneously, other crews are in the process of setting up temporary work facilities and shelters. Despite the crane crew's best efforts at analyzing the hazards, when they get onsite and operations commence, one of the spotters realizes there may be a possibility that the crane boom and tower section may pass over the other crew preparing the site for the temporary shelter. He may not be completely sure if this will happen, but if it does, it could result in damage or injury. In this case, the team leader may conduct a PTA activity, pausing the crane operations, gathering the affected teams together (including the crane and the shelter preparation crews) to discuss the updated information, potential hazards and effects, and developing a new plan to safely conduct the operations. This could mean moving the shelter crew out of the way, moving the site for the shelters altogether, changing the approach pattern of the crane and tower section, or some other solution that reduces risk while accomplishing the job. While the actual process would probably be much more complex and detailed than described here, this should provide a basic understanding of how changes in job performance and situation updates may be used to maintain an ongoing focus and anticipate tasks and changes, and their impacts on future performance.

Causes of Degraded Focus during Operations

While this chapter has discussed some of the potential causes of degraded focus, attention, and awareness during operations, by learning more about the sources and ways to either prevent or minimize these causal factors, team leaders and team members alike may be better prepared to create and maintain higher levels of focus and awareness when operations commence. As described, initial planning often sets the stage for awareness when the job begins. A lack of planning in low-hazard environments may result in business disruption, embarrassment, or degradation in processes, but in high-hazard environments a lack of planning could result in catastrophic failure. In these operational conditions surprises are generally not well received. A lack of planning can lead to dangerous surprises, and when teams are caught off guard, mitigating these hazards will often be a lot more difficult. When teams are highly prepared and briefed on hazards when going into an operation, they will generally be more organized and better equipped to deal with hazards as they are encountered.

While planning may seem like a simple task, it is often quite involved. Despite the level of detail required in planning operations, leaders and team members often take it for granted, simply assuming that the operation will "take care of itself." Leaders can help teams improve their focus and awareness through detailed planning, but this approach must begin with the right attitude. Team leaders' and team members' attitudes play a large part in the planning process, particularly during routine operations. When teams conduct recurring tasks over and over and fail to encounter the consequences of hazards they may feel as though the detailed planning that goes into these routine tasks is not worth the effort. After all, why should they spend so much time planning when nobody gets hurt very often and mistakes don't seem to have much of an impact? This dismissive attitude is not uncommon, and team leaders must set the tone by modeling the attitudes and behaviors they expect out of their team members. Simply because a mishap has not occurred does not mean it will not occur, and it could very well be the case that mishaps and accidents were avoided in the past because of the detailed planning and hazard mitigations put in place by the teams. As a team leader you must continually remind your teams of these issues.

The right attitude by itself, however, will not create effective plans, so team leaders must develop planning strategies and techniques to help create repeatable planning processes. One strategy to help create consistent, detailed plans is to use a planning template or guidebook, which can be used to identify crucial operations and safety areas that must be addressed prior to work commencing. As the template is used and lessons are learned, the template may be adapted over time so that it becomes more useful and appropriate to the specific operational environments where teams work. The planning template should be a living document that is continually updated and improved, and this guide can actually be used to provide input into operational team briefing templates, guides, or checklists.

Another cause of degraded focus and loss of situational awareness is task overload, where team members and/or team leaders are overburdened with too many duties to handle. This is the reality in many high-hazard operations and is often the result of human, material, and financial resource constraints. Oftentimes, due to economic pressure, organizations are forced to do more with less, resulting in team members doing the work of more than one person. This can be mitigated in several ways, including using cross-functional teams, where team members share job responsibilities. This may be effective when certain employees are complete with a specific portion of their duties and must wait on resources or other team members before they can proceed with the rest of their tasks. In these cases, their down time may be utilized by helping other team members who may be somewhat overloaded. As a team leader you should be cognizant of the way your team members are utilized and consider ways to load the team in a level fashion so work levels are balanced. This may also require the work system to be evaluated and redesigned using a system approach, so rather than team leaders making all of these decisions on their own, the organization may be able to help with resource planning and identify strategies to help team leaders when these situations occur. This way, there is a degree of standardization to the process of task loading and assignments.

Similar to task overload, time compression can also contribute to a loss of focus, difficulty concentrating on tasks, and decreased awareness of current task status and potential future impacts. Time compression may occur when the task requirements for a given operation are fitted into a short period of time, often too short for the individual team members to accomplish. Simply put, this is when there is not enough time to get the job done, and this is often a result of poor planning or the effects of resource constraints. Customers may want their project completed "yesterday," or abnormal events (such as storms and subsequent power outages requiring immediate rectification) force teams to conduct a lot of work in an extremely short period of time. Time compression often results in employees rushing through their tasks, potentially skipping steps (intentionally or unintentionally), or performing the steps incorrectly. Both of these effects can have serious outcomes, such as poor quality that leads to catastrophic loss if the job is not performed to the appropriate standards, or personnel injury if the omissions or errors result in hazard occurrence while team members are exposed.

Organizations can help operational teams avoid time compression through the job/project planning and resource allocation process by properly estimating job requirements, anticipating potential changes in the job, and assigning supplemental resources in a reserve capacity (such as additional personnel to be called in from a standby status if the job requires their participation). Operational team leaders can help teams avoid the effects of time compression by maintaining awareness of the overall job status and changing demands during execution, anticipating potential team member needs, and understanding when certain phases of the job will begin to require a great deal of work in a short period of time. By understanding varying workloads versus the time available, team leaders may be able to shift certain time-compressed tasks into lower workload periods. Many jobs have periods with lower and higher workloads, and the higher workloads in many cases include tasks that must be completed in limited amounts of time. Using their leader–manager skills, team leaders may be able to reprioritize tasks and shift some of the tasks that would typically occur in the high-workload/time-compressed phases into the lower-workload phases. Even if some of the tasks must be executed during the time-compressed phase, it may be possible for some of the preparatory planning activities to be completed earlier, which may help reduce some levels of time-compression. While this reorganization may be feasible at the operational team level, it should also be conducted using a work system design process, so that impacts and any unanticipated consequences can be addressed in a systemic fashion.

In many operations, change is a normal part of the job and teams must be prepared to adapt when the work commences, but the effects of changes on task execution may be compounded in high-workload and time-compressed situations if prior preparations have not been made. Therefore, in anticipation of the high-workload situations and possible need for adaptation, teams should try to conduct advance preparations (such as equipment setup) if feasible, rather than waiting to make preparations once the time-compressed stage begins. After the preparatory work is completed and when the high-workload phase begins it may be easier and less time-consuming to make minor changes as necessary during the execution of the steps, since a lot of the work to prepare for the task steps has already been completed.

Another strategy to help teams contend with time-compression is to embed certain task coordination steps into SOPs. For example, if crews must arrange equipment and verify that the equipment is set up correctly prior to operations commencement or between task phases during execution, a SOP that includes specific instructions and requirements for each team member, including the verification of equipment status, may help to alleviate the effects of time compression. When the workload increases and time is critical, team members may execute their steps according to the SOP, rather than trying to determine their own ad-hoc ways for setting up and confirming the equipment status. Checklists may help keep the team members' focus on the SOP items. When using this approach, the SOP or checklist items should be taught well in advance of operational execution and this training should include a process where team members become highly familiar with the SOP and checklist items, rehearse their actions, and achieve qualification through an evaluation process.

Task overload and time compression are often related to upstream resource constraints, and another related impact of resource constraints is team leader span of control. Span of control relates to the number of direct reports (subordinate team members). While there are often varying opinions regarding the optimal number of employees that team leaders must supervise, ultimately the number is largely dependent on the nature of the work, the consequences of improperly executed tasks, and the potential effects of hazards when team members are exposed. In low-hazard environments a large span of control may mean that team leaders spend a great deal of time providing oversight to various administrative functions and if errors in supervision occur this could result in lost productivity, a lack of quality, and failure to meet customer requirements. These are all unacceptable results for any business striving for excellence, but in high-hazard operations the effects of supervisory and leadership failures are much worse. In those environments when team leaders' span of control is so large that they cannot properly oversee task execution and hazard mitigation the effects could be disastrous, including personnel injury or accidents, or major equipment or environmental damage.

Needless to say, organizations that work to find the optimal balance between the number of team leaders and the number of direct reports may set their teams up for a higher likelihood for successful outcomes. One way to optimize span of control is to develop sub-team leaders who can assist with team leadership activities. This strategy has been used effectively in certain military units for years. In the US Marine Corps, at the small unit level many team leaders have approximately three to four direct reports, and in some cases these direct reports are also subordinate team members who lead several direct reports. In this decentralized leadership fashion, additional team members are empowered to supervise and lead small teams, which reduces the span of control requirements from the overarching team leader. While military models are not a panacea for commercial and non-profit organizations, they do offer potential benchmarks for other organizations to design span of control strategies. If team leaders must only oversee three to four sub-team leaders, rather than checking on the job status of every team member, it can free up time for other leadership duties, such as communicating with other organizational agencies or departments, sourcing of job or project materials, hazard abatement, and making decisions regarding overall team requirements, schedule status, and safety performance. This span of control approach requires high levels of technical and leadership competency on the part of the sub-team leaders, as well as high levels of trust among the team and organization.

Two often-overlooked causes of decreased focus, attention, and ability to detect negative impacts to performance are task interruptions and changes to the order of task steps. In many industries these are fairly common occurrences, so their impacts can be under-analyzed. Task interruptions can occur for a number of reasons, including missing equipment during execution, other team members requiring assistance, and reprioritization of job requirements and personnel duties. A related situation occurs when the typical task steps are changed, resulting in steps being performed out of sequence. Reordering task steps may occur when equipment or tools are not available, and the line operator, rather than pausing, decides to continue performing other steps while waiting on the equipment. This seems innocent enough, right? The employee wants to be a productive team member and rather than taking time off and waiting for the supplies, which may cause delays, he decides to keep going with other steps and intends to complete the skipped steps at a later point in time. Some jobs that are highly standardized may not allow steps to be executed out of order, but other jobs may allow some flexibility, and this flexibility can actually be beneficial in some cases. However, this flexibility strategy is not without its challenges.

Earlier in the chapter, some of the benefits of task reordering were described. This concept can be helpful in some cases, particularly when some tasks can be shifted from highly time-compressed situations to phases when there is more time available, which may help to ease the burden on the team. However, caution must be used. One problem with task or sequence changes is that when tasks are interrupted or steps are completed out of order it can be easy for team members to forget where they left off or what task steps still remain. These occurrences may not always be eliminated because task interruption is a reality in many industries, yet there may be ways to help employees get back on track and regain focus and awareness of task status, so the job may be completed properly and safely. First, teams may be able to prevent interruptions due to equipment non-availability by planning and ensuring the resources are available prior to job commencement. Additionally, when interruptions or reordering of task steps occurs, employees may be able to use checklists to keep track of the steps that were completed and those that remain. They may also use other team members to provide backup support and help them remember where they left off in their task performance. Optimally, teams would be well suited if these interruptions did not occur, but in many industries that is simply not reality. So, while these strategies are not foolproof solutions, they may help teams contend with the negative effects of task interruptions and reordering.

Another cause of degraded focus is the development of procedural workarounds. If inadequate systems or tools are not provided to help teams perform their jobs adequately employees will often find workarounds. Team members may improvise by using different tools, or by creating their own procedures and modifications to make do with the tools and equipment that have been provided by the organization. This can reduce their ability to focus on the job because the workarounds themselves may require an inordinate amount of concentration. So, rather than focusing on the job itself they may end up dividing their attention between the task steps and ways to modify their procedures and the ways their equipment is used to complete the tasks. While this may result in successful job completion in many cases, it can introduce unrecognized hazards into the operating environment. Organizational-level managers should work with operational team leaders to ensure that employees have the correct equipment and tools for the job, that this equipment is maintained in proper condition, and that any damaged equipment is replaced prior to use. As will be discussed later, workarounds can be a beneficial source of information, but if allowed to go unchecked, can potentially result in unintended consequences and unrecognized hazards.

Another often-downplayed factor that degrades focus and awareness is fatigue. Fatigue may be cumulative, building over a number of days, or can be more acute, occurring over numerous hours during a long work shift. High levels of fatigue can impair team members' ability to focus on tasks and can impact their ability to think through the results of actions and the impacts on other team members, and to anticipate future effects. Fatigue can be overlooked because it is often viewed as a fact of life in many high-hazard operations. For example, in heavy human-centric operations where crews are required to conduct difficult and challenging hands-on work to get the job done, it is expected that they will be tired. In mining, oil and gas, medicine, and many other industries, long hours are very common and fatigue is a continuous challenge. While many industries, such as military and commercial aviation, have developed procedures to help mitigate some of the risks associated with fatigue, there are opportunities for improvement in other industries.

Several strategies may be used to help minimize employee exposure to excessive fatigue-inducing situations. Job rotation, where certain team members are temporarily rotated out of one job and into another, can help provide short reprieves from certain physical work. Additionally, managing team rotation schedules to ensure work time and off time are balanced, limiting the maximum amount of cumulative work days, and placing maximum hourly caps on work days may help to limit fatigue. Each industry and organization must decide for itself what level of fatigue and associated risk is acceptable in the operating environment, but ignoring fatigue as a source of risk and decreased situational awareness will more than likely result in less-than-optimal performance.

While much has been discussed up to this point about ways to maintain focus on operations and safety during task execution, teams must be prepared to recover from decreased attention situations. Even the most well-prepared teams will likely face situations where at least one team member experiences lapses in attention during task execution at some point and potentially fails to project task implications into the future to determine overarching impacts. So, as an operational team leader, what can you do to help your teams recover from decreased attention events? The R–A–R strategy may help, but the team may need to mobilize as many resources as needed to help regain focus and rebuild situational awareness. These resources may include other co-located team members or crews from other job locations who may have high levels of expertise or experience, measuring devices or equipment, such as gauges, Information Systems or displays, or equipment manuals, which may help team members compare their perception of the environment with actual data and information, so that decisions can be made to rectify any deficiencies. Team members should work through a process of explaining what they think is happening, or may happen in the near future, and ask other team members if they have differing opinions. One of the key points to remember is that if there is a doubt about task status, rather than ignoring the doubt team members should check and verify the status prior to moving forward, particularly if serious impacts could result from incorrect status.

Error Detection

Focus and attention are key requirements in high-hazard operations, and where a heavy amount of hands-on work takes place there is a potential for errors and mistakes, which are sometimes the precursors to degraded levels of focus and attention and the inability to accurately predict the effects. While preventing errors is ideal, it is unlikely that operational teams will maintain continuous performance over time without making some types of errors. Whether these are errors of omission (where team members fail to perform certain tasks or steps) or errors of commission (where a task or step is performed incorrectly), at some point they will likely happen. So, teams should attempt to prevent as many errors as feasible, but since some errors will occur, a diverse approach for dealing with them also includes detecting errors and correcting them before their effects escalate. Organizations and operational team leaders should devise strategies to help teams apply all of these techniques.

Technical proficiency may help to shape an environment for error minimization and teams must understand the technical aspect of the jobs and be able to execute the job in the operational environment. A high level of technical proficiency may also improve a team's ability to detect errors when they do occur.

When team members understand what task or task step is supposed to take place at a particular time, and what the result should be for each step, this provides them with a means for measuring the actual outcome and comparing it to the expected outcome. If there is a variance, then team members should understand that an error has occurred.

While this may sound simple, it is not always an easy undertaking, so certain techniques may be used to assist with the error detection process. One such technique is the use of operational and safety checklists. While checklists may seem like an extremely simple tool, if used correctly they can be highly effective at helping teams actively manage operations, including error detection. To be as effective as possible deliberate steps must be taken to design checklists to adequately cover the required task steps and to train teams on how to manage the checklist itself. As described in Chapter 4, Team Communications, checklists may be managed in several ways, including Challenge–Action–Reply or Action–Challenge–Reply. When using the Challenge–Action–Reply format with a team-based task one team member calls out the challenge step, then the other team member completes the task step (or verifies the step has been completed properly) and also replies with the appropriate response. In a single-person task, the same person would perform each challenge step, action, and reply, and the reply might be conducted orally or mentally, and may or may not use a set of check boxes to confirm in writing the step has been completed. With the Action–Challenge–Reply format, teams may conduct pre-rehearsed task steps from a SOP and after the step or steps are completed, one team member calls out the challenge statement to describe the specific task step and the appropriate team member who completed the step(s) confirms the status and replies with the appropriate response. In all of these cases, the checklists are not simply a book of perfunctory words that team members simply read off without putting deliberate thought into what they are saying and why they are saying each statement. The checklist should be designed and managed during task execution to help team members complete all of their required task steps, to verify that the steps were completed appropriately (and to detect the errors if they were not), and to verbally and mentally confirm the status to raise situational awareness. If, during the course of task execution, the checklist reveals errors of omission or commission, the checklist should be stopped and the procedural step should be corrected (or a corrective action plan should be developed) before the checklist is continued. In some cases checklists may be designed to include a section for notes on the job status as well, which may be helpful with single-person tasks.

In distracting environments, such as those with high-noise or where frequent interruptions occur, deliberate attention to the checklist itself must be maintained. Otherwise, the checklist will likely fail as an error detection tool. For example, when non-standard situations occur and normal task flows are interrupted it can be easy for team members to become distracted and lose their place in the checklist, potentially forgetting to complete a step, but thinking it has been completed. This can cause confusion when teams attempt to regroup and determine where they stopped a specific procedure. This could also result in uncertainty regarding the status of certain equipment or important mode settings on critical technology.

While hazard elimination and engineering controls are often favored over behavior-based solutions, which may be less effective for hazard mitigation, in the hands-on operational environment behavior-based techniques may be a highly effective tool for detecting and correcting errors, particularly if there are no automated or engineered safety features to automatically detect these errors. Checklists are typically managed using a top to bottom flow and a behavioral strategy is to either keep a thumb or finger on the checklist item until the task step has been verified, or to use a writing instrument to check a box after verification. Using this strategy, when distractions or task interruptions occur a team member may hold a thumb or finger in place (or use the checkboxes to place a mark) on the last checklist item completed. Although more time consuming, another technique is to begin the checklist again from the very first step, verifying the status of each item until the checklist is completed. While not foolproof, these techniques offer a means to assist teams with staying on task in distracting environments.

Error Trapping, Correction, and Recovery

When a team recognizes errors of omission or commission have occurred, they should take action to prevent the error from escalating. Particularly in high-hazard operations, if errors are not trapped (and potentially corrected) they could result in cascading failures, ultimately leading to catastrophic loss. So, teams must deal with errors in some way. After detecting errors, if time permits and the conditions allow it, team members may consider pausing momentarily to think about the situation before diving into immediate corrective actions. They can then diagnose and trap the error, and determine what corrective actions might be needed. If the error is a simple task omission and it can be corrected, then it might be a simple fix, but if the error is more complex the teams may need to go further into troubleshooting procedures. If standardized procedures exist then teams typically execute these procedures, but if no procedures exist, then team members must use their individual and collective knowledge, available documentation, operator's manuals, and other resources to stop the effects of the error from progressing further. Teams should also be accustomed to performing real-time hazard analysis and time-sensitive risk management activities so they can diagnose specific threats, employee exposure, and potential consequences (such as employee injuries or fatalities, or major equipment damage/environmental loss). This assessment should include a process for elevating high-risk situations to appropriate levels of authority within the team (such as sub-team leaders, or the overall operational team leader) or higher within the organization.

Oftentimes, when errors do occur they may impact more than one isolated area of operations. If errors are not detected, trapped, and corrected they can lead to more serious consequences. If errors result in compound emergencies (where multiple simultaneous hazards occur) this can dramatically reduce focus and attention levels, and cause a great deal of confusion as teams attempt to determine the source of the emergencies and remedial actions. For example, suppose that a team is performing maintenance on a piping system that contains flammable liquid. If an error or equipment failure triggers a pipe rupture and an ignition source is present this could result in both a flow of flammable liquid and a fire, and could have potential downstream effects of employee injury and major equipment and environmental damage if recovery actions are not taken. In some cases there may not be prescriptive pre-existing procedures to cover the exact situation. When compound emergencies occur and specific pre-defined emergency procedures do not exist, one strategy may be to focus on the most critical steps to trap and correct first. This rapid assessment may be based on the potential for injury, equipment loss, or environmental damage. Team members must also know who is in charge, and this might require the immediate assistance of the team leader and the assignment of FLs to help control the situation.

As errors escalate into emergencies, the focus shifts from trapping and correcting to containment and recovery so that damage may be minimized, and team leaders may need to assign specific team members to specific roles. These roles may become second nature, particularly if the emergencies are well-understood and roles have been pre-assigned, such as mine-rescue crews who may need to respond in certain mining emergencies. In other cases, this may require on-the-fly assignments as team leaders begin to serve in the capacity of an incident commander (at least temporarily).

Optimizing the Operational Environment through Work System Design

Up to this point we have spent a great deal of time describing strategies and techniques team leaders and team members can use to improve focus and attention, and to help improve a team's ability to maintain higher levels of awareness, including mentally projecting the results of actions into the future. While the ability to actively manage focus, attention, and situational awareness is a critical aspect of leadership and teamwork, this capacity may be enhanced when organizations make deliberate efforts to design the work system so that hazards are reduced, and the work environment is improved, ultimately lessening the burden of maintaining focus and attention (at least to some extent). By identifying hazards (and distractions that may lead to hazards) organizations can then work to either design these out of the work system or to provide mitigating methods to protect operational teams. Using this approach there may be less reliance on the team to detect and mitigate hazards on their own, freeing up mental capacity to focus on their tasks. Using a simple example, suppose a construction crew is conducting elevated work using scaffolding. If the organization fails to design adequate safety measures with the scaffolding, despite the fact that it is more than likely violating regulations, it places the crew in a position to use inordinate measures to actively manage their own safety, which pulls their focus away from their operational tasks. On the other hand, if proper scaffolding construction procedures are followed and higher safety levels are achieved, the crew will still need to maintain safety awareness, but there will be less overall reliance on these crews as the source for safety creation, allowing them to use more of their mental and physical capacities to focus on their work. By taking steps to mitigate risk through a risk assessment and design-for-safety process, the organization can help facilitate an operational environment that reduces error potential by placing team members in a position where their attention is less divided so they can perform at optimal levels.

When organizations use a hierarchy of hazard control methods to reduce risks to acceptable levels and, through a combination of technology and task analysis, devise ways to help employees conduct their work more effectively or efficiently, operational teams may realize these benefits at the point where the work is performed. They may find it easier to get their work done, and the organization may recognize the long-term benefits of improved efficiency, productivity, and reduced operational losses. For example, when a high-hazard task is examined, the organization may look to eliminate some of the risks altogether or modify the way the work is performed, then a combination of engineering controls, such as barriers or automated lockout systems or guards, may be used to protect employees from risks that cannot be eliminated or designed out of the work system. Additional strategies that include warnings and cautions, procedural or administrative controls, and PPE may also help. In some cases a combination of controls may be used to reduce the probability of injury while attempting to protect the employee if the hazard occurs. As part of this risk-reduction strategy, organizations should examine sources to make the job of the individual team member and the team as a whole easier, less cumbersome, or less labor-intensive, perhaps through automated technology to assist them with their work or through the use of improved tools and equipment.

Some additional considerations for optimizing the work system include ensuring equipment and tools are adequate for the job, that tasks are designed using a system approach, including operations, safety, ergonomics, and human factors specialists, and that when these tasks are designed they are tested with teams to determine their effectiveness and their potential to either enhance or reduce focus and attention during operations. All of these efforts should be designed to reduce risks and place the team in a position to perform its job well, which includes maintaining high levels of focus and attention, and situational awareness. While the costs associated with the work system design or redesign efforts may seem high, when monetized over time, the benefits should be realized. Additionally, there may be ancillary benefits of happier employees (and the employees' families), which may also help the organization with sustainable growth.

Shaping and Managing Situational Awareness through Safety Information Systems

Although it may be considered part of the work system design process, the role of Information Systems can play a substantial part in shaping the operational environment for improved safety, focus, overall attention, and situational awareness. Information Systems can take many forms, but for the purpose of our discussion we will consider them as automated or manual methods for collecting and transmitting information to enhance the safety levels of job performance. Since operational performance and safety should be inextricably linked, these Information Systems may include both elements and should be designed to cover multiple phases of operations, from pre-job planning, to debriefing and lessons-learned.

- Pre-job planning systems: As previously described, comprehensive planning is an important factor in helping teams gain and maintain situational awareness. Therefore, if used properly, pre-job planning systems that help teams identify operational, communications, logistics, and safety requirements may help team leaders and members begin to build the framework for successful performance. These planning systems should include a standardized and repeatable process for helping teams input key information, including (but not limited to) performance requirements and timelines, overall task descriptions, goals and definitions of success, Leader's Intent, safety goals, hazard identification and controls, emergency procedures, communications systems and procedures (including primary and backup methods), and ways to coordinate team activities and provide situation updates. These pre-job planning systems can also include a method for producing a pre-job or pre-operations brief, which operational team leaders can then use to brief the team before commencing operations.

- Operational Hazard Analysis and Hazard Tracking Systems: Two components related to the pre-job planning system are the Operational Hazard Analysis and Hazard Tracking Systems. These systems provide a comprehensive approach to identify the objects or conditions that could cause harm to operational teams if they occur. The hazard analysis portion may identify the harmful objects, events, or conditions and may help determine human exposure. It may also help determine the probability of the hazardous condition actually occurring and the potential severity or consequence to people, equipment, and the environment if the hazard actually occurs. The output of that process is a list of risks (hazards explained in terms of probability and severity), which are evaluated for mitigation requirements. As the organization goes through the process of controlling the risks, the Hazard Tracking System is updated to reflect the new status. As an operational team leader planning a job, you should make a concerted effort to review the Hazard Tracking System prior to conducting operations. You should also encourage feedback from your team members related to hazards as they are identified during operations so that you can help determine safety levels. As new hazards are identified, you should ensure they are entered into the Operational Hazard Analysis System for further evaluation and entry into the Hazard Tracking System. While this is an organizational responsibility, and may in some cases fall on the shoulders of the safety department, the organization often relies on the "eyes and ears" of those doing the work at the sharp end.

- Near-miss reporting tools: Sometimes referred to as near-hit reporting tools, these systems provide a means for team members to report incidents that occur during any phase of operations where an employee was almost injured. While some may consider this a lagging indicator identification tool, because it identifies events that have already happened, it can actually be seen as a form of leading indicator identification tool because although an event took place, if no injuries occurred the information may be used to help identify hazards and to develop methods to help prevent future, more serious occurrences. Near-miss reporting tools may help organizations learn about hazards that could cause harm by themselves or when combined with degraded focus and attention. If every employee is viewed as a safety representative and provided with a means of accessing these reporting tools it may provide the organization with the ability to identify more hazards and threats to attention and situational awareness.

- Debriefing and lessons-learned systems: As a final asset for post-operations learning, organizations should develop and implement debriefing tools, which team leaders can use to capture information immediately after jobs are completed regarding what went right, what went wrong, and what could be improved. Additionally, this information should be entered into a lessons-learned system, which can help the organization as a whole become a learning organization. This system can also be an effective way for transferring knowledge from experienced employees to more junior employees, which can be particularly helpful when senior employees approach retirement. As operations are conducted, hazards are identified, and threats to attention and situational awareness are recognized, they should be input into the lessons-learned system. Prior to operations this system can be queried to determine if any of the previous lessons and recommendations apply to the new operations. In this fashion, debrief points and lessons are fed forward into future planning to help reduce risks, create opportunities for improved performance, and to reduce the potential for degraded focus and attention. While lessons-learned systems may be similar to Operational Hazard Analysis Systems and Hazard Tracking Systems, they may actually go into a more detailed narrative about the events surrounding the aspects of the operation and do not necessarily focus solely on the hazards. The lessons-learned system tells a story in a way, by including key details that may not be part of hazard analysis and tracking systems.

Modeling, Simulation, and Training

Earlier in this chapter we discussed some of the ineffective strategies for building attention and situational awareness. By telling employees to "pay more attention" you are not necessarily solving the problem of reduced attention or focus, particularly when the operational environment inherently contains hazards and error-inducing conditions. Situational awareness can be a difficult skill to teach, and often improves with time and experience. However, most organizations cannot simply wait for employees to gain more experience in order to maintain high levels of focus and attention and to be able to project the effects of their actions into the near future. They must be safe and aware from the moment they begin their work.

In the absence of experience, organizations may try using modeling and simulation techniques to help employees experience situations similar to what they may find during actual operations. First, the model is created to represent the version of work the organization or team leader wishes the employees to experience. This might include developing a scenario that places the team members or the entire team in their working environment to complete a specific job. After the model is developed simulations may be conducted where sample distractions are introduced, such as employees asking for help, broken or incorrect tools or equipment, or changes in the work conditions after the team members arrive "on site." As the teams work together to complete the job and maintain focus, different simulations may be introduced to determine how teams cope with the situation, including an evaluation of their communications, teamwork, and real-time risk assessments. The simulation sessions should be monitored by experienced observers who may pause the simulation to provide feedback, and who will debrief the team members after the simulation sessions are complete.

Simulation scenarios should be as realistic as possible, and should include all required team members and team leaders who would normally be present on the job being modeled. The scenarios should be pre-defined to help expose the teams to different situations requiring divided attention while completing their tasks, and during the simulation all team members can role-play as if they were performing their regular jobs to make the training as realistic as possible. Some of the goals might be to help teams detect and mitigate hazards, handle error-inducing situations (including the use of error detection, trapping, and correction strategies), and gain proficiency executing simulated emergency procedures, and error/emergency containment and recovery tactics. The debrief portion should be conducted in an open forum using a coaching format as opposed to aggressive corrections for poor performance. These simulations are learning sessions and should be designed that way. If no simulation facilities exist and it is too risky to conduct these simulations in a live operational environment, the organization may consider scenario-based classroom discussion and what-if scenarios. While the modeling and simulation strategies won't create instant situational awareness, they may help operational teams develop awareness of the challenges associated with attention and focus in high-hazard environments, may accelerate the learning curve, and may also help prepare teams to cope with error-inducing situations when they do occur.

Operations and Production Pressure

The pressure to meet key organizational performance demands exists in nearly all industries and can be so embedded into the fabric of the organization that it may be missed as a source of risk. Production and performance pressure can have such an impact on safety, operations, and the ability of employees to maintain high levels of attention, that it should be discussed as a distinct subject. Regardless of the industry or sector, organizations have goals to meet. Whether the goals are to provide a certain level of service, produce a specific number of products at certain intervals, or to meet specific sales targets, the pressure to meet these goals often flows throughout the organization. Like a stream of water flowing through cracks in rocks, eventually it will make its way to each member of the organization in one way or another. Oftentimes, particularly in high-hazard environments, the biggest impacts of production and performance pressure are felt by those closest to where the work is performed and those at the sharp end actually doing the work.

This influence may be realized in the form of time pressure, when team members are forced to complete a job in a minimal amount of time. Time pressure can often result from potential negative stakeholder or customer impacts, which could occur if a job is not completed on time. This pressure is often woven throughout the organization, and funneled down through various managers and supervisors until it reaches the operational team.

Another reality may be the requirement to meet a certain quota, such as the number of units built or installed. While this pressure will typically exist to some extent, organizations should attempt to balance performance-oriented goals with safety and quality goals as well. If this balance is not made explicitly known, it may leave team leaders and team members in a position to make real-time choices and trade-offs, often to the detriment of safety. What might normally be a safety-related decision, where safety is the overriding decision criterion, could unintentionally become a production or performance quota decision, where the pressure to complete the task overrides safety and/ or quality. This shifting emphasis could lead to a loss of focus on the safety requirements that should be designed into operational tasks associated with the job. If production is given such a higher priority than safety, to the point where risk exceeds acceptable levels, it could ultimately result in operational losses in the form of accidents, injuries, or equipment and environmental damage. In those cases, any performance gains would be negated by the other operational losses.

Another challenging source of production and performance pressure is in the form of financial incentives, such as performance bonuses for reaching the required targets. These bonuses, while often effective for motivating employees, may induce unintended consequences in the form of increased risk. When team leaders push their teams and employees push themselves beyond their abilities to safely complete tasks it may result in decreased focus and attention. While financial incentives may be appropriate in certain circumstances, unless they are balanced with safety and quality goals, operational teams may lose focus and may set their minds on achieving the incentivized goal rather than thinking through the impacts of their tasks and the overall effects on the team. This emphasis on incentives may also cloud their judgment and reduce their ability to think through and anticipate potential downstream impacts and consequences.

A somewhat covert form of pressure is sometimes referred to as "perceived pressure." This term refers to how employees perceive the performance goals set by the organization. In some cases the organization may attempt to convince operational team leaders and employees that any pressure that could possibly be the result of production goals is simply part of employees' perception and is not really being pushed by the organization. While different personnel will perceive and react to production goals and pressures in different ways, if the ultimate effect of these goals includes employees who perceive that they must sacrifice other important goals, such as safety and quality, in order to meet the production schedules or quotas, then this perceived pressure becomes real pressure. The end state is the same; employees potentially cutting corners and experiencing lower levels of attention as they work under the pressure to achieve the production goals.

So, in today's competitive society when time is money and schedule delays or missed production quotas can reduce profits and potentially even lead to layoffs, what is an organization to do when faced with multiple competing goals, such as production, quality, safety, and reliability, particularly when production is seen as king? The first step may be to make sure top-level leaders within the organization understand the existence of pressure and the effects production pressure can ultimately have on operational teams. This pressure might not be as critical in low-hazard environments, such as certain administrative jobs with low exposure to hazards or where consequences for poor performance are not likely to result in major catastrophic failure. However, in high-hazard operations the potential for employee injuries or fatalities, major equipment or environmental losses, serious disruption in processes, or catastrophic damage as a result of mission failure is escalated, so this understanding between leadership and employees is critical. The process of developing a shared understanding between the organizational levels starts with an open and forthright conversation between top-level leadership, production department heads, and operational team leaders. When the organization begins to understand the demands excessive production pressure places on teams it could help to reshape perspectives and goals, particularly if it is possible to link the potential effects of excessive production pressure to operational losses. The organization must understand that to realize long-term sustainable growth, production must be balanced with additional key performance goals, including safety, quality, reliability, and social responsibility.

Team leaders should also attempt to insulate employees from undue pressure when able, taking action at their level before the team is impacted. This might mean working with operations/project schedulers and quota decision-makers, who design production goals, and helping to determine more realistic and achievable performance targets. In this capacity, the team leader serves as a buffer between excessive performance pressure and the team itself. If this pressure can be cushioned through the efforts of the team leader, employees may not feel it at the same levels, which may help them maintain focus and attention to their tasks in an effort to produce quality results. Above all, team leaders should understand that a "mission accomplishment at all costs" mentality will be detrimental to efforts at achieving operational excellence, which is attained in more ways than simply meeting production goals. After all, is finishing the job on time with injured employees or environmental damage really the definition of success?

In order to balance incentives and production goals in a way that enhances team members' abilities to maintain focus during operations, organizations may seek ways to encourage and reward safety and quality targets along with performance goals. In this manner, if the team meets the production goals, but the work includes numerous errors, team members fail to abide by safety requirements, or if the job fails to meet quality requirements, incentives may not be distributed or may be reduced in some manner. Using this model, organizations will likely need to agree on some type of reduction in production objectives that still helps them meet long-term profitability goals because operational teams may be able to reach the lofty production goals, but may not be able to reach them with the same levels of safety and job quality. So, organizational leaders should agree to a blended goal that perhaps reduces production slightly, and maintains the appropriate levels of safety and quality that would typically be expected.

Incentives and production goals could also be tied in with leading indicators and proactive safety behaviors, such as near-miss reporting and lessons-learned reporting, as well as the generation of ideas for helping to improve safety and operational performance. In this fashion, when on-time performance or quota completion is met with proactive reporting of incidents or near-miss events (where employees come close to, but escape injury) and with the sharing of valuable lessons-learned to help improve operations, safety, and quality, performance incentives and rewards may potentially be increased. An added strategy may be to use a tiered goal approach rather than all-or-nothing incentives. This way employees would at least earn some form of reward along the performance goal curve (even if it was not the full amount), as long as they got close to the target production objectives and as long as they met the other key metrics related to safety, quality, and so on. This approach may help reduce the amount of pressure to cut corners, which can potentially result in a loss of focus and degraded awareness.

From an individual standpoint, team members may feel performance pressure in numerous ways, particularly if they are singled out in an open manner. For example, if operations departments track and openly post individual employee performance numbers, where employees are compared against each other, this could add pressure on team members who feel they need to perform higher amounts of work to look good on the charts and to potentially receive the recognition and approval of their peers and supervisors. This can drive competition and have potentially negative impacts on safety. This may be particularly true if production reports highlight employees in varying colors to show levels of performance, from deficient to superior.

Team members may feel added pressure to move up from the "red zone" to the "green zone." Some employees are naturally slower and more methodical about their work, maintaining a higher degree of attention to their work and their surroundings. This isn't an excuse to reward deficient performance, but is a way to help employees remain somewhat insulated from the operational production pressure so a total system focus on performance, safety, and quality may be obtained.

Equipping employees with strategies to help them stand up to undue pressure or unsafe decisions that could potentially be the result of excessive performance pressure may go a long way in helping organizations mitigate the negative consequences of this pressure. Designing policies, such as a SWA, that encourage employees to speak up in the face of unsafe situations may help to provide a standardized platform which employees can refer to. A formal written policy may bolster their moral courage since this policy is written down and backed by the organization. Team members should also be encouraged to become FLs, elevating problems to their team leaders. This can be a particularly effective strategy when high risks limit their ability to make safety-related decisions themselves. Risk decisions should be made at the right level and if team members do not possess the authority to make those decisions, they should not be placed in a position to do so. By designing formal policies for risk-informed decision making, organizations may help alleviate some of the effects of production pressure on line employees.

As a final strategy, even if organizational leaders do their best to minimize tight deadlines and excessively high production goals, sometimes, due to circumstances beyond their control, they may find themselves in untenable circumstances requiring aggressive operational performance requirements to meet short-term quotas. For example, a utility company may need to respond rapidly in order to restore power after a natural disaster. In this case the demands from customers may be so heavy that organizational leaders are left with little choice but to ramp up performance requirements. In the military this is sometimes referred to as a surge in operations, where performance requirements are temporarily increased. Figure 5.2 shows an example of how surge operations can potentially affect safety levels, and when safety levels are reduced the potential for a loss of attention and focus may result, leading to errors, failures, and potential mishaps.

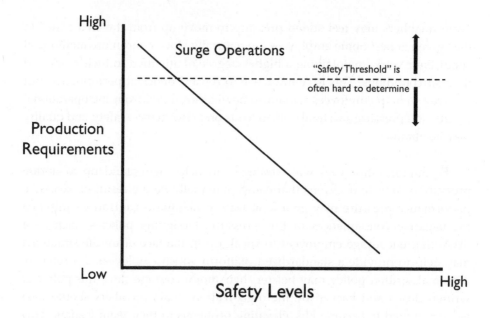

Figure 5.2   Production surge and safety levels
Note: This figure is illustrative only and does not reflect actual reference data.

Since it is understandable that production surge requirements will take place in some instances, the organization will be well-served to conduct planning in advance to determine its surge capacity, identifying what human and material resources will be available if or when a situation requiring temporary aggressive production goals arises. As part of this asset identification and planning process, leaders should also develop guidelines to determine how long the organization can operate safely at that surge capacity and set those time limits in advance. They should also identify surge capacity safety limits in specific terms (such as maximum work hours and work days and any safety guidelines which may have been relaxed to accomplish the surge goals). These limits should become a safety threshold, beyond which the organization will not drift. The safety threshold can be extremely challenging to identify, as it is often a moving target, and during surge operations, as a team leader it is very important that you remain vigilant of hazards, and the effects of the surge operations, which may induce fatigue and loss of attention and situational awareness. Lastly, organizations should ensure they identify the required actions to be taken after returning to normal operations to rebuild the human and system capacity, which may have been stretched towards very thin safety margins during the surge. This might mean downtime for employees (who may need rest) and equipment (which may need extra maintenance and repair after being pushed to its limits).

Employees are often the last line of defense in the effort to mitigate hazards, but they should not be the only line of defense. Comprehensive strategies to minimize the impacts of performance pressure are warranted, but since production pressure is a reality nearly every business lives with, it will not likely be an easy task to eliminate all of the negative effects. However, if the potential adverse effects of excessive production or performance pressure are weighed against the gains, it may help organizations to understand that a "production first" mentality may not always work, particularly in high-hazard operations where the consequences of failure can be disastrous and have the potential to harm personnel and damage organizational credibility. When short-term production goals and associated reward and incentive programs are matched with other key performance criteria, such as safety and quality, organizations may have a higher probability of long-term success. With these strategies, although short-term profits may be lowered, if operational performance targets are designed using a total system approach to determine the total potential positive and negative impacts, the organization may realize gains in safety performance, reduced operational losses, and more longer-term, sustainable growth.

Conclusions

High-hazard environments pose unique challenges for operational team leaders and the team members they lead. While it may seem convenient to blame employees for lapses in attention and accidents, citing human error as the cause, in order to truly understand the causes of degraded attention and focus, and decreased situational awareness organizations must examine the nature of the operational environment and the associated hazards. These operating environments often include harsh and stress-inducing conditions, hazards, and job requirements that force employees to divide their attention as they attempt to perform their work. Ideally, if organizational resources were limitless and leaders were not constrained by economic factors, they might be able to eliminate the majority of hazards and error-inducing conditions that drain the attention of operational teams. This would place teams in a position to constantly maintain the highest possible levels of focus, attention, and situational awareness. The reality, though, is that all organizations face some type of resource constraints. To some extent, operational teams will typically be exposed to at least some degree of risk and to operational environments that require proactive approaches to maintain adequate levels of situational awareness.

In order to place teams in an optimal position to maintain focus on operations tasks while maintaining appropriate levels of safety, organizations should use a combined approach to mitigate hazards and error-inducing conditions. By eliminating some risks, implementing various levels of hazard controls, and training teams in ways to handle error-inducing conditions, distractions, and hazards as they occur, operational teams may be in the best position possible to develop and maintain sufficient situational awareness and to complete their work according to quality and schedule requirements while avoiding injuries and accidents.

Each of the strategies and techniques explained in this chapter offer ways to potentially improve focus, attention, and situational awareness, but they may not be appropriate for every organization and job. In some highly standardized process-oriented industries several of these strategies may not be feasible. Any organization attempting to design these types of strategies into their work systems should take a system-oriented approach and also verify that these strategies do not violate any compliance-related regulations or policies. Ultimately, it is up to the organizational leadership to work with operational team leaders to decide the pathways for improving focus on safety and operations in their organizations. If a concerted effort is made to identify error-inducing and hazardous conditions, and corresponding corrective strategies and techniques, organizations may realize the benefits of improved efficiency, safety, and long-term sustainability.

Chapter 6

Job Planning and Execution Analysis

Excellence in safety and operations begins well in advance of the commencement of work. Although some teams that perform routine operations may think it is acceptable to show up at the job site and begin work without much forethought or planning, organizations that truly seek exceptional operations and safety performance should invest in job planning strategies and techniques. Regardless of whether work is routine or unique, all teams that operate in high-hazard environments should conduct a thorough operational planning process prior to commencing work and ongoing reassessment as operations unfold. As an operational team leader, it is part of your responsibility to make sure your teams are conducting these activities so that safety and preparedness will be infused into your tasks when work commences.

While there are many strategies to assist organizations with job planning and execution analysis, the process should start by examining operations as a system and designing policies, procedures, and work methods to help team members complete their jobs as safely as possible, given the operating environment and the goals of the organization. Additionally, team leaders and organizational policy developers should understand that work is rarely static, and as work methods are designed, they should be analyzed and improved over time as employees learn what works and what doesn't. Some of the information in this chapter will expand upon the material in Chapter 5, while additional information will provide strategies to help operational teams and organizations to become more innovative as they plan for effective and safe operations.

Work System Design

Prior to work commencing, operational teams should work through a comprehensive planning process to ensure the job requirements, risks, schedules and timelines, logistics, and other related factors are well-understood.

This planning process can help set teams up for successful operations and consistent outcomes. However, that planning process is unlikely to mitigate serious shortcomings associated with the design of the specific work processes. By examining work from a system perspective, where the inputs, operational processes, and outputs are analyzed and scrutinized against the conditions associated with the high-hazard operating environment, organizations may be able to take more proactive steps to plan the way work is conducted. If this is done well, by the time operational teams conduct their own downstream pre-job planning, they should be in an optimal position to achieve safety and performance goals.

So, then, what is a work system and how does it apply to job planning? First, let's examine the basic components of an open system through the lens of operational work as a reference point. An open system generally consists of some type of inputs, transformational processes, outputs, and interaction with the environment (Katz and Kahn 3). From an operations perspective, a work system also contains inputs (job requirements identification, and human and material resources), operational processes (the actual work that is performed to develop products or services and which helps the organization accomplish its goals—examples vary by industry, but may include performing maintenance functions, producing manufactured goods, operating on sick patients, and extinguishing wildfires), outputs (the final product or service that is either delivered to a customer or stakeholder or used as an input to other work systems), and interactions with the environment (this not only includes the physical location and weather conditions, but also hazards that may exist). From this perspective, a work system includes human and material resources, and also considers individual operator performance capabilities and limitations, the work to be performed, and the limitations imposed on the operational team by the high-hazard environment itself.

In labor-intensive and/or hands-on operations, one of the goals of effective work system design should be to optimize the process for the human performing the work. Since the human should be considered the most important component within the system, the overall system around the team should be designed to place the team in the best position possible to do the work of the organization. This means that inputs are properly identified so the team has the appropriate resources, the objectives are clearly defined so the team and team leader understand when they have achieved success, and the tasks are designed to make it as easy as possible to do the work while mitigating hazards, complying with safety rules, and minimizing the effects of distractions.

When organizations seek to design the work system properly they should include all required operations staff members, team leaders, and employees who will actually perform the work. This way, those who are most familiar with what really goes on "in the trenches" can help provide input to the work system design process. As a team leader, how much worse can it be to have a set of work procedures handed to you by those who have never done the work and who sought no input from you or your teams? Oftentimes when work systems are designed in that manner the procedures may be developed in such a way that makes it excessively difficult for teams to do their jobs. On the other hand, if only operations personnel are involved in the work system design process they may miss critical non-operations elements, such as logistics and supply-chain issues, financial processes and requirements, risk management goals, and safety compliance requirements. By bringing in a cross-functional team the organization can design the work systems so interdependencies are identified in advance to help avoid unintended consequences and impacts that may otherwise be missed. Using this methodology, when the team completes pre-job planning and commences work, it can capitalize on the experience and expertise of the individual team members who can focus on their tasks as opposed to creating workarounds, ad-hoc procedures, and hazard mitigation strategies to make up for shortcomings in the work system itself.

Work system design is an iterative process and even after the systems have been designed, they must be tested and revised. Following a design–develop–test–implement process, the work system may be created and then tested in a controlled environment with those who will be doing the work to ensure it works effectively. Feedback is obtained and input back into the design phase until the work system meets the needs of all parties involved. Then the work system is implemented into the operational environment and used by all required teams. Feedback should be obtained again, particularly from the operational teams closest to the hazards and doing the work. Ultimately the work system should support those teams, so their feedback is essential.

While it would be nice to think this process would be finished after the implementation phase, in reality it should never stop because the organization is constantly adapting and changing, so the work system should simultaneously adapt, change, and undergo incremental improvements. As often happens after work systems are implemented, the teams realize there are better ways to perform their tasks and that some of the compliance requirements and safety rules may not fit with more efficient methods for doing the work. If work system design iteration is not made a priority gaps may emerge between the way operational teams conduct their work and the formal procedures.

When these gaps are created violations of compliance rules and safety policies often occur, and even worse, injuries and accidents can result. This is not to say that the operational teams are right or wrong for their perspective on the best way to do the work, but the process itself must be monitored and updated, aligning the operational procedures that are actually used and the formal policies that are created. This methodology is neither an appeasement of operational teams doing the work, nor excessive conciliation with the rule makers creating formal policies, but is a way of ensuring all the requirements are aligned in such a way as to keep the teams safe, effective, and efficient while ensuring the organization itself remains in compliance with obligatory regulations. In this fashion the gap between actual work and policy can be closed (or at least narrowed) while adhering to compliance and safety rules. This iterative alignment process should also work to ensure that risks remain within acceptable levels.

If this method is to be truly effective, all levels of the organization must support this work system design process, and operational team members should not be reprimanded for speaking their minds and providing feedback on what works, what doesn't, and what needs to be changed. By learning from their experience with the work systems, employees may actually discover better and safer ways to execute their operational tasks and procedures. Therefore, honest feedback and improvement recommendations should be sought from teams. If this process is not followed, teams may ultimately end up secretly modifying their work in an attempt to meet production and performance quotas as efficiently as feasible, even if it means cutting corners and neglecting some safety rules. Since operational teams may not fully understand all of the hazards associated with the divergence from the original work system, this drifting process may place teams in a perilous position when work commences and could ultimately result in injury, accidents, equipment or environmental damage, or other operational losses.

Operational Analysis and Job Planning

After the work system has been designed and the procedures have been implemented the operational teams become a part of that system and use many of the system components to do the actual operations work for the organization. Although the work system design process is not truly linear, in some ways the operational team picks up where the work system designers leave off. It is at this point where the team takes the results of the design process and puts them into practice. However, before the work begins, the team leader should lead the team through the operational analysis and job planning process.

Operational planning is essential because it often helps build a structure to facilitate successful mission outcomes. The planning process should also follow a system approach, examining each aspect of the operation. While it may seem out of order, by first examining the desired outputs, which are the operational goals, it may help teams identify some of the requirements for other system elements. By determining clear objectives and measurable goals the team will be able to understand the definition of a successful operation. After all, in order to know if you have achieved success, you must understand what defines a successful operation. After identifying the expected outcomes teams can then identify the required inputs (resources) required for the job. These resources often include human resources (the required personnel in terms of crew position, experience, expertise, and availability), material resources (such as tools, machinery, equipment, vehicles, and PPE), financial requirements, and scheduling tools. Additionally, the actual work procedures should be reviewed for correctness and fit for the particular operation to ensure that all team members understand the tasks that need to be performed, including the order and type (linear and concurrent tasks). Finally, as part of the planning process, the team should assess the operational environment and the team's interaction with this environment. This includes assessing weather and temperature conditions, internal workplace safety conditions, dormant hazards that could become active and cause harm (including hazards that occur in the operational environment), organizational or safety culture aspects that could affect the operation, and any potential changes in the environment that could impact the work. As the operational environment is assessed and hazards are identified, the risk management process can help to identify additional input requirements for hazard control and mitigation.

As an operational team leader, you may wonder how you can set your teams up to conduct this type of consistent planning. There may be numerous approaches, but one common format is to use formalized job planning tools. Sometimes referred to as a Job Hazard Analysis (JHA) or a Job Safety Analysis (JSA), these tools assist planners with identifying key operations and safety requirements that will assist the team in accomplishing its goals. While job planning tools by themselves will not necessarily make the operational environment safer, more effective, or more efficient, they provide a structured format for helping teams to ensure important components and resources are not missed or overlooked. Job planning elements can include (but are not limited to):

- Customer/stakeholder requirements, expected outcomes, and definitions of success: A key component of job planning should include ways to determine if the work has been completed satisfactorily. This may include production or performance quotas, but should provide planners, team leaders, and team members with Key Performance Indicators (KPIs) to help them understand when the team has met its objectives. These objectives and desired outcomes will often drive some of the required input planning as well, such as human resources, equipment, and tools.

- Timelines: Team leaders should be able to explain to the team each phase of the job from briefing through execution to debriefing. An accurate timeline helps job planners estimate resource requirements as well.

- Hazard identification and risk assessment: If used correctly the pre-job planning risk assessment tools can help crews identify hazards that may exist in the operational environment, assess those hazards in terms of probability and severity, make decisions based on operational and safety requirements to determine acceptable risk levels, and develop controls to mitigate those risks.

- PPE and risk control requirements: A key part of risk management includes the identification and selection of appropriate risk controls, which may either 1) reduce the likelihood of the hazard actually occurring or 2) minimize the damaging effects of the hazard if it does occur. In many cases a combination of hazard controls may be used in a defense-in-depth approach to reduce the likelihood and severity. While higher levels of safety may be achieved if certain risks are eliminated or less hazardous methods or procedures are substituted in order to complete the work, in some cases this approach may not be feasible and may actually prohibit the organization from accomplishing its mission. Engineering controls may be used in some cases to help remove or limit the team members' exposure to the hazard or to preempt a hazardous condition from leading to harm or damage. Warnings and cautions may also be used, as well as administrative controls (often found in safe work procedures that prescribe certain behaviors and actions to be taken to protect employees). As a last line of defense, PPE, such as flame-resistant clothing, helmets, gloves, eye and hearing protection, and respirators may be used to prevent or minimize harm to employees. The job planning tools should help leaders determine risks (hazards defined in terms of probability and severity), identify and implement the required risk controls (including PPE requirements), and gauge whether or not the final risk levels after controls have been implemented are acceptable. This is a recursive process and the job planning tools can help.

- Team composition and personnel requirements: The planning tools can help team leaders identify the members who should be assigned to the team (which may be based on their documented training, qualifications, proficiency, and experience).

- Right mix of skills and experience level for crew scheduling: As part of the team member identification process, team leaders and planners should understand how the right proportion of skills and experience levels may be used to complement the team. While there are advantages to having highly experienced team members on the job, such as technical and problem solving capabilities, if team leaders never bring in junior personnel, how can these younger employees be expected to learn and help to develop the next generation of experienced professionals? In many industries on-the-job knowledge transfer from older and more experienced employees to junior employees is critical and helps organizations to become more sustainable. On the other hand, having too few senior members on the team could limit technical expertise and diminish error detection, correction, and recovery capabilities and emergency management functions. Job planning tools should serve as a scheduling aid to help teams develop their future capacity, yet balance the crew composition to account for quality and troubleshooting requirements.

- Scheduling conflict mitigation: While team leaders may want certain line operators on their team, based on experience, prior working relationships, or qualifications, scheduling conflicts may exist, resulting in the assignment of a team member who is unavailable. In some cases, scheduling lapses could place certain team members in a position to push the limits of fatigue, particularly if they are just coming off one lengthy job and are scheduled for another job without adequate rest. A set of well-designed job planning tools should provide steps or reminders for planners to check proposed team member schedules. Organizational fatigue risk management policies may help with this process. In this fashion, the job planning tools serve as a scheduling checks-and-balances system.

- Identification of machinery, equipment, and tool requirements: During routine tasks, the material and equipment requirements may be well-understood, but in non-routine operations (or even in routine operations with variations) job planning tools should help planners and team leaders to understand the machinery, equipment, and tool requirements as well as any automated systems that may be necessary to effectively complete the job. If, during routine operations, this step is left out, teams could arrive at the job site and realize that what appeared to be a routine job includes slight variances, requiring a specific tool that was overlooked. Part of the planning process may also include identifying tools that can be staged as part of a reserve equipment kit, remaining in a standby capacity unless/until needed.

- Impact of the high-hazard environment on the work procedures: While teams may become highly familiar with their typical tasks, the high-hazard environment may deliver unexpected changes and should be examined to determine areas of uncertainty, potential variances from what normally occurs, and compensation strategies. For example, if teams have been conducting routine operations on a pipeline installation project over the course of several cool and rainy weeks they may not be accustomed to the need for high fluid intake to stay hydrated. If the weather is expected to change, including unusually dry and warm weather, the teams should prepare for increased hydration needs and an increase in rest breaks. In many organizations that conduct labor-intensive, hands-on work the environment can throw unexpected surprises and if teams are unprepared they could end up struggling to adapt to the changes after they have occurred. Job planning tools should include a thorough examination of the operational environment and ways to prepare for uncertain or unexpected changes.

- Communications requirements: Operational planners and team leaders should understand the nature of the operating environment and ensure that proper communications resources and methods are identified in advance of job commencement. The need for verbal and non-verbal communications should be well-understood and plans should be developed to help the team know when it may be required to shift from one form to another. For example, if verbal communications are being used to direct tasks and the environment becomes excessively noisy the team may consider switching to non-verbal signals. The time to plan for these requirements is not in the middle of a hazardous task. Teams should also identify critical backup resources, such as extra radios or batteries, in case the primary resources fail. As part of the communications plans, any signage and signal requirements should also be reviewed.

- Check-out and check-in procedures: If any team members will be working alone or in small groups at remote locations during high-hazard operations, the team should deliberately plan methods for them to check-out with fellow team members or supervisors when work commences, to check-in at pre-defined intervals to let the team leader know they are okay or to request assets, and to perform a final check-in when the work is complete so the team leader is aware of their status.

- Specific permit requirements: Some jobs may require specific work permits prior to work commencing to ensure that adequate safety measures have been identified. Permit-required confined space entry is one example. Some permitting requirements may include a degree of lead time so these areas should be identified as early as possible.

- Abnormal operations activities and emergency actions: While teams will work to help ensure activities are conducted safely and predictably there may be cases where process upsets, abnormal operations, or emergencies arise. In high-hazard environments operational teams must be prepared in case these situations occur. Pre-defined emergency procedures or actions should be part of the planning process, and organizations should also help to develop an overall emergency management framework that helps teams to take action in the absence of prescriptive step-by-step procedures.

Pre-Operations Briefing

After the operations are planned and as much information as possible has been obtained to identify the mission goals, the resource inputs, work processes and procedures, operational hazards, and factors associated with the operational environment, the pre-operations brief can be developed. This brief often follows a pre-defined template (with some room for variation if required) to help ensure all required outputs from the planning process are input into a standardized format and that key items are not omitted. The brief (also known as briefing) should provide a general overview of the operation, working from general to specific and provide a high level of detail for safety-critical or mission-critical functions. The pre-operations brief sets the stage for building a shared, collective expectation and understanding of the mission objectives, required resources, activities, timeframes, communication procedures, risks, and risk controls, and helps begin the process of developing situational awareness. Since the brief is conducted with all team members present it allows the opportunity for each employee to speak up, ask questions, or raise concerns about the job or associated risks. While the brief should be conducted by the team leader, he or she may turn over certain sections of the brief to other team members or FLs to address specific technical areas. In this fashion, the team leader still maintains overall control and responsibility for the brief. Additionally, in some industries after the team leader has completed the overall brief, individual team sections may break out on their own to conduct sub-team specific functional or technical briefs and discuss their specific tasks.

While job briefing templates will likely differ from industry to industry, some general briefing requirements may include (but are not limited to):

- Roll call and team member introductions: Prior to the commencement of the briefing the team leader should ensure everyone is present or accounted for. While in most cases all team members should be present, there may be some circumstances that make this infeasible (preferably this would be the exception, not the norm). The roll call helps the team leader to know who is present and if anyone is not in attendance, and this helps identify potential needs for re-briefing certain personnel if they are absent from the brief. In many industries, and particularly in small organizations, the team members may already know each other, but in very large organizations or those with a distributed workforce it could be possible for team members to meet for the first time during the pre-operations brief. This is a great time for introductions and to help new members feel welcomed, which can help to build camaraderie.

- Time sync: Many operations require team members to maintain awareness of time so that certain activities can be performed at specific times. In some industries timing may be more critical than others, but overall, it is a good idea to ensure each team member understands the current time, particularly if employees have arrived at the job site from different time zones.

- Crew day and fatigue: The expected hours required to perform the assigned work should be explained so all personnel understand the expectations. If organizations have a policy that limits the total work hours it should be clearly explained so all team members understand the maximum limits. Additionally, during this portion of the briefing team leaders can discuss the effects of fatigue on work performance and its influence on risk. If team members are overly fatigued this is an opportunity for them to bring this to the attention of the team leader.

- Overall description of the operation with emphasis on goals and Leader's Intent: This section of the brief should include a broad overview of the work to be performed by the team and should include targets or goals that the group must reach to achieve success. Leader's Intent is typically conveyed through a written and/or oral statement, and explains what needs to be accomplished, but not specifically how to do it. A strong Leader's Intent Statement can help set the tone for the job and provide general guidance about the desired end-state, or what the team leader expects to see when the job is finished. In the absence of prescriptive orders teams may use Leader's Intent to decide what actions to take or not to take in order to accomplish the goals (*Command and Control* 72). If you are a team leader, you may think of Leader's Intent as a description of what you would like to see at the end of the operation in terms of production, safety, and quality, but you are not directly telling team members specifically how to perform each and every step required to achieve those goals in the Leader's Intent Statement.

- Discussion of procedure flows and team member responsibilities: This is where the briefing begins to move from general to specific. Sometimes referred to in military circles as "walking the dog," this portion of the brief includes a start-to-finish description of the activities that will take place in chronological order. If certain tasks will be performed concurrently these can be described as well. The team leader should describe each aspect of the work, the individuals or sub-teams assigned to the tasks during certain phases, and the roles and responsibilities of those individuals and/or sub-teams.

As a team leader briefing this portion, just think of this as if you are mentally projecting the tasks and leading your team along the path from start to finish. The team members depend on you, so make sure you lead them along the mental path with helpful descriptions of the work to be performed and what they are expected to do. This helps to build a mental model and shared awareness of the tasks to be performed.

- Mission-critical and safety-critical tasks: If certain tasks must absolutely be performed in order to avoid serious negative operational consequences (such as loss of production) these may be considered mission-critical tasks and should be emphasized. Likewise, if certain tasks must be performed properly to avoid serious safety consequences (such as employee injuries or fatalities) they should be deemed safety-critical and should also be emphasized (*Department of Defense Standard Practice for System Safety* 7).

- Authority, responsibility, and distributed leadership: The operational team leader should be the overall DL in charge of the operation, with the authority to direct team actions as well as the one who is responsible for safe mission accomplishment at the team level. However, if sub-team leaders are to be used for oversight of specific functional responsibilities this should be explained. The expectations of FLs should also be explained so each team member understands their potential role as a leader on the team, at least for brief periods of time. The team should leave the briefing with a clear understanding of who is in charge and to whom risk decisions should be elevated.

- Resources available: The outputs from the pre-job planning efforts should be well-defined and should include all of the required human resources (team members, technical experts, supervisors, and sub-team leaders (if applicable), material resources (machinery, equipment, Information Systems, tools, and communications devices), and logistics resources (such as routine or rapid supply chain ordering processes, hydration and meals, or other supply-related resources). In many mission-critical or safety-critical tasks Single Points of Failure (SPF) may lead to unacceptable consequences, so backup resources may be required. The primary and backup resources should be described.

- Description of normal procedures, abnormal procedures, and emergency procedures: The team leader should specify the procedures to be used throughout the job. Oftentimes these procedures will be well-understood by the team, and may simply require a brief comment, but in other cases unique jobs may require specific procedures that may be less familiar, and in those cases the team should have a more detailed discussion. If necessary, lengthy discussions regarding specific techniques to be performed by a sub-team may be tabled for a side-bar discussion after the overall brief. In some cases, as operations progress, the team may realize the procedures typically used are not working or that due to unrecognized hazards or equipment failure the job has progressed into a mode known as abnormal operations. The teams should pre-brief actions to be taken in certain situations where pre-defined abnormal procedures exist, or should discuss general actions to be taken (such as time-sensitive risk management) if the situation is not covered by any procedure whatsoever. The team leader should also explain emergency procedures that may be implemented if hazards escalate to the point where an emergency occurs. The team should also talk about general actions to be taken, such as sounding alarms, protecting and/or evacuating employees, and calling for assistance for certain levels of emergencies, or if an emergency occurs that is not covered by pre-defined step-by-step prescriptive procedures.

- Detailed hazard analysis/risk discussion: The team leader should describe the hazards that were identified during the pre-operations planning process and the overall risk rating (probability of occurrence and severity or consequence). If necessary, the team leader may bring in a functional expert, such as a safety manager, to assist with this discussion. The risk discussion should describe the implemented controls (or the plan for control implementation), acceptable and unacceptable levels of risk, and any uncertainties that still remain. The teams should emphasize the need to maintain awareness of the hazards and the danger of letting their guard down and becoming complacent. This may be of particular importance if the team has been performing routine operations for many days in a row and has not experienced any injuries. Also, while it may be tempting to focus on the most-likely hazards to occur, the team leader should also emphasize awareness of low-probability high-severity scenarios. The team leader should clearly explain who is allowed to make decisions based on the level of risk. For example, it might be the case that line employees may only make risk recommendations for low-level risks and only the team leader can make risk decisions for moderate-level risks, while more serious risk conditions must be elevated to higher levels of authority within the organization. These policies may vary by industry and/or organization and must be decided by the organization as a whole and made explicitly clear to the team. These policies should be developed ahead of time, and reemphasized during the brief.

- Communications procedures: Communication is an Essential Component of effective teamwork and performance, and should be discussed with enough detail to give the team a solid understanding of sender and receiver responsibilities, and feedback requirements. Verbal and non-verbal communication procedures and techniques should be discussed, including primary and backup techniques. If any signals are to be used they should be confirmed for uniformity and understanding across the team.

- Administrative and logistics: Any unique administrative or logistics issues affecting the team, such as supply chain ordering and lead-times, component swap-outs that may require shipment, hydration and meals, logistics request procedures, and any other supply-related issues should be discussed here. This section is more descriptive about the tasks associated with administrative and logistics issues than the Resources section of the brief.

- Turnover plan: In many shift-based operations work can span many hours or even days, and the crews that start a job may not necessarily be the ones to complete it. Therefore, it is critical to clearly explain how information from one team will be passed on to the team that relieves them. The turnover plan should emphasize how important mission-critical information, safety-critical information, changes to the original plan, and production accomplishments and goals will be explained to the oncoming teams. The turnover plan should help to provide a seamless transition between the shift teams. As an additional point, the oncoming team or shift should conduct the same type of pre-operations brief as the team that commenced the job.

- Debrief time and location: A productive debrief is essential for organizational lessons-learned. The team leader should specify the time and location for the debrief and who should attend (typically the entire team).

• Questions or concerns: As a final action before closing out the overall team pre-operations brief the team leader should open the floor for questions, concerns, or discussion of safety issues. If you are a team leader conducting this brief, this is a time to assertively explain your expectations of team members to raise concerns. You may also explain to the team that if anyone is uncomfortable speaking up in public they may speak with you in private after the brief is complete.

Ongoing Analysis throughout Job Execution

The term "job planning" (often referred to as "pre-job planning") may not be a truly fitting term because it seems to imply that planning is only conducted prior to work commencing, but planning is actually an ongoing process. Operations assessments should continue even after the initial job plan is developed and the team is briefed and, in this fashion, planning is actually an ongoing endeavor.

After the pre-operations brief teams will often move to the work area. In some organizations, this may not be a far movement. For example, in hospitals a medical team may work in the same facility where the brief was conducted. In other organizations, such as oil refineries, field engineering, or mining environments, the movement could be to a work site that is slightly further away from the briefing location. When work commences the team will likely encounter either planned or unplanned changes and in many cases some of the information that remained uncertain during the pre-job planning phase may become clearer as the work unfolds. Therefore, teams should periodically compare actual conditions to what was expected, planned, and briefed to determine if any aspects of the plan are different compared to what is actually encountered. New or updated information should be fed back into the original plan to see if any parts of the plan (such as human or material resources, or procedures) must be changed in order to accomplish the work safely and according to the organizational goals and success criteria. Additionally, any team members affected by the new conditions should be informed of the differences so they, in turn, can take appropriate action. In some cases, portions of the briefing may need to be updated and re-explained to the team. Additionally, if time permits an operations log or shift log may be used to document these changes. Depending on the organization and operational environment this log could take several forms, such as a physical logbook or a web-connected electronic Information System. This documentation may also help to facilitate an effective debriefing session, capturing of lessons-learned, and shift turnover information.

Checklist Design and Management

A great deal of information regarding checklists was described in Chapter 5 because well-designed and properly used checklists can be an extremely effective tool to help teams maintain focus during operations and can help them to identify errors during task execution. While checklists may seem like a very simple item in the job planning toolkit, if implemented properly they can become a highly functional administrative control for managing risks by helping teams to keep jobs on track, detect and correct errors before they become hazardous conditions, and recognize when the operational environment may have changed compared to what was originally expected. While a checklist can be extremely helpful for job planning by providing a structured planning and team briefing framework, using checklists in real-time during job performance takes their value to a new level. At the highest level the checklist itself and the actions associated with its use become an essential part of task execution and real-time safety management.

Some organizations use checklists to keep track of overall stages or phases of operations. These checklists are often used by military units and are referred to as execution checklists. They are used to ensure procedures are followed in order and that key items are not skipped. Another more detailed checklist is similar to the execution checklist, but contains specific tasks or steps that must be completed during the job itself as well as specific challenge and reply items to be spoken out loud between team members, or reviewed mentally or orally if work is done by one team member. Since complex jobs often include multiple sets of procedures, a well-designed checklist can provide teams with a means for staying on track and ways to identify if errors have occurred during task execution.

Since checklists are often designed to help teams perform complex tasks, they should be created with enough detail to help employees understand what is required, but not so much information that they become overly burdensome, to the point where they degrade mission performance. Using this concept, checklists should be designed in two formats. The first format is an expanded version of the checklist, which is used for training, and describes each item on the list with the appropriate explanations of the tasks to be completed. If challenge and reply statements are required, the expanded version should list the specific team members required to state the challenge portion and the reply portion, along with the required challenge and reply statements to be read out loud. The next checklist format abbreviates the expanded version into task items, challenge and reply statements, and perhaps associated cautions notes. This format is often much smaller and can be used in the operational environment because of its smaller size and weight.

In some industries (particularly military aviation) these abbreviated formats are referred to as pocket checklists because they often fit in the pockets of the uniforms worn by aviators. Pocket checklists often assume that the users have already read, understood, and been evaluated for adequate understanding of the expanded checklists. Therefore, users must be highly familiar with the expanded checklist requirements or else the pocket checklist items may confuse them. In addition to the specific task items and challenge and reply statements, the checklist should include a method for confirming that all tasks or procedures on the list have been completed. Oftentimes this will include a final statement requiring a team member to verbally confirm the checklist is complete. In a team-based environment, other team members should be primed and ready to hear that statement, and should be prepared to challenge the team if they do not hear the completion statement or if all items have not been completed. Generally speaking, with sequential tasks and checklists, teams should not commence a new checklist until the previous one has been completed, or if there is a reason any items cannot be completed the team should explicitly acknowledge this, including any risks associated with non-completion, and develop a plan to complete the skipped items if necessary. Figure 6.1 is a sample format for a pocket checklist, which includes abbreviated steps.

Procedure A (Checklist Name)

"Procedure A checklist"—verbal announcement

– Task 1
- • Challenge Item .... Reply-Team member(s)
– Task 2
- • Challenge Item .... Reply-Team member(s)
– Task 3
- • Challenge Item .... Reply-Team member(s)
– Task 4
- • Challenge Item .... Reply-Team member(s)

"Procedure A checklist complete"—verbal announcement

Figure 6.1   Sample abbreviated/pocket checklist template

Even the best checklists require conscientious management or their effectiveness will be diminished. Just like any other tool for a job, the checklist must be used the way it was designed in order to be truly effective. If it is left in the toolbox, coveralls pocket, or lab coat, how can it be effectively used to manage task flows and as an error detection instrument? Checklist management is a critical responsibility for team leaders and team members alike. From a team leader perspective you should ensure your team and sub-teams are using any applicable checklists, and from a team member standpoint, you should be responsible for using checklists to manage your activities. Checklist management includes a start and end point and is often referred to as "running the checklist." In a team-oriented task, one employee runs the checklist (meaning he or she reads each item and manages the checklist pace or flow) while the other employees conduct their work. One person on the team should be responsible for ensuring the employee running the checklist actually performs this function. The team member running the checklist typically holds the checklist, tracks each challenge and reply item as they are completed step by step, and holds the team accountable for specific reply responses to verify that the work is done correctly. Additionally, this employee needs to keep the team informed if any checklist items must be performed out of order, and explain how the team will maintain awareness to ensure these items are not omitted. Running the checklist is usually not the only function for this team member, who may also perform job-specific technical duties, and who may be required to reply to certain checklist items related to his duties as well.

In practice, a team supervisor calls for a checklist to be used at the start of the job. The task items integrated into the checklist include a natural flow, so the employee running the checklist reads the challenge items out loud and the other team members reply after their work is complete. The employees' replies match the checklist and are a verbal confirmation that the work has been completed accurately. Let's use an example to illustrate how this is done. In order to keep this broad enough for all backgrounds, rather than choosing an industry-specific example, we'll use a notional piece of equipment, a basic three-person operational team, and a checklist entitled "Equipment Setup Checklist." Suppose this three-person team is preparing to operate heavy mechanical equipment to perform a field engineering or maintenance activity. The crew consists of a supervisor, who is also serving in the capacity of Equipment Operator (EO), an Equipment Technician (ET), and an Assistant Technician (AT). In this case, the EO operates the equipment and the ET ensures that all equipment is properly maintained and set up correctly (including electrical connections, hydraulic fluid, engine oil, and fuel). The AT supports both the EO and ET with their duties and also performs multiple checks to verify the condition of the equipment, such as electrical connections, cooling fluids, and so forth. The EO is in charge of this specific task and the ET is running the checklist. The AT assists both the EO and ET. Prior to work commencing, the equipment must be inspected, and placed in the proper condition, with all connections in place, all fluids at the right levels, adequate fuel for the job (and perhaps with some in reserve in case the job takes longer than planned), additional maintenance and support tools in place, and any additional supplies (such as water for the crew) on hand. Each team member has individual task requirements he or she must perform on this job.

Equipment Setup Checklist

1. Equipment status ....Inspected and ready (ET)
2. Tool status ....Inspected and ready (ET)
3. Fuel level reservoir ....Checked, (state level) (ET)
4. Fuel level gauge ....Checked, (state level) (EO)
5. Hydraulic fluid level ....Checked, (state level) (AT)
   reservoir
6. Hydraulic fluid level gauge....Checked, (state level) (EO)
7. Oil level ....Checked, (state level),
                                            cap secured (AT)
8. Oil pressure light..................Off (EO)
   CAUTION, if the oil pressure light is illuminated
   DO NOT PROCEED with the PRE-START CHECKLIST
9. Generator ....Checked, Set (AT)
   "Equipment setup checklist complete"(ET)

Figure 6.2   **Equipment setup checklist (for figurative system)**

The sample abbreviated/pocket checklist for equipment setup in Figure 6.2 includes the checklist items, including the challenge items (on the left side of the page) and the reply items (on the right side of the page). The reply items also include parentheses to indicate which crewmembers are required to provide the stated reply. Checklists may be conducted using an Action–Challenge–Reply format, where each team member conducts the specific actions required by the checklist item, then the employee running the checklist calls out the challenge item, and the corresponding team member states the appropriate reply. Alternatively, checklists can be conducted using a Challenge–Action–Reply format, where the person running the checklists calls out the challenge item, the appropriate team member performs the specific task item, and then the appropriate team member states the required reply. If appropriate, it may be feasible to include warnings, cautions, or additional notes to assist checklist users. The equipment setup checklist in Figure 6.2 includes some basic steps to ensure the equipment is in the right condition prior to use, and this checklist includes challenge and reply statements.

While this abbreviated/pocket checklist might seem intuitive, it is helpful, both for training purposes and for reference on the job, to have an expanded checklist that explains the detailed steps required by the pocket checklist. Having already been trained with this checklist and evaluated for proper understanding and usage, teams should already be familiar with this expanded checklist prior to commencing work. However, it does provide an added level of support during operational execution if teams have the expanded checklist on hand while work is being conducted. Taking Figure 6.2 and expanding the items into more detail, we find there is much more that goes on behind the scenes of the pocket checklist. Figure 6.3 shows the expanded version of the equipment setup checklist. This checklist is typically run by the ET, who will call out the start of the checklist and each challenge item on the left side of the pocket checklist. The EO, ET, and AT are each required to provide the proper checklist reply (listed on the right side of the pocket checklist) once their task items have been completed.

Equipment Setup Checklist

EO calls out, "Run the Equipment Setup Checklist."

ET states, "Equipment Setup Checklist."

1. Equipment status

The ET inspects all heavy equipment and associated components for proper condition according to operator's manual and replies, "inspected and ready." If there are any problems the ET will raise the concerns to the crew.

2. Tool status

The ET inspects all tools that are used to support, maintain, and repair the heavy equipment and associated components for proper condition according to the

---

operator's manual and replies, "inspected and ready." If there are any problems the ET will raise the concerns to the crew.

3. Fuel level reservoir

The ET visually inspects the sight gauge on the fuel level reservoir and states the specific level in terms of reservoir markings and replies, "Checked, (states level, for example—Full, three-quarters tank, half tank, and so on)."

4. Fuel level gauge

The EO visually checks the fuel level gauge in the cab. Emphasis should be placed on comparing the level of the reservoir in step 3 with the level on the gauge, and any variances should be noted. The EO replies, "Checked, (states level)."

5. Hydraulic fluid level reservoir

The AT visually inspects the sight gauge on the hydraulic fluid level reservoir and states the specific level in terms of reservoir markings and replies, "Checked, (states level)."

6. Hydraulic fluid level gauge

The EO visually checks the hydraulic level gauge in the cab. Emphasis should be placed on comparing the level of the reservoir in step 5 with the level on the gauge, and any variances should be noted. The EO replies, "Checked, (states level)."

7. Oil level

The AT visually inspects the oil level markings on the dipstick, replaces dipstick cap and verifies that the cap is secure, and states the specific level in terms of dipstick markings and replies, "Checked, (states level), cap secured."

8. Oil pressure light

The EO visually confirms that the oil pressure light is not illuminated and states, "Off."

CAUTION, if the oil pressure light is illuminated DO NOT PROCEED
with the PRE-START CHECKLIST, WHICH FOLLOWS THE
EQUIPMENT SETUP CHECKLIST.

---

9. Generator

The AT checks the generator for proper condition, verifies it is set for startup, and replies, "Checked, set."

ET confirms completion of the checklist by stating, "Equipment setup checklist complete." If all items have been completed satisfactorily the team may move on to the Pre-Start Checklist.

Figure 6.3   Expanded equipment setup checklist (for figurative system)

As you can understand, the expanded version of the checklist includes much more detail, and should be derived from and validated with any industry-specific procedures or procedures required by operator manuals/handbooks. Rather than deviating from sound operating procedures provided by manufacturers, operational checklists should be aligned with those procedures to help ensure they are conducted properly and they are in sync with the operational work processes. Also, these checklists are not a substitute for equipment manufacturer instructions and must also not take an organization out of regulatory compliance. So, when examining checklists from a system standpoint, we can see that what seems like a simple solution is more complex when we dig deeper. These examples provide sample generic checklists for normal operations, but in many industries, checklists may be used for managing abnormal operations (when typical processes do not go as planned or expected) and emergency operations (when normal procedures exceed safe boundaries, such as overpressure situations, fires or explosions, gas leaks, engine failures, or other industry-specific emergencies). Organizations seeking to design effective checklists should include diverse representation from all affected parties in the development process to ensure proper design, adequate performance for the tasks considered, and appropriate levels of safety.

Standardized Callouts

As part of operational planning and ongoing execution, team members are often required to maintain a high level of awareness and coordination between each other so that each team member understands what the others are doing, and that equipment modes are set correctly. The sample notional abbreviated/

pocket checklist in Figure 6.2 and the expanded version in Figure 6.3 described challenge and reply items, explaining how the replies should be read back verbatim, or variances explained. Using this reply concept and expanding it even beyond checklists, standardized callouts may be used by team members to request and confirm actions between each other and between team members and equipment (such as mode settings). Surprises in high-hazard environments can often bring with them devastating consequences, so by identifying clear expectations regarding task status and equipment modes (such as ON, OFF, STANDBY, and so on) team members can help coordinate their actions, and develop a higher degree of awareness regarding how other team members and equipment should behave and react, potentially minimizing the number of times surprises occur.

As with the sample checklists, perhaps an example of a notional callout exchange between two crewmembers will help. In this notional example, let's suppose two of the three team members from the example used in Figure 6.2 are operating a piece of machinery (again, we will use a generic, non-industry specific example to make it easier to understand). The following verbal exchange describes how one employee calls for a certain setting while the other one performs the action and/or replies with a standard reply:

Initial Callout (EO)	Reply Callout (ET)
1. "PPE set"	1. "PPE set"
2. "Clear the area"	2. "Area clear"
3. "Connect power cable"	3. "Power cable connected"
4. "Standby for power"	4. "Standing by"
5. "Set power switch to ON"	5. "Power switch set to ON"
6. "Power Confirmed ON"	

While this format could be written down into a unique checklist, for some procedures the checklist may not be appropriate or feasible, or perhaps for some job-specific reason the procedures must be memorized. In addition to the memorization, they could also be embedded as sub-tasks within a checklist. For example, this verbal exchange could be a memorized task flow embedded in a checklist called the "PRE-START CHECKLIST." This information exchange helps keep the two team members "on the same page" and assists with the development of shared expectations and awareness. This format helps hold employees accountable to each other, because, like checklists, these task flows and callouts provide a means for team members to correct each other if the proper response is not delivered and also help them understand the correct modes and status of certain equipment. In high-hazard environments this can be especially critical because risks often emerge in non-obvious ways, such as through errors in coordination and equipment/automation modes. If these errors in coordination and human or equipment status/modes are not corrected they could escalate and lead to downstream failures, with the potential for injury, damage to equipment or the environment, or other operational losses.

In the present age of technology design, design-for-safety is becoming more prevalent, and many forms of equipment and machinery contain built-in safety controls (often referred to as engineering controls) to prevent operators from inadvertently setting incorrect operating modes or from inadvertent exposure to hazards. While these forms of controls can be highly effective and in many cases should be designed into the equipment, there may be situations when using standardized callouts prior to the activation of a specific engineered safety device may be applicable. When callouts are used in this format team coordination becomes a type of administrative hazard control layered on top of the engineering controls designed into the equipment or systems. For example, many modern aircraft are designed with autopilots and automated control features, which allow pilots to pre-select altitude settings. When operated in certain modes the aircraft will alert crews when within a certain altitude (such as 1,000 feet prior to the pre-selected altitude). This automated alerting is a safety feature designed into the aircraft system to help aircrews maintain awareness. In the US Marine Corps KC-130J Hercules aircraft crews actually call out the approaching altitude before the automated system provides the alert. They still use the automated system, but rely on each other to make the callouts when approaching an altitude before the aural system, rather than simply relying on the automation.

This doesn't negate the importance of engineering controls, but can provide a heightened sense of awareness for team members. Rather than letting their guard down and relying on the engineering controls or automated warnings to catch an error, standardized callouts can be used as a way of maintaining correct procedural execution and operational performance, which may even help teams avoid an error or hazard situation before the engineering controls are activated. With this concept the engineering controls can become a backup to the administrative controls (standardized callouts), providing a defense-in-depth strategy while potentially even raising situational awareness.

Checklist Management Discipline

Even the most well designed checklists, operational procedures, and standardized callouts are only as effective as their users. Checklist management and enforcement can be a big challenge. As a team leader, you should work with your teams to develop sound checklist discipline. It is easy to drift away from checklist usage, particularly if this concept is new to the organization or team. Additionally, some team members may initially be uncomfortable with challenge and reply statements, especially if they are used to working alone.

As part of the cultural transition to using these types of checklists, team leaders must take charge and set the example for employees. After all, if you are serving in the role of the team leader and want your employees to use the checklists, you have to show complete buy-in and embrace the process. This includes attending any type of training classes to ensure you understand how the checklists should be used so you can properly supervise and enforce proper checklist usage and motivate your crews using your leader–manager skills. Even if you do not perform the actual duties that require a checklist, you should understand how the checklists are to be used by the line employees so you can identify if they are being used correctly. This knowledge should help you to make on-the-spot corrections if you determine that the team is not using the checklists the way they were designed, and may also empower you to solicit feedback from your team about the checklist effectiveness and impacts on efficiency and safety so they may be improved.

Real-Time Risk Management and Operational Drift

Despite the most detailed planning, the most judicious use of checklists, and adherence to standardized callouts, some degree of uncertainty about risks will always be present. Even during routine operations, like snowflakes, no two jobs are exactly the same. They may seem highly similar, but there are almost always some variances. Therefore, part of ongoing job analysis includes reassessing previously identified risks in real-time to determine if the planned risk controls are effectively maintaining appropriate safety levels. As a team leader, one of your responsibilities should be to ensure that operational risks are identified and controlled, and that if risk levels escalate beyond acceptable levels, you take action. By conducting time-sensitive risk management activities, which may be led by the team leader (or conducted by other team members if she is not available), hazards may be rapidly assessed and real-time risk-informed decisions made to implement risk controls, which may also include pauses in work or stoppages until acceptable levels of risk and appropriate levels of team safety can be assured.

One area that deserves special attention is the way employees perform their work. This chapter has described a great deal about standardization and control, yet if the operational environment is constantly changing and if no two jobs are identical, how can teams be expected to perform their work in the same way, every time, all the time? When work systems are designed, they must be tested and then implemented, but as the operational teams determine what works and what doesn't, and how standardized procedures either support or degrade their ability to meet production goals, they may slowly begin to modify their work to get the job done. This is normal in many organizations, and can have positive and negative impacts. As operational teams begin to stray, or drift away from the work procedures that were designed, they may be introducing inherent risks into their work processes. A shortcut here, a skipped step there, all in the name of improved speed or efficiency, can introduce systemic risks that may not be well-understood by the team members. In some cases, the team members may understand these risks very well, yet from an organizational risk decision-making process, this may not be their decision to make. Decisions made locally by the team may also have downstream impacts on other parts of the organization, which may not even enter into the minds of the team members (which is yet another example of why work should be planned and updated using a system approach).

If left unchecked, this operational drift can become the new, normal (and informal) way the crews conduct their work. Any undetected risks may emerge in new ways and result in injury or damage. But is all drift bad? What if the employees are actually finding better and safer ways to perform the work? What if their methods actually *are* making the work safer? This is why, as a team leader, you must earn the respect of your teams so they will explain these issues to you. As their senior representative to the organization, you become the voice of the team about the risks they face, the way they perform their work, and any policies and procedures that need to be examined for adaptation and change.

So, how can the organization capitalize on the innovative and creative capacity of operational teams who are very good at what they do? Ignoring drift won't solve the problem, yet constantly trying to enforce procedures that don't work is not likely to solve it either. However, when an organization can develop openness, honesty, and trust between teams, team leaders, and organizational staff (including policy designers and safety staff members) they may begin to find new ways to work together to close the gap and keep the drift from expanding too far. By creating innovation teams and methods to allow employees to work with policy and procedure designers, organizations may be able to capitalize on the wonderful diversity of thought, creativity, and thoroughness that a well-balanced team provides. This requires the organization to view itself as a system of teams that must work together, regardless of specific technical functions. As an operational team leader, you are the representative for your teams to become part of this process and you should be adept at communicating with and translating between management, top-level leadership, and operational team members so that the gap between designed work and actual work is kept as narrow as possible.

Debriefing and Lessons-Learned

Since job planning is continuous, it should be carried into the post-operations debrief using a lessons-learned process. While this may not immediately seem like ongoing analysis, if the debrief points are captured in a lessons-learned system they can actually be fed forward into future job planning. Immediately after work is completed and the team returns to a safe and comfortable area where they can talk, the team leader should lead a debrief session. The debrief should be an open and honest forum to allow all team members the opportunity to discuss what went right and what went wrong with the job, what may be improved, and ways the improvements may be made. The debrief is part of a lessons-learned process that helps teams and organizations with continuous learning and, if used properly, mistakes, errors, and failures from the past may potentially be identified and avoided in the future. Additionally, lessons-learned systems can help teams identify what aspects of past operations helped teams achieve success. While it is easy (and tempting) to focus on what went wrong with an operation, oftentimes teams can learn as much about safety and production by studying what went right as they can by studying what went wrong.

The debrief should be built into the work day, as opposed to an add-on duty. In order to capture critical feedback during the debrief, as a team leader you may be required to put on your tactical leadership hat. Oftentimes the crews are tired and ready to go home, and a lengthy debrief may be the last thing on their minds. This is why you must encourage them, seek their input, and let them know how valuable their feedback is to the safety and production process. One technique you can use to facilitate feedback is to coach your team through the process, beginning with an oral review of the job phases, working chronologically from start to finish and asking team members what went right, what went wrong, and what can be improved (both from a safety and production standpoint). While the lessons-learned process is not foolproof and will not guarantee the same problems will never reoccur, it can help teams find ways to improve over past performance by identifying failure points and designing strategies for success.

Conclusions

Production and safety performance are inextricably linked. Job planning that simply focuses on operations and production goals will likely expose teams to unnecessary risks. Conversely, if planning focuses too heavily on safety, the operational team may not achieve organizational objectives, leading to downstream financial failures, which may ultimately degrade safety in other less obvious ways, such as layoffs or reductions in safety investments. Job planning should begin well before the operational team meets, and should be embedded within the organization as part of the work system processes. If organizations take this concept seriously, and work to design standardized procedures, develop highly-disciplined teams that can execute checklists with a high degree of coordination and acumen, and include methods for capturing lessons-learned to improve the work system, sustainable long-term safety and production may be the result. As an operational team leader you are the link that binds these larger concepts to the team and it is up to you to work with your teams and the organization to achieve this continuous improvement.

Chapter 7

Resilience, Adaptability, and Adaptive Capacity

Resilience is a ubiquitous word and generally brings up images of people bouncing back from tragedy, or rebuilding after losses have occurred. Resilience can be collective, as when communities survive the effects of a natural disaster and rally support to rebuild, or personal, as when individuals survive devastating illnesses to emerge seemingly stronger and then encourage others to do the same. The world is filled with stories about resilience. Perhaps that is why it is so applicable to team leadership, and particularly to teams that operate in high-hazard environments where adversity is part of everyday life.

Rather than focus on a single definition of resilience, let's consider resilience as a range of capacities. While some degree of resilience probably exists in everybody and every team, developing resilience to increasingly greater degrees may help teams to work at their highest levels of sustainable safe performance. In order to reach these levels of resilience operational teams must develop the ability to adapt and should view this ability as an essential function, or perhaps even as a skillset, which should be cultivated and improved over time, just like technical job skills. Since the world is constantly changing, including the economic and regulatory environmental system surrounding the organization, operational procedures must constantly adapt and change as well. Adaptability is the aptitude which individuals, teams, and organizations possess that enables adaptation, and adaptive capacity may be viewed as the amount or level an individual, team, or organization can adapt before safety, performance, quality, and reliability are negatively impacted. By building in resilience, adaptability, and high levels of adaptive capacity at the individual and team level, the organization stands to become stronger as well because the employees and teams are the most critical part of the organization. Through the creation and cultivation of resilience, adaptability, and adaptive capacity, operational teams (and therefore, organizations) may be better positioned to anticipate and react to unexpected risks, thereby helping them stay a step or two ahead of failure. While organizations may want to feel like safety is a static goal that is achieved once and for all, in reality it is a quest and a continuous process that should last as long as the organization exists. Resilience, adaptability, and adaptive capacity work to support this process.

What is Resilience?

Imagine for a moment the victims of natural disasters whom you have seen on television interviews. Can you picture their faces? Can you hear the sadness in their voices as they demonstrate the resolve and determination to push forward and recover? Stories of human resilience abound and are a great testament to the human spirit. From earthquakes, hurricanes, or wildfires, natural disasters are a reality that humanity must face. Additionally, there are so many tragic stories of people stricken by severe illness, which not only affects them, but their families and friends as well. Yet, in so many cases, we can find the will and determination to recover and thrive. Despite the tragedy, devastation, and emotional toll experienced by these people, who could easily give up, they push forward and fight to recover. These are great stories of collective and personal resolve, and this is often what comes to mind when we think of resilience. People often associate resilience with the ability to bounce back or return to an original state (or perhaps an improved state) after being subjected to extreme conditions. In mechanical terms this might be seen as the ability of an object to return to its original form after being stretched to (or past) its operational limits. From a personal standpoint it could also mean recovering from illness or depression.

Generally speaking, however, organizations may not typically think of resilience as a safety or an operational attribute. In a safety and operations context, resilience may be thought of as the ability of an individual employee, team, or organization to accomplish operational goals with consistent performance and adequate levels of safety, despite the existence of hazards, uncertainty, and risk, and while being exposed to constant external and internal pressure and unexpected disruptions and threats. This description does not necessarily make one think about catastrophic loss and recovery from adversity, such as more traditional connotations of resilience, but why is that? Perhaps it is because in the most resilient organizations, teams and individuals are constantly adapting with micro-variations to continuously manage safety and production, so that rather than breaking under extreme adversity or pressure, these systems are able to bend, flex, adapt, and eventually emerge as good as (or better than) before. And, yes, there are times when disaster will happen, catastrophic failures will occur, and the organizations will need to rebound (following the traditional notion of resilience), but if organizations consider adaptability and resilience as necessary attributes (and integrate them into the definition of performance), catastrophic failure as a result of operational processes and degraded safety may be limited.

Resilience may be thought of in terms of levels. Rather than considering organizations as either resilient or non-resilient, it may be more helpful to determine how resilient a team or an organization is and the level of adaptive capacity that exists. After all, it is unlikely that organizations and teams exhibit no resilience at all, and by identifying where they are on the resilience, adaptability, and adaptive capacity scale, leaders will have a baseline for improvement.

- Surviving: The first level of resilience may be thought of as Surviving. This is often seen in small businesses that lack a large staff or budgets, and may not have an abundance of resources to invest in planning. These organizations may be comprised of very small teams and often rely on "heroes" to get the job (often many jobs) done. The leaders' hope is that eventually they will "make it" and be able to invest more resources into contingency planning, safety systems, and additional human and material resources, which will help them to be more equipped to handle external pressures. If they can just wait it out long enough, and avert catastrophic failure until they succeed they will have enough capital resources to invest in more robust systems. The problem exists in this last statement. What if they do not avert catastrophic failure? What if they are stretched so thin they cross safety margins and experience a devastating injury or major equipment failure? This is a big what-if question that many leaders in Surviving organizations hope they do not have to face. They hope failure and accidents will not occur and they also hope the organization will be able to recover if catastrophe does occur. The problem is that if an organization is barely surviving, making payroll, and relying on heroes to get the work done, teams may be closer to a mishap than they realize, and if catastrophic failure does occur, they may or may not be able to mobilize the resources to recover. Without well-defined backup and contingency plans and resources, recovery options are a guessing game and leaders really cannot determine with any degree of certainty if they will be able to rebuild after a significant financial, operational, or safety loss. Another problem with the Surviving level is that although some teams and organizations may have the capacity to move beyond this level, they may still rely on the old habits developed during the Surviving stage of resilience.

- Planning: The next level of resilience is probably something many teams and organizations are quite familiar with. They expect failure to occur at some point and through resource accumulation and planning, have created ways to reduce the effects of failures so that the organization can rebound and recover from failure without completely losing its ability to operate. They may have a core set of functions that can still be performed even if they experience devastating losses. This is still a somewhat reactive mode, but at least teams are prepared for certain scenarios so they can react appropriately instead of trying to come up with recovery plans after a catastrophic event has occurred.

- Sustaining: The third level of resilience builds upon the Planning level by including all of the attributes associated with that level, but also by incorporating methods to contend with the constant internal and external pressures faced by operational teams, which require them to continually adjust their performance. A key requirement for achieving the Sustaining level of resilience is the creation of adaptive capacity within the organization by developing individuals and teams that possess adaptability as a key job performance skill. Sustaining organizations are able to adapt when faced with new demands, which are subsequently placed on the operational teams that will carry out the procedures to achieve the goals associated with these new demands. They also employ leaders who are highly capable of determining when performance must be adjusted in favor of safety goals over performance when they realize operational teams are precariously close to the edge of safety boundaries. Sustaining organizations tend to deal well with unexpected changes and maintain composure during conditions of uncertainty because they are able to mobilize incredible amounts of human thought leadership to devise strategies for safely executing new operational functions. They are also adept at predicting how failure may occur and attempt to either stay several steps ahead of failure to avert catastrophe or to reduce the level of damage that occurs through adequate planning measures. Sustaining organizations tend to perform well over time because, rather than ignoring the impact of external and internal demands and changes, and constantly telling employees to follow the old rules (even though they won't work under the new demands), these organizations embrace change as a way of life, and develop the capacity at the individual and team level to effectively deal with these changes using a system approach. Leaders continually assess new demands, compare these demands to as-designed work processes to see what works and what doesn't, and lead teams in the redesign of work systems or in the design of completely new systems. Table 7.1 summarizes the characteristics of resiliency levels.

Table 7.1   Characteristics of resiliency levels

Resilience Level	Characteristics
Surviving	• Lack of resources
	• Relies on "heroes"
	• Hope that mishaps or major failures will not occur
	• Limited or no contingency or backup plans
	• Highly reactive
Planning	• Expecting some level of failure to occur
	• Resource accumulation and planning to develop ways to mitigate the effects of failure
	• Planning methods for rebound and recovery from failure without completely losing ability to operate
	• Moderately proactive with slight reactive tendencies
Sustaining	• Builds upon Planning level
	• Includes methods to contend with the constant internal and external pressures faced by operational teams
	• Continually adjusting performance to meet demands
	• Developing adaptive capacity
	• Ability to adapt when faced with new demands
	• Tendency to deal well with unexpected changes and maintain composure during conditions of uncertainty
	• Highly proactive, plans for the need to react, and develops adaptability as a skill that helps employees react in a controlled manner

Resilience Maturity

So, as a team leader, how does this impact your ability to safely and effectively lead your team as you work to accomplish the goals set forth by your organization? First of all, if after reading this you realize that you are operating at the Surviving level of resilience you may have some work to do, including some challenging conversations with your bosses. However, the good news is that it is possible to move out of the Surviving mode, and organizations truly seeking excellent performance should strive to reach the Sustaining level of resilience. This requires employees and teams to mature over time as they learn how to adapt to changing demands while balancing safety, production, and efficiency. Part of this maturation process should include planning for how to reach the Sustaining level of resilience (which may take some time to achieve, and requires constant vigilance to maintain).

If your goal is to become a Sustaining organization, start out by seeking areas for improvement. Are there ways to improve the way work is performed? Are there ways that safety can be improved at the individual and team level? When new demands are placed on the team (either increased production requirements or emerging requirements) are there ways that the team can effectively adapt to these changes while planning for potential failure, so that if these changes result in losses, your teams can continue to function, even in a reduced capacity while adequately protecting your personnel? As new procedures are introduced, are your teams adept at detecting new risks and providing feedback into the lessons-learned and work system design process? These are all guiding questions you may consider when determining your level of resilience and ways to help your teams and organization reach higher levels of resilience.

Adaptability and Adaptive Capacity

"Improvise, adapt, and overcome." Have you ever heard this maxim? Often used to describe military approaches to adversity, this phrase has become somewhat commonplace in society to describe ways to address hardships. It sounds like a great slogan, but is it really that easy to improvise, adapt, and overcome the challenges faced by operational teams? Maybe it is, but in the process of improvising and adapting in order to get the job done, undetected risks can sometimes emerge in new ways. While improvisation and adaptation are important capabilities for operational teams conducting high-hazard work, if used incorrectly the process of improvising and adapting can bring negative consequences, which will probably not help the operational team or organization overcome its obstacles.

Adaptability may be viewed as the capability of an individual, team, or organization to adapt to external and internal changing conditions. External conditions may be economic or regulatory demands, requiring the organization to make changes to the way work is performed. Internal conditions may include the downstream demands on operational teams that result from the external changes. Adaptable organizations are better prepared to react to changes. Adaptive capacity may be considered the degree to which individuals, teams, and organizations can adapt before crossing a safety boundary into catastrophic failure. To further explain the concept of adaptability and adaptive capacity, perhaps an analogy will be helpful. Think of adaptability as being like a container designed to hold a liquid, such as water. A pliable or flexible type of cup may be able to adapt and slightly expand to hold more water. A paper cup may not be very adaptable because it can only flex a little bit. However, a hydration pack, such as those with flexible drinking straws worn by endurance athletes or soldiers, are quite flexible and can conform a bit to fit around the shape of the body. A hydration pack may be considered highly adaptable when compared to the paper cup. Now think of adaptive capacity like the size of the drinking container. There are various sizes of containers. Smaller cups hold a smaller volume of liquid and larger cups hold a larger volume of liquid. Individuals, teams, and organizations that have low levels of adaptive capacity may be like a small cup. The capacity to adapt is smaller, and when the cup overflows, mishaps or failures occur. On the other hand, individuals, teams, and organizations that have higher levels of adaptive capacity may be like a large container that can handle large volumes of water before overflowing and experiencing a mishap or failure. A large hydration pack would be both adaptable and have a higher level of adaptive capacity than a small cup, which is less adaptable and has a lower adaptive capacity. Adaptability and adaptive capacity directly support resilience, and, like resilience, it is unlikely that organizations are not adaptable at all. It is more likely the case that adaptable organizations fall on a continuum, having low to high levels of adaptive capacity, and are comprised of teams and individuals whose adaptive capacity ebbs and flows from day to day.

In order for operational teams to be adaptable, individual employees must be able to adapt to changing environments, react appropriately using mitigation efforts when unexpected hazards are encountered, and be able to change operational approaches when plans become ineffective. Therefore, a high degree of adaptive capacity at the individual level is a core component for building team resilience. Additionally, in order for organizations to be adaptable, individual employees who possess high levels of adaptive capacity must be well-integrated with other team members to form adaptable teams. Through the collective teamwork process operational teams are then able to adapt to changing conditions and operational environments, proactively anticipate and plan for risks, and work together as a group to change operational approaches when they no longer work, when original plans become ineffective, or when unexpected situations emerge.

In most high-hazard environments work is often performed as a team, so it is not good enough for organizations to simply hire and develop individual employees who are adaptable and flexible, without considering the operational team. Adaptable teams with high adaptive capacity levels are a core component for building resilient organizations. If left unchecked and without direction, individual adaptability may result in a lack of direction, so as a team leader you should encourage team-based approaches to adaptability and for developing higher levels of adaptive capacity. This provides teams with direction and helps individual members understand that their adaptive decisions must be directed towards the shared objectives of the team. This concept can be expanded further, from an organizational perspective. Top-level leaders must ensure that departments harness the adaptive capacity of their teams and staff so that any plans and decisions that are made through an adaptive approach are in line with the overall vision of the organization, because ultimately, individual, team, and departmental actions must be consistent with the overall vision and corporate objectives in order to meet production and safety goals.

To illustrate the concept of adaptability and adaptive capacity we'll use two examples. The first is a US Marine Corps aviation squadron and the second is a hypothetical broadcast tower construction and maintenance company. In the US Marine Corps, aviation crewmembers are trained early on in their careers to follow step-by-step procedures for their aircraft crew positions. For example, pilots are trained to follow aircraft operations checklists as well as technical procedural manuals to ensure they operate the aircraft correctly and safely. At the same time, in practice, they are trained to become adaptable; to learn how to adapt their decisions based on the changing operational environment. Additionally, at the beginning of the aircraft operating manuals there is an explicit statement claiming the procedures contained in the manual are not a substitute for good judgment. What this means is that crewmembers are expected to think and adapt if the procedures in their manuals will not work, particularly if following the procedures will make them less safe under certain conditions. So, at the individual level aircrew are able to adapt. When multiple crewmembers are placed together as a team (such as the pilots, crew chiefs, loadmasters, and so on) each member supports the team's ability to adapt by providing feedback based on the changing mission dynamics and the operational environment, balanced with the shared team objectives. The organization itself (the squadron) builds this adaptive capacity into operational planning by providing these crews with the additional resources they may need in case external demands change, such as the need for additional aircraft to meet the mission objectives. So, adaptability and adaptive capacity exist at the individual crewmember level, the crew level, and the organizational level.

Using the second example and working in reverse order (organization to individual) to demonstrate adaptability and adaptive capacity, suppose a wireless tower company is faced with an increasing demand to install additional towers or to upgrade towers with new equipment to meet changing customer requirements. The data needs of customers may be increasing so rapidly that in order to keep pace with that demand, the organization must schedule more and more construction and maintenance activities. From an organizational perspective, adaptive planning may consider forecasted needs and project the required number of human and material resources to meet those needs, including the use of a surplus, or reserve capacity, in case there is an additional surge in demand that must be met. At the team level, there should be well-trained individuals who understand the operational goals set forth by the organization. Therefore, when the skilled individuals, who are extremely technically competent, find out that a procedure is not working or that they need to adjust their work based on the team goals, they can interject their opinions and ideas into the ongoing planning and analysis process to help the team adapt and meet the goals passed on to them by the organization. This is not to say they create their own procedures or violate safety rules to get the job done, but they work within the operational and safety boundaries promulgated by the organization, while adapting to the demand through additional resource requests, scheduling changes, or formal requests to modify techniques to get the work completed accurately and safely. In some cases this may be through debriefing/lessons-learned and the work system design process, but the process may need to be conducted rapidly in order to satisfy demands, particularly if time is of the essence. This is why adaptation must be examined using a system approach, so that decisions are made using input from multiple experts, which in turn helps support resilience.

Support Structure for Enabling Resilience

Resilience, adaptability, and adaptive capacity often start with attitudes. When leaders and employees shape their attitudes and then model the behavior they wish to see in others it can help start the process for building deeper levels of resilience, adaptability, and adaptive capacity. However, attitudes and behaviors must be backed by organizational structures, which provide everyone with the needed support to lean on when attempting to build this capacity. While there may be numerous models to examine when trying to develop higher levels of resilience, developing a support network with the types of programs shown in Figure 7.1 may be a great starting point to begin the resilience development process.

Figure 7.1   Resilient program structure for safety and operational performance

- Management system for leadership and employee involvement: At the organizational level, a program should exist that facilitates the management of activities that promote leadership and employee involvement in safety and operational performance. This is a system for managing how employees and leaders alike get involved and remain involved with the way operations are conducted and the way safety is planned, implemented, and improved. This involvement could include such activities as committees, planning and improvement teams, or safety councils. While there needs to be a balance between the number of committees in an organization and the amount of work to be done (in order to avoid the getting overly burdened with meetings), without a system for managing this type of involvement, participation may be highly variable, and results may be highly inconsistent. This system can also help to guide the organization as leadership and authority strategies are created.

- Quality management: In many organizations quality management probably already exists in some form. Attaining quality management certification may help organizations refine their processes for achieving quality goals, and these goals must be promulgated to the operational team level. Operational team leaders, in turn, should make these quality goals explicitly known. Otherwise, in the face of high-hazard environments, where errors and distractions must be managed, and decisions must be made between production and safety, how are sub-teams and individual employees supposed to determine if they have met their quality goals when work is complete?

- Operations, standardization, and compliance: While some organizations may view standardization and compliance as safety requirements, organizations should consider the possibility of placing some of the burden for achieving these goals on the operations department. For example, compliance with safety regulations is often seen as the responsibility of the safety department, yet it is the operational teams that must comply with many of these regulations as they perform their work. For example, the safety department may create a policy for fall protection, requiring employees to use a fall protection system, but the compliance responsibility in practice really falls on the teams as they do their work. Standardization may also work well if managed as an operations program by the operations department, since the operational teams are the ones who must conduct the work and follow standardized procedures. Consideration should be given to sharing some of these overall responsibilities by the operations department and teams, but this will require top-level support of the team leaders, who are often in charge of ensuring production demands are met.

- Safety management system and safety engineering: A safety management system creates the structure for managing all of the organization's safety activities and can actually work to integrate some of the already-existing committees and councils into the safety management process. Safety engineering, which is a related function, should serve to implement many of the components of a safety management system, and should emphasize the participation in hazard identification and risk assessment processes, work system design (from a safety perspective), and methods to design hazards out of operational systems. These functions should serve to support the operational teams and assist them with methods for conducting their activities as safely as feasible.

- Communications strategies and topologies: Communication is oftentimes one of the most challenging aspects of organizational effectiveness. Many other programs and policies rely so heavily on effective communication, yet organizations may not even consider deliberate communication strategies, or if they do, it may be an afterthought once the programs and policies are designed. By thinking through the way information should be communicated and designing topologies that clearly show (visually and in writing) the proper flow of information, organizations may be able to minimize the amount of confusion that takes place and maximize the capability of the teams to perform their work, identify needed changes, and communicate those needs to critical parts of the organization. This way, rather than getting bogged down trying to identify who needs to know what and when, a communication framework can help team leaders to quickly send information and receive feedback to make faster and more accurate decisions.

- Learning and reporting systems: Identifying leading indicators is a crucial function for organizations that conduct operations in high-hazard environments. Leading indicators are often pieces of information that help provide leaders with data points and explanatory information that potentially indicate how catastrophic failures could happen in the future. A lessons-learned system is a key feedback tool that allows operational teams and organizations to understand significant information about past operations. While learning what went right or wrong in the past may appear to be a lagging indicator rather than a leading indicator because it points to historical data, the learning process can actually facilitate the detection of errors, operational drift, and small failures before they escalate into bigger disasters. If used effectively, lessons-learned systems can actually help organizations identify and act on small indicators when they are revealed and feed this information forward into future planning to help teams avoid potential negative consequences. Near-miss (or near-hit) reporting tools are also an essential element of resilience because, like lessons-learned systems, they allow organizations to identify potential failure points when they are smaller and to identify dormant hazards that could become actualized if the conditions are different in the future. Sometimes a near-miss is one step away from a serious mishap and by identifying these situations before an accident or major failure occurs, organizational leadership may be better prepared to understand the ways things can fail, the associated conditions and context, and the necessary adaptations that must occur to remain ahead of failure as much as feasible. One of the main contributions of leading indicator systems is that they help organizations learn, adapt, and grow. If organizations are constantly looking at lagging data and only correcting the conditions that caused injuries or accidents in the past, without thinking about how to actually prevent mishaps in the future, they may be missing opportunities to learn, become proactive, to make small adaptations, and build resilience to stay ahead of hazards before they occur.

- Work system design and feedback: When external demands placed on organizations cause them to change internal policies or production demands on employees, operational teams will often find ways to meet these new demands, even if it means cutting corners or skirting around safety requirements. Unless a conscious effort is made by top executive leadership and department leaders to understand how the changes will impact the way work is performed, there will be a gap between existing rules, regulations, and policies and the way operational teams do their jobs. For example, if new customer demands force organizations to ramp up production, this will have an impact on employee schedules. Jobs that may have taken ten hours to complete could take 12 hours or more to complete in order to deliver more product or additional services. If the organization has work day limitations this could force operational teams to violate the rules in order to meet the production requirements. Otherwise, if they comply with the existing rules they may fail at meeting the production goals.

Neither of these choices is fair, and the situation places the operational team leader in the uncomfortable position of having to choose between the two options, yet both are losing propositions. It is the organizational leadership's responsibility to avoid putting team leaders and employees in this position. If you are an operational team leader this may require push back from you as you attempt to manage the safety of your teams. Unless organizational leadership understands the repercussions and works to either staff the teams with additional employees, balance production demands against schedules (such as by stretching out the schedules slightly to avoid work day violations), or modify the work system altogether to allow operational teams to conduct the work more efficiently, a gap between policies and actual work procedures is likely to emerge. Work system design processes should allow input from key organizational departments as well as feedback from line operational employees so that everyone can get a true picture of what works and what doesn't, particularly as the teams strive to adapt to new changes. Using this process, the organization may think ahead and proactively plan, which should enable judicious adaptation rather than hasty decision making that lacks a system approach. Work system design processes that include employee input and feedback facilitate resilience by helping the organization deliberately stretch and flex to meet changing demands, rather than acutely pushing past safety boundaries.

- Innovation and experimentation: Related to work system design processes, innovation and experimentation are a vital part of adaptation. Programs that facilitate testing new policies, procedures, and work methods/systems and allow employees to try new and innovative techniques in a controlled environment can help organizations push their adaptive capacity to deeper levels. In highly-controlled organizations that do not allow innovation, change to official work processes often happens very slowly, even while the external environment is adapting and forcing new demands on the organizations to produce better products in shorter amounts of time. So, when red tape and bureaucratic policies prevent teams from innovating and trying out new methods for adapting to the new work demands, mismatches emerge between what the organization needs to do and what they allow employees to do. Organizations can design formal innovation and experimentation programs and facilities (such as engineering labs and simulation systems) that support the testing of new ideas to see what works and what doesn't, particularly compared to emerging demands. These programs can enable resilience through proactive planning, design, testing, and implementation of new methods, and should be tightly integrated with the work system design process. This integration should also include the previously described safety engineering activities, which may help to provide innovative risk controls.

There may be some overlap between the structural elements, but the common link between all of these program components is leadership behavior and the activities leaders perform. Unless leadership at all levels of the organization supports a deliberate resilience development structure and efforts to build adequate levels of adaptive capacity, resilience development is more likely to fail. If the structure fails to function properly, efforts at maintaining resilience may falter and employees, teams, and departments may fall back into their old habits. When this happens managers tell employees to adhere to the old procedures, employees create ad-hoc workarounds and keep them hidden from management, teams rely on heroes to get the job done, and the organization itself hides from the reality of internal and external demands, the need for adaptability and greater adaptive capacity, and the necessity for greater levels of resilience, all the while moving closer and closer to failure. Leadership is the common hub that binds each program together, and all of the programs and policies in this structure require unquestionable buy-in and support from all levels of leadership. When supervisors and line employees see the activities senior leaders perform and the behavior they model, they may in turn mimic those behaviors, so it is crucial that leaders behave and act in ways that encourage employees to do the same.

Standardization versus Adaptation—How Can You Have Both?

If adaptability and adequate levels of adaptive capacity support resilience, yet standardization (which enables consistent performance) is a requirement for operational teams, how are these ostensibly diametrically opposed concepts reconciled? As a team leader if you are telling your teams to be standardized using checklists, and conduct the same procedures all the time, yet at the same time you are telling them to be flexible, adaptable, and to develop deeper levels of adaptive capacity, how can they reconcile these conflicting goals? Be adaptable, but do things the same way. Does that make sense to team members? It might not at first, but if they are trained right, they should begin to understand how and when to standardize and how and when to adapt. Over time, organizations that do these things well and know how to standardize procedures and then adapt those procedures when needed may show higher levels of resilience, which is essential for sustainable growth.

Standardization and adaptability may seem like contradictory terms. Standardization requires uniformity and commitment to doing the same thing every time. Adaptability allows for change and improvisation. Standardized procedures build the framework for consistent performance and shared expectations among team members, and standardization may be required on many levels. Whether integrated into SOPs and checklists, briefing templates and guides, work system design processes, or operational work tasks, standardization provides a structure to build common knowledge across teams and to create consistent performance. It can help new employees integrate well on high-functioning, well-established crews or teams and help align team members "on the same page."

This shared collective understanding through standardization allows a common reference point for adaptation if or when it is required to mitigate risks associated with the dynamic operating environment. When employees understand the standardized processes for conducting their work they may begin to understand how risks can impact this work and how the work may potentially be modified in order to mitigate risks and maintain adequate levels of safety. In this manner, standardization provides a baseline or foundation from which to adapt. This foundation can facilitate adaptation and a shared understanding across the team, rather than uncontrolled ad hoc adaptation by individual team members, which can induce chaos. When new threats emerge employees and teams may be more resilient and able to adapt and continue operations rather than shut down completely.

Consider the following example: Suppose a team is conducting construction operations and a standardized checklist requires the removal of a physical barrier at a certain point in the operation. Due to increased production demands another employee (who is part of a completely different team) is assigned to an additional job, working adjacent to the construction team. If the team removes the barrier it could potentially expose the new employee to hazards. So, when the team realizes the additional employee could be exposed to physical hazards, they conduct a PTA activity, reassess risks using the time-sensitive risk management process, and decide to wait to remove the barrier until the new employee completes his task. After this operation, the debriefing, rapid feedback, and lessons-learned process could lead to the addition of a note to the

SOPs or checklists so that in the future, before the barrier is removed teams will be required to ensure all personnel have cleared the area and if other personnel are present, teams remove the barrier at a different time, providing protection to any employees who have not cleared the area. In this fashion, standardized procedures are locally adapted and then this adaptation is integrated into future versions of the procedures, which are then standardized to include the new information. This is one way standardization and adaptation can be reconciled.

For operational team leaders it may be helpful to have a roadmap or a loosely structured method to assist teams through this process. Operational team leaders may use the following guidelines to help guide their teams through the process of adapting standardized procedures:

- Determine which procedures or tasks are modifiable: Many procedures are etched in stone and may not even be slightly modified without a lengthy bureaucratic process. These may be safety-critical procedures that must be followed exactly for correct and safe operation of a system. Other procedures may have some "wiggle room" for modification. This might mean that steps may be changed or fine-tuned slightly to make them better. In many cases, older and more experienced workers may be a great source of knowledge, as many of them have already figured out better, more efficient, more effective, or safer ways to accomplish their work. As a team leader you should work to gain their trust so they will share this knowledge with you and the other team members. It is better for the team if this knowledge is shared and integrated into a standardized process for everyone to use than to keep it hidden. When faced with changes in the operational environment or changes forced on the operational teams by the organization as it reacts to external pressure, knowing which procedures can be modified will help speed up the adaptive process. In some cases overarching procedures must be specifically followed, but allow for minor individual techniques to accomplish the standardized procedures. For example, a technique may be a way to accomplish the procedure while allowing individual improvisation, as long as the procedural requirements are not violated. In Step 3 of the Equipment Setup Checklist from Figure 6.2 in Chapter 6 the ET is required to check the fuel level in the fuel reservoir by examining the reservoir sight gauge, and is then required to confirm that it has been checked and state the fuel level. However, if this sight gauge is notorious for getting grease and debris stuck on the outside, which may limit the ability of team members to see the fuel level, the ET might apply a simple technique of wiping off the sight gauge every time the reservoir is checked. Does this violate any part of the procedure or was any item skipped? Not at all. This is just a simple example, and your specific organization may have numerous areas where this approach may be applied. However, whether or not this process is allowed may vary by industry and organization, so open and honest conversations about procedures and techniques must be part of the debriefing, lessons-learned, and work system design process to make sure all team members understand techniques versus procedures, what can be amended, and what would actually be a rule violation. As a hint, removing a safety guard from hazardous machinery to perform work faster is not a technique, and is likely a safety violation.

- SOP and checklist review: Review SOPs and checklists on a regular basis and compare the policies and procedures written in those documents with what you have observed on the job. If your operational teams have devised more efficient, more effective, and safer methods for conducting the work, they should be formally reviewed and perhaps considered as best practices. Finally, the SOPs and checklists can be revised based on these best practices. One advantage to this process is that it can help standardize methods across the organization, so that all teams performing the same work at multiple locations do it the same way. This helps avoid multiple disparate policies and procedures being used at multiple work sites, which can sometimes be confusing for employees traveling from site to site. This review and updating method should be integrated into the work system design process, which would also include risk assessments of the proposed changes.

- Develop a refinement process flow: By working with the organization and operational teams it may be possible to map out a defined flow for adapting to changing conditions through policy or procedure changes. Following a design–develop–test–implement (and document) process can help operational teams and the policymakers who create rules align their expectations and work methods in an organized fashion. Documenting the results of changes and distributing the changes to all affected parties is a key part of the process. How frustrating will it be for a team to get to a work site and have no idea about the changed procedures or revised policies they are expected to follow? The aforementioned communication strategies and topologies may help streamline this information dissemination, which is why they should be considered a key element for resilient organizations.

- Develop rule boundaries with upper and lower limits if appropriate for certain tasks: Operational team leaders and key department staff members should spend time identifying which rules are absolutes and which contain zones. There may be cases when some of the rules that have been followed for years can actually be adjusted to allow a range of compliance, including an upper and lower limit, without affecting safety. For example, suppose at one point in time a rule was created that required employees to wear a certain level of PPE. This may have been because there were no other methods to control hazards. Over time engineering controls may have been implemented and the work methods may have been redesigned to make the work safer for employees, so that the PPE levels could actually be reduced without affecting acceptable levels of risk. However, unless the original PPE policy is examined, employees may be complying with an absolute rule unnecessarily, simply because they are told to do so. In this situation, perhaps the PPE requirements could be reexamined to determine a range of conditions and corresponding PPE requirements. For example, if all the engineering controls are installed and operating correctly, the teams could have the option of wearing the minimum PPE as specified in a lower limit, yet if for some reason those engineering controls are not functioning properly they would be required to wear a maximum level of PPE as specified in the upper limit. This is one example, and it is likely that your organization has other examples of rules that could be developed into ranges. This range or zone approach to rules can help to balance safety with efficiency because it provides teams and team leaders with concrete tools to use for determining how to do their jobs as effectively and efficiently as possible while maintaining adequate levels of safety. This process will require a great deal of trust because many organizations feel that the best approach is to simply choose the option that appears to lump the highest amount of safety on top of their teams, but in some cases this approach can actually degrade operational performance, place employees in very uncomfortable positions, and trade off apparent safety in one area with degraded safety in other areas as employees develop personal methods for working around the potentially excessive safety tools. Also, if this boundary-based approach to rule making is going to be used, care must be taken to avoid operational drift. When teams get comfortable using the lower limits they could fall into the habit of always complying with the lower limit, regardless of the actual conditions, and then over time perhaps even attempt to drive this limit even lower. As an operational team leader, keeping an eye on the pulse of the team is essential, and may require your consistent effort at helping them stay at the appropriate level within the rule boundaries.

Each of these options must fit within the organization and a high level of trust must be developed between policy/rule makers within the organization, operational team leaders, and employees. Without this trust, rule makers may feel that employees will always skirt the policies if they are allowed to and employees may feel like rule makers do not understand what it is like to actually do the work. However, if this trust can be built and a total system approach is used to detect risks and adapt to changing conditions the organization may be better prepared when faced with new threats (or even opportunities) that force them to adjust their work. Training teams to continuously reexamine operational risks and using the work system design process may help them find opportunities for adaptation of their work systems, methodologies, and procedures to counter emerging threats. Earlier recognition and risk-informed planning, rather than late recognition and reactive patching may also help teams maintain higher levels of safety. By acknowledging initial ambiguity about risk, closing the gap between knowledge and uncertainty as small hazard signals are detected, implementing hazard controls, and adapting standardized work methods, operational teams may stand a much better chance of successful short-term adaptation as they build deeper levels of adaptive capacity through learning and knowledge application. Ultimately these processes help build resilience and longer-term sustainability.

Unexpected Risk and Conditions of Uncertainty

A key characteristic of resilient organizations is the ability to proactively manage risk, to respond appropriately to unexpected risks when they emerge, and to balance uncertainty and risk-informed decision making with operational goals. This ability is enhanced when all levels within the organization are trained at developing anticipatory skills for identifying potential failure points. If anticipatory skills can be honed at the individual, operational team, and departmental level, the organization will be much more adept at detecting impending failure when the signals are weak (as opposed to waiting for the larger signals that often come in the form of big failures or mishaps). It is normally far better (and often easier) to deal with and ameliorate the risks before accidents happen than to deal with the aftermath and recovery, which can include much higher costs. Developing anticipatory skills can also enable the growth of corrective skills, so as employees become more proficient at detecting risks they may understand ways to mitigate those risks as well.

Risks can fall into a range of categories, with varying degrees of uncertainty (and there will almost always be some degree of uncertainty, even if it is minute). In some cases operational teams know the risks they will face and understand how to mitigate them. For example, military combat aviation aircrews may understand that an enemy threat includes bullets and shrapnel, so protective armor is installed on their aircraft. In other cases, the teams may understand the hazards they will face, but lack true clarity on the projected probability or severity, so mitigation strategies become more challenging. Using the previous example, if aircrews lack adequate military intelligence, they may not understand how likely the threat of enemy gunfire will be and they may not be sure of the types of weapons the enemy will have. They know there is a possibility of one of those threats occurring, but they don't know how likely or how severe it will be. This makes mitigation efforts harder, because they may take so many precautions that safety efforts could actually inhibit their ability to conduct the mission efficiently. Finally, there are situations where operational teams may lack clarity on the types of hazards they face and may have a high degree of uncertainty. Have you ever heard of the expression, "You don't know what you don't know?" In these cases it is nearly impossible to truly mitigate the exact threat when the teams do not even know what the threat might be. Using the military aviation example a third time, if an aircrew is about to fly into enemy territory for the first time and has no idea of the types of weapons the enemy may have, nor a clear picture of where the enemy might be, there is a lot of uncertainty about what to mitigate and if they don't understand what to mitigate it is extremely difficult to develop ways to mitigate the threats. While military aircrew attempt to minimize uncertainty as much as possible, there have been numerous times throughout history where militaries have engaged in warfare and faced new risks that had not been anticipated. Additionally, although these three notional examples are drawn from the military, other types of organizations that consistently push the boundaries of technology and production, and that delve deeper and deeper into uncertainty in the quest to remain industry leaders may face these types of risks on a regular basis.

The last category, sometimes referred to as unknown unknown risks, can be the most difficult type of risk to deal with because operational teams may have to guess at the types of hazards, and since organizations do not possess unlimited resources, they cannot mitigate every conceivable risk. One of the major problems is that even if teams have numerous resources, time constraints could impede risk control implementation, and since hazards are not pre-identified, a range of hazard controls may be required (such as a heavy defense-in-depth approach) to provide adequate protection against a range of potential threats. This control strategy could hamper operational performance to the point where the teams cannot accomplish the mission at all. So, the reality is that there will always be some type of limitations on risk management activities, whether they are resource constraints (time, personnel, financial, equipment availability, and so on) or operations-oriented limitations.

While this does not paint a promising picture, does this mean that operational teams are left without a method to detect and mitigate risk? Not necessarily, but it does mean that to improve resilience, organizations must make operational employees the "eyes and ears" of the risk assessors so they can help detect risk early. By training employees in hazard analysis and risk assessment, the organization can help build a foundation to develop risk mitigation strategies when the risks become more salient. In many of these risky operations where the types of risks may have not even been imagined, hazards may begin to show themselves in a variety of ways, even in non-obvious manners. If teams are trained in the importance of paying attention to weak signals, such as variations in the operational environment (compared to what was briefed, and/or expected to occur) and communicating those variances or weak signals to those who need to know and who may be affected, adaptive capacity may be improved as the teams learn how to mitigate these emergent risks. This approach is also directly tied to the lessons-learned process. As a team leader, you probably understand by now that processes for identifying unexpected risks are not foolproof and perhaps some risks will be missed, but engaging all employees to act like an army of hazard identifiers may help improve your chances of gaining more clarity on unknown risks and lessening the amount of uncertainty. This clarity should help you and your organizational leadership make risk-informed decisions based on probability and potential consequences so that risk controls may be implemented and refined.

Tight versus Loose Coupling

Even the most conscientious organizations may fail to identify certain hazards, may misidentify or mis-categorize certain risks, and ultimately experience some form of loss as a result of a hazard actualizing. If a serious hazard occurs in the presence of human exposure, injuries or fatalities could result. Even if humans are not exposed, catastrophic equipment failure or environmental damage could dramatically impact the organization from an operations disruption and financial loss standpoint. How, then, is an organization supposed to deal with the uncertainty that exists, and willingly progress into high-risk operations knowing there are threats they haven't even imagined, and how can organizational and operational team leaders devise strategies to minimize the effects if these risks do materialize?

One concept is to create soft linkages between key operational areas that can be closed off or redirected if necessary in order to protect employees and keep at least some level of operations functioning. In tightly coupled work systems, operations may be so closely linked that a failure in one area can rapidly cascade throughout the work team and associated systems and equipment, resulting in multiple failures. However, more loosely coupled processes may provide opportunities to deal with errors and accident consequences, so rather than allowing small errors and accidents to grow and impact multiple areas, certain work functions may be shut down or routed to different parts of the team. In highly linear processes or procedures, errors in Task A can affect Task B and then Task C, and damage can potentially occur at each step in the failure chain. These may be somewhat obvious and easier to detect and mitigate, but in highly complex processes or procedures, with non-linear interactions and numerous interdependent and interconnected parts (including distributed work teams, mechanical systems, or equipment), the way failure affects the total operation may not be so easy to detect. Rather than cascading in a linear fashion, failures can have more of a ripple effect, expanding in several directions. Both of these conditions should be considered when trying to design more loosely coupled systems. For example, in a non-linear fashion, a single power source could provide electricity to several critical pieces of equipment that are being used for multiple disparate functions. If the single power source fails this could disrupt multiple operational processes and cause several downstream impacts, each with their own unique consequences. A safety-related example of a tightly coupled system would be a generator used in a confined space that powers both lighting and ventilation. If the generator fails, the air supply may become hazardous and crews may not be able to see to find their way out. When considering methods to deal with tightly or loosely coupled operational processes or procedures, each scenario must be considered to determine ways to respond to unexpected risks.

When dealing with the uncertainty of risks, the interdependencies between sub-teams and equipment should be examined to determine where employees, teams, and components are so tightly coupled that a failure in one area is likely to cause a failure in another area. If these are detected, consideration should be given to determine if methods can be created to design "safety gates" that can interrupt mishap sequences through either shutting down certain functions or equipment and/or redirecting those functions elsewhere in the team. Safety gates may be thought of from a conceptual standpoint as ways to stop errors and accidents from cascading to downstream work (in a linear fashion) or rippling throughout the operational area (in a non-linear fashion). Developing methods to move from tight coupling to loose coupling may provide opportunities to deal with unknown risks as they emerge, and while it may not prevent a hazard from actually occurring and affecting the team, it may help to minimize the impact and may help the teams adapt in real-time to prevent failures from escalating. For example, if the team identifies one or more Single Points of Failure (SPF), this could be an indicator that multiple rippled consequences could occur if that equipment fails. Considering the single power source scenario and developing it further, suppose the scenario includes a single generator in use during an excavation operation. If the generator supplies power for both equipment operation as well as water pump-out functions, generator failure could result in power loss to the team's operational equipment and simultaneous shutdown of the water removal functions. This tight coupling could be loosened by designing in safety gates to block or redirect the mishap sequence. For example, perhaps an automated switching system could be designed to automatically switch power to a standby generator and/or backup generators, or multiple power sources could be installed at the point where the teams are working, and emergency pumps with their own power supply could be installed. In these cases, there are multiple barriers that can uncouple the SPFs from the work, so that one failure would be unlikely to affect multiple functions. SPFs do not necessarily need to be mechanical devices. They can occur in the form of financial, scheduling, and human SPFs as well. In fact, any area that relies on one entity or object has the potential to induce cascading or ripple effects if it fails. From a human SPF standpoint, team leaders should determine if operational teams rely on one (and only one) employee to perform a mission-critical or safety-critical function. If you are a team leader, ask yourself, "What would happen if that person was hurt on the job and could not perform that function? What would happen to the team or the work?"

These types of questions may help provide hints for how to address tight coupling and to identify ways to create new safety gates and looser coupling.

Also, as a general rule, always "leave yourself an out" by trying to avoid making decisions which are irrevocable and have catastrophic consequences if the decisions turn out to be wrong. This is like painting the floor in a room with only one door and painting yourself into the corner of the room with no way to get out except for walking through the paint. This will ruin your work. In a painting operation this may not be a serious consequence, but in high-hazard environments not leaving you and your team with a way out can potentially be catastrophic, particularly if a high degree of uncertainty about risks exists. As a team leader, when you make decisions always try to leave yourself with recovery options so if the original decision fails or leads to potential damage or injury you have an escape plan to protect the team and yourself, and potentially to continue operations (even in a reduced capacity, and if feasible).

To illustrate an example, consider the following scenario. In the US Marine Corps the KC-130 Hercules is used to perform refueling and transport missions. This aircraft has four engines, and can generally operate and maintain level flight on three engines if one of the engines fails. If two engines fail the aircraft may or may not be able to maintain level flight, depending on the aircraft weight and environmental conditions. If one engine experiences a minor mechanical problem and is shut down as a precaution and then a second engine experiences a more serious problem, the aircraft commander must consider options. If both engines are shut down the aircraft may start descending under certain conditions. Is it feasible to restart the first engine before shutting down the second one (to maintain three-engine operation)? Is it possible to operate either the first or the second engine at a reduced power setting to avoid complete shutdown? These are all questions that should be considered before simply shutting down both the first and the second engine without thinking through the consequences. By adapting and implementing safety gates, potential tight coupling may be rearranged into a more loosely coupled fashion, providing more safety options and potentially giving the aircrew with a way out if the aircraft cannot maintain level flight on two engines. While the options described would be temporary and would likely be chosen only to help the aircrew reach a point to land the aircraft safely (not for continuous operation), they illustrate how adaptability, time-sensitive risk management, problem solving, and decision making could be used to maintain resilience.

These scenarios are just a few notional examples. Regardless of the industry or organization, many of the actual scenarios will vary, depending on the situation and severity of conditions. Determining ways to design safety gates to make processes more loosely coupled will require teams that are adaptable and have a high degree of technical knowledge about the systems and operations, and who are comprised of effective communicators. Each organization will have to determine for itself what level of tight coupling is acceptable and at what point loose coupling and safety gates can potentially begin to exceed the resources available. However, if used as part of an overall risk mitigation strategy this approach may provide operational teams with the ability to mitigate the effects of uncertain risks if they do actually occur.

Conclusions

Adaptability is a key component of resilience and organizations that are able to develop appropriate levels of adaptive capacity at the individual, team, and organizational level may be able to plan for and react appropriately to changing conditions. Resilience is a way to build options to mitigate risks, plan for potential failure, design recovery options, and to create long-term sustainability. Organizations with the highest levels of resilience are able to consistently maintain safe operations while anticipating risks, creating options to deal with the uncertainty of risk, and using these strategies to adapt as they explore new ways to meet customer demands. Rather than allowing risk to diminish their capacity to adapt and create new or better products or services, they acknowledge this risk and make risk-informed decisions to intelligently move forward for sustainable growth. While resilience will not offer complete protection from hazards and risks, and it is likely that some failures will occur at some point, these strategies may help minimize the impacts. Learning should be a continuous process and is a necessity for resilient organizations. Team leaders play a vital role in this process, as they are the link to key organizational staff and the workers who must ultimately deal with the effects of risk-informed choices.

Chapter 8
Decision-Making Techniques for Operational Teams

Making decisions is a routine part of business operations and often occurs with little thought about the decision-making process. In some cases, this may work well, considering the operational environment, but in other cases a structured approach may be required. In many situations a large influx of information, a lack of clarity about objectives, time-compression, and the consequences of risks may all affect operational team leaders as they search for the most appropriate Course of Action (COA). By describing the decision-making process and the relationship between leadership, risk, and decision making, operational team leaders may be better prepared to face the difficult decisions required on a regular basis, even under conditions of uncertainty, and may develop more clarity on the impacts to personnel and the organizational mission through the process.

What is Decision Making?

Making decisions is an everyday part of life. We may make personal decisions, such as what we will eat for breakfast, what types of products we will purchase, and what sports teams we will watch compete on television. In professional situations decisions are also made daily. These could be decisions for product purchases, employee hiring, or where to hold a meeting. Many professionals have an intuitive decision-making process they have developed and refined over years of practice, but this process may not work for every situation. For younger or less-experienced team leaders, this method may not come naturally, and the learning curve required for operational team leaders may not afford them years to practice and refine the decision-making process. Additionally, decisions that are made in high-hazard environments often have vastly different impacts than those made in low-hazard environments, and the consequences of ineffective decisions in high-hazard situations can have serious repercussions. Therefore, a structured approach to describe decision making and methods for explaining the decision-making process are necessary to provide team leaders with a framework to consider when faced with the multitude of operational choices and subsequent decision-making requirements.

> *Decision making may be defined as the ability to choose a course of action using logical and sound judgment based on available information. This process requires situational assessment, information verification, solution identification, anticipation of decision consequences, making a decision, informing others of the decision and rationale, and evaluating the decision.* (NATOPS General Flight and Operating Instructions 3–17)

Using this definition, it would appear that decision making is a skill, a characteristic, or an attribute. If this is true, then team leaders should view decision making as a job skill requiring an individual ability to assess a situation, select from a range of options, make a decision, and keep others informed, all the while considering the potential impacts. Additionally, decision making uses a feed-forward approach because, if decisions are consistently evaluated, team leaders should be able to assess the level of effectiveness and develop personal lessons-learned which are fed into their future decision-making situations.

Elements of the Decision-Making Process

The decision-making process should ultimately help team leaders select a COA to achieve one or more goals. The term Course of Action (or COA) will be used interchangeably with the term decision because a decision may not necessarily simply be the selection of an object (even if the decision is related to a product purchase), but oftentimes includes associated elements required to actually implement a decision (including any product or service selected). The decision-making process requires team leaders to perform several steps. If this process becomes well-understood and is developed as a skillset by team leaders they may realize their method for making decisions becomes more efficient because, even if this process is only used as a loose guideline, it provides common reference points leaders can use repeatedly. Rather than struggling to find out where to start and what to do along the decision path, following a roadmap with integrated decision-making elements can help them to consistently work through a natural progression for selecting the best choice to meet the needs of the situation. This process should include the following elements:

- Situation assessment: Before leaders can make a decision they must first assess the situation, but what does that mean, and what goes into a situation assessment? A system-oriented approach may help leaders assess the overall situation by linking decisions with desired objectives (or outputs), inputs, work processes, and the ways operational teams interact with the internal and external environment. During a situation assessment operational team leaders should consider the overall desired end-state and goals. By identifying the goals, leaders can then begin to identify a range of solutions and the inputs (resources and/or constraints) that may affect those options. Input considerations may include time, financial, or personnel resources or constraints. For example, if a team leader knows the desired goal and understands three COAs that could be selected to achieve the goal, but time or personnel constraints make two out of the three options impossible, this narrows the decision space significantly. The work methods themselves will often be well-understood, and the available choices should be evaluated against the work methods or procedures to make sure they don't overly inhibit a team's ability to perform their work. Lastly, by understanding the team's interaction with the internal environment (such as cultural aspects or policies) and the external environment (including error potential, hazards, and risk mitigation strategies and options) the operational team leader may gain more clarity about how a possible COA will impact the team. Additionally, other parts of the organization that could be affected (such as departments, divisions, or business units) should be considered as part of the environment assessment as well. Ultimately it will be the desired end-state that will start the COA selection process, so understanding what the team must accomplish is a key part of situation assessment. Figure 8.1 illustrates the situation assessment process.

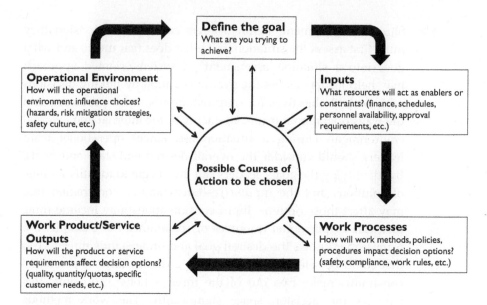

Figure 8.1   Decision-making situation assessment

- Information verification: While the situation assessment progresses, information must be continually verified for accuracy, and updated information must be fed into the situation assessment process. Nearly all decisions will lack some clarity and will include some level of uncertainty, but as a team leader, you should strive to identify the most important information requirements (such as operations-critical functions, and safety-critical functions), determine the level of uncertainty that exists, and develop methods for obtaining as much of the information as possible to either verify or refute your expectations or assumptions and reduce levels of uncertainty where feasible.

- Solution identification: Figure 8.1 illustrates COA options at the center of the situation assessment process. This is because many times a range of possible options will be known or quickly obtained early in the decision-making process, and the available options may influence the system components, and vice-versa. Key decision criteria should be matched up against possible choices, and may consist of such attributes as operational performance, cost, safety levels, quality, availability, schedules, and numerous other characteristics. As the operational team leader reviews the components of the situation assessment, the range of choices will likely decrease to the point where only several (or perhaps a single choice remains). This may also require trade-offs and sacrifices because it is rarely the case that one single COA can satisfy every single resource enabler or fit within all of the constraints. Narrowing the options down to a handful can help the team leader avoid getting unnecessarily bogged down in an attempt to satisfy every single criteria associated with the system components in the situation assessment cycle.

• Review of possible solutions for potential positive and negative impacts: When possible options are examined, they should be compared against the goal(s) to determine the degree to which they will likely satisfy those goals and should also be reviewed for any adjacent affects or impacts on other parts of the operation, other teams or sub-teams, or other parts of the overall organization. Additionally, as a team leader, you should be highly adept at anticipating the outcomes of the decision and any negative or unintended consequences that could develop. These may not be well-understood at the beginning of the decision-making process, but as you examine each possible COA you should think through ways that negative impacts could affect downstream processes or other parts of the organization. It will help if you build a diverse team to help you work through this analysis process as you narrow down your range of options. Particular attention should be paid to the potential for introducing additional hazards into the operating environment. If the decision creates a greater hazard than already exists (even if it is a different type of hazard), then you should probably consider striking it off the list. This highlights the importance of conducting a risk assessment for each possible solution.

• Choosing from the list of options: By this point the list of possible choices or COAs should be narrowed down to a few options. At some point you will have to make a decision and understand that it may not seem ideal. This is why it is so important to explicitly state the decision criteria. However, if the selected COA is aligned with the operational goals, meets the decision criteria, preserves the safety of employees, is ethically responsible, and supports the organization's mission and values then it may be the best choice, even if it is not perfect.

- Keeping key personnel and teams informed: As an operational team leader you should make it a point to inform your team and higher-level leaders and managers within the organization about the decision and the reasons behind that decision. Sometimes knowing why a decision was made can go a long way to build morale, even if the decision is unpopular. As a team leader, you should place a priority on the well-being of your teams and should also attempt to keep the organizational network of other affected departments and leaders informed as well. They will likely need to know how the decision will impact them or their departments, particularly if it will affect their operations, work processes, or safety.

- Implementation and follow-through: After the decision is made, the implementation process should begin. This timeframe may vary, depending on the complexity of the decision and any logistical issues, such as long lead-time items to be ordered. However, the decision should be evaluated as implementation takes place and the results begin to take shape. Any good team leader should consistently evaluate the decision-making process, the decision itself (to determine if it met the goals or objectives and if the unintended consequences were more than the organization or team should have to endure). From a personal standpoint, team leaders should consider keeping a personal decision-making journal to track their proficiency over time, and from an organizational standpoint, decisions should be captured in a lessons-learned system and distributed to other employees and leaders to assist with organizational learning.

Resources and Constraints

Oftentimes, many factors affecting the decision-making process are both resources and sources of constraints as well. Although not exhaustive, the following list provides some examples of possible resources and constraints that may affect the decisions available.

- Personnel: Specific COAs may require employees with unique technical skillsets, such as installation or operation of equipment, or support personnel who understand ways to obtain needed logistics assets. Organizations who can mobilize these personnel can use these as human resources, and if the right number of employees for the specified COA exist, then this may help the selection process. On the other hand, if the required number of employees cannot be met or if the team is not able to find the correct employee skillsets, personnel issues can also become a constraint and may inhibit the selection of certain COAs.

- Material: Whether supplies to be used directly in work processes or raw material that will be used to construct a manufactured system or for tool fabrication (such as by in-house engineers/fabricators), material resource availability may affect which COAs are available. If the right material resources are available, it can help decision-makers add certain COAs to the list of options. However, if the desired material does not exist or is unobtainable during the required decision timeframe, then material availability can function as a constraint that inhibits certain COAs.

- Communications: Communication is a vital part of any operation, and certain COAs may require specific communication resources to be successful and to accomplish the goals of the operational team. If the correct type and amount of communication assets are available, such as radios, cellphones/smartphones, land lines, web-enabled laptop computers or electronic tablets, these can serve as enabling resources during COA selection. Alternatively, if these assets are not available they may restrict a team leader's ability to implement certain COAs, and therefore communications constraints may cause some COAs to be removed from the list of options.

- Financial: Nearly every decision includes a cost of some sort, and even if costs are not obvious and direct, there are typically costs involved at some level. The finances available for COA selection can greatly enhance the decision options (if adequate funding is available), or restrict the number of COAs (if funding constraints render some options inaccessible).

- Risk control: Hazard analysis and controlling risk may be viewed as forms of decision constraints because any selected COA must conform to the organization's acceptable risk policy, providing adequate protection to limit probability of hazard occurrence, reduce the effects of hazards if they do occur, or reduce both the probability and severity. However, each organization will likely have some form of risk controls (whether administrative/procedural controls, engineering controls, warnings and cautions, and PPE) and since these controls serve as assets to employees they should also be seen as a resource to draw from when considering different decision options. From a constraint standpoint, if a COA involves the design of risk controls which may not be immediately available or which have a highly negative impact on the work processes the COA may not be feasible.

- Time: Although it can be very difficult to put a price on time, it can be one of our most precious resources. When we have a great deal of time at our disposal it may not be immediately evident that time is a resource because it can be taken for granted, but lessen the amount of time available (such as when rapid decisions must be made) and the value of time becomes evident. So, like many of the other resources, the more time available, the more it may serve as a resource, yet in time-compressed situations, where a lot of work (such as selecting a COA to solve a complex problem) must be done in a short timeframe, time quickly seems to become a constraint. The amount of time available to analyze, plan, and implement a COA will directly affect which COAs may even be practical. For example, even if a COA seems logical in many respects, if long-lead items are required and delivery time will exceed the time available to make and implement the decision, this could remove that particular COA from the list of choices.

There are numerous other sources of resources and constraints, and while this list is not exhaustive, it describes how resources and constraints can both impact available COAs. In many cases numerous constraints will intersect, further reducing some decision options and possibly removing them from the list. For example, if one possible solution involves the design of risk controls which may not be immediately available and will take a great deal of time and personnel to develop and test the controls, then risk control, time, and personnel constraints will intersect, magnifying the level of constraints associated with one COA. While this may seem obvious after the fact, if each resource and constraint is looked at individually and COAs are selected before considering all constraints, what should be obvious may be obscured during the decision-making process. A diverse team using collaborative efforts and expert judgment may be able to help team leaders avoid the surprises that can emerge later in the decision-making process.

Leadership and Decision Making

Leaders at many levels face a unique responsibility because oftentimes they are expected to make correct decisions consistently. But what is a correct decision? By reviewing the decision-making process it would seem that a correct decision is one that accomplishes the goals associated with the problem the team is trying to solve. However, team leaders often interact with numerous employees who have their own individual perspectives, and this definition may seem overly simplistic (and sometimes callous). Leaders are faced with the pressure to make accurate decisions that take many factors into consideration and in many cases these considerations are not understood by others. However, this is why the role of the team leader is so critical and why decision making is such an important skill. Others may not understand all the factors you must consider as a leader when making a decision, but it is a necessary part of your job duties.

Leadership has a direct relationship to decision making. Leaders must be willing to make difficult decisions and must determine the right balance between safety and production. They must also balance the tension that often exists between long planning processes and the apprehension with making a decision and rapid judgment when a time-sensitive decision is required. On the one hand, with lengthy decision-making timeframes you may be concerned with missed opportunities and failures that could occur as you deliberate over potential COAs, yet on the other hand you may want to avoid the negative consequences associated with knee-jerk reactions.

It should be apparent by this point that decision making is a critical, yet challenging and often very difficult job requirement for leaders, and although some decisions may be very uncomfortable, this does not make them any less necessary. This is another reason why leadership is such an important responsibility and why organizations should be very selective about which employees are selected for key leadership positions. Particularly in high-hazard environments, the effects of decisions can be magnified and if they include numerous unintended consequences and additional hazards, they can place operational teams in a worse position than before the decision was made. So, while it is a responsibility to hire, promote, train, and mentor competent leaders, it is the responsibility of operational team leaders to mobilize resources to help them solve problems, including organizing teams in a collaborative fashion to assist with the situation assessment and overall decision-making process.

These teams should be as diverse as feasible, because diversity of thought can lend itself to balanced input. Oftentimes, if leaders surround themselves with like-minded thinkers they may limit creativity and key dissenting opinions, which are often necessary to avoid groupthink and the possible mistakes associated with single-mindedness. If decisions are made in a vacuum and all required stakeholders (including other team members, key departmental staff, and those affected by decisions) are not included this may limit expert input. Additionally, if leaders fail to include those in charge of resource allocation, they could make a decision that cannot be implemented, yet may not know it until it is too late to choose an alternative COA.

In some cases lower-order decisions must also be made by sub-team leaders or line operator employees. As a general rule, decisions with potentially high negative consequences should be made by those leaders in higher positions of authority, so the decision-making magnitude is commensurate with job position. However, in some situations sub-team leaders and team members may be required to make decisions in high-hazard environments, particularly if they directly affect their tasks, so training employees in hazard analysis and decision-making strategies may help to distribute some of the decisions closer to those doing the work. One strategy to help employees, which was described in Chapter 2, is to use a well-defined Leader's Intent statement. This overarching broad objective can help provide sub-team leaders and team members with a guideline to work with. Since it provides them with a goal, or desired outcome, they can use that as a vision for the desired end-state and work through the decision-making process, even if it is on a smaller and more rapid scale. The Leader's Intent and objectives will drive their decision-making processes and provide them with space to act in the absence of direct, prescriptive orders. While some organizations may be hesitant to allow this type of process, in many organizations employees and sub-team leaders will make decisions regardless of whether or not they are trained or provided with a strong Leader's Intent. So, isn't it better to at least provide them with some guidelines in advance?

Time-Sensitive Decision Making

The decision-making process includes many steps (and many sub-steps) and it would appear that actually making a decision is labor-intensive and takes a very long time. However, if you are an operational team leader and are faced with the need to make a decision rapidly, how can you use such a seemingly long method? In high-hazard environments there may be some scenarios where hesitation can result in injury, illness, catastrophic failure of equipment, or environmental damage. In some cases the consequences of not making a decision may be worse than rapidly selecting and implementing a COA, so team leaders must be able to discern when time is a significant constraint to the decision-making process and must balance the safety of personnel with decisiveness, while maintaining awareness of the consequences associated with a poor decision.

Time-sensitive COA Analysis is one method used to narrow the options and to help leaders make decisions in a more rapid fashion. Using this process, leaders consider the goals or objectives and rapidly work through the situation assessment and identify potential solutions, with particular emphasis on determining the best fit from the range of options, based on the most important criteria. Then, narrowing the possible COAs down to three available options can help reduce the analysis requirements. While it may be helpful to conduct a quantitative risk assessment, including historical injury data and possibly product manufacturer failure rates, in time-sensitive situations team leaders may not have that luxury. In many cases, a qualitative risk assessment, based on best-case scenario, worst-case scenario, and most-likely case scenario may help set upper and lower severity boundaries. For example, based on the information available case-based scenarios could include a prediction of the end state in terms of operations success and risk consequences. This may require rapid expert judgment and, if possible, gathering information from a lessons-learned database. If a lessons-learned database is designed properly (including ease of search methods), connected to the Internet, and accessible through wireless devices, such as smartphones, this may help in some situations. Additionally, expert judgment and input from team members, including FLs and key technical personnel may help to provide qualitative input regarding risks and potential successes. Using this qualitative assessment, the team leader may be able to estimate which of these three COAs has the best chance of success and the lowest chance of failure and vice-versa. Then, the option with the highest chance of failure and the lowest chance of success (which may include too many unintended consequences or potential risk severity that exceeds acceptable limits) is dropped off the list. At this point the team leader must select from the remaining two options. While this may not be an easy process, it provides a set of guidelines to help team leaders and employees who must make quick decisions in time-compressed high-hazard environments.

In a perfect scenario team leaders would have unlimited resources and all decisions would accomplish the desired goals without any negative consequences. This would be great, but all decisions have impacts, both positive and negative. Decisions can often affect personnel, operational processes and production capacities, equipment, the environment, and the organization's reputation. Gaining clarity about risks may help leaders make risk-informed decisions, rather than "going with their gut," or basing decisions on single factors (such as cost). While an intuitive, experience-based decision-making process may work in some cases, and leaders often have a gut feeling about what to do in certain routine situations, in many unique circumstances a decision based on gut feeling may omit the consideration of certain risks, including impacts that are not easily identifiable. An additional concern is that leaders may succumb to biases based on their prior experiences, even if those biases are not appropriate in certain situations. As a team leader, if you can work to elucidate risks by planning in a methodical manner and gain clarity through comprehensive assessments and discussions to help avoid biases, you may be better equipped to make sound decisions in a consistent manner and may have the added benefit of gaining confidence about your decisions. Additionally, since the decision-making process includes communicating the decision and explaining the rationale to others, using a consistent process may help you defend your position, if (or when) required.

Risk-Informed Decision Making: Impacts on Personnel, Mission, and Organization

Since all decisions have impacts and each decision-making scenario is far from utopian, understanding the relationship between risk, loss, and gain may help to empower team leaders as they weigh their COA options. In high-hazard environments, the level of risk the organization is willing to accept is likely higher than in low-hazard environments. For example, in oil exploration, mining, fire service, or law enforcement organizations leaders may be more likely to accept higher risk levels than in well-controlled, static manufacturing environments, which have fewer impacts from the external environment and often include an inherent ability to install more protection mechanisms on certain types of equipment. Maximizing safety performance by reducing risks to a level as low as reasonably practicable should be a goal of the organization in every situation, but it would be naïve to assume that all decisions can be solely based on risk avoidance. If organizations attempted to achieve zero risk (which is impossible anyway) they would probably need to halt their operations altogether, shut the doors, and divest the company. So, team leaders must understand how to balance risk and reward, loss and gain, and short-term and long-term sustainability.

Organizations exist to perform a mission, function, or set of functions. While safety is (or should be) a highly valued goal along with production performance, organizations do not exist to simply remain safe or to remain in a state of safety. If organizations design safety into their operations to the detriment of performance (meaning safety performance requirements are so stringent the organization can no longer achieve its mission), then safety efforts will often be misguided. Lofty safety goals are commendable, but if not balanced with operations performance requirements, safety and organizational leaders may be unaware of the negative consequences associated with the safety programs. In these cases, the organization must shift its mission or production goals so they are aligned with safety goals. From a safety standpoint, there may be nothing wrong with this approach, but from an organizational sustainability perspective, this could potentially result in a significant loss of business. So, oftentimes what happens is that safety and operational goals are developed apart from each other, placing employees in a position to choose which goal to pursue. One of the most challenging situations for employees and team leaders is contending with competing safety and production goals, especially when they are extremely far out of alignment. This puts workers in a position of choosing either safety or production and either following safety rules and risk not accomplishing their work or meeting production or performance quotas and risking the violation of safety rules and requirements. Both are losing propositions. Rather than placing employees and team leaders in lose–lose situations, it is better to develop safety and production goals together so that all affected personnel will be in a position to safely accomplish their goals. From a risk-informed decision-making standpoint understanding loss and gain and their relationship to risk can help team leaders with this process.

Risk-informed decisions are often based on the goal of minimizing safety risks (minimizing loss potential for people, equipment, and the environment). Standard risk matrices are used to determine probability of hazard occurrence and severity of impact on personnel, equipment, and the environment. Oftentimes this is where the risk assessment process stops and decisions are made based on loss potential without considering the larger impacts. However, the other side of the two-sided risk coin includes maximizing operational gain, but risk is often not viewed from this two-sided perspective. As an operational team leader, along with minimizing loss, how often do you examine the potential gain in terms of production and performance? How often do you consider the potential gain side of risk, such as unique opportunities for improved organizational performance, with the potential ripple effects associated with large payoffs, including future hiring potential and the ability to enrich the lives of employees and customers through continued growth? Alternatively, how often do you consider emphasizing safety over production? For line operational team leaders or supervisors you may consider the immediate production goals quite frequently because that is often what is demanded of you, but you should also place a high priority on risk minimization and the safety of your teams. However, considering the long-term potential gains associated with decisions you must make on a regular basis may provide added perspective when trying to balance safety and production. If you are a top-level executive or department head, it is your responsibility to effectively communicate all of these goals to your operational team leaders so they can be in the best position to make decisions for the benefit of their teams and the organization, from a safety and productivity standpoint.

One way to assist leaders with gaining this two-sided perspective is to consider the risk associated with performing an operation compared to not performing an operation. Examine the scenario in Table 8.1. From this perspective cost equals a loss and payoff equals a benefit or gain. If a COA is selected and the decision is made to perform a specific operation, there are certain costs associated with it. These costs are listed in terms of potential loss risk to personnel, equipment, and the environment. On the other hand, if the operation is performed there is the potential for monetary gain, improved operational performance, and improved organizational reputation with customers. The other side of the matrix includes the potential cost and payoff associated with not performing the operation. In that case, the potential losses are identified in terms of giving up the potential monetary, performance, and reputation gains and the potential payoff includes the preservation of employees, equipment, and the environment. Notice that during the decision making and risk assessment process, each of these situations is based on potential cost and potential payoff (not actual). There is no way of truly knowing what the actual cost and payoff will be until the operation is over and hindsight is used to assess the results. However, while hindsight is a necessary and useful tool, it can be a double-edged sword when assessing performance. In some cases if an operation is not performed in favor of protecting employees and hindsight reveals that the identified hazards actually did not occur, it would appear that employees would not have been harmed and the organization wasted an opportunity for potential gain. This could result in reactive decisions to pursue future operations of a similar nature, but this does not guarantee employees will not be harmed in the future. Alternatively, if the risks to personnel are assessed as low (or within acceptable limits), the operation is performed, and personnel are injured this could result in a knee-jerk reaction where the organization decides to never perform that type of operation again (without putting any thoughtful analysis towards reassessing risks or determining if operational conditions could be different) and potentially giving up operational gain. While this seems like a simplistic scenario (and many decisions fall along a range of options rather than binary Yes/No, Perform/Don't Perform options), it helps to illustrate the point that for every decision you make as a team leader you are sacrificing other options. As challenging as this may be, it is part of your job as a leader.

Table 8.1   Loss–gain analysis

Perform Operation	Don't Perform Operation
Cost: Risk of loss impact on people, equipment, environment	Cost: Lost opportunity to achieve payoff in terms of monetary gain and improvements in performance and organizational reputation
Payoff: Monetary, performance, reputation, and so on	Payoff: Preservation of the safety of people, equipment, and the environment

In many cases the decision to perform or not perform an operation will be based on the importance of loss versus gain. For example, if the potential cost of not performing an operation is seen as worse than the potential loss associated with performing the operation, then operational leaders may decide to perform the operation. In ostensibly callous terms, this may be viewed as potential harm to personnel, equipment, or the environment being worth the risk because the impact of operational loss if the operation is not performed is greater than the loss if it is performed. In reality this perspective is not that simple and leaders in many high-risk industries go to great lengths to protect employees and minimize loss potential. While situations where mission accomplishment is placed above personnel safety may not be a common occurrence in many organizations, there are numerous industries where leaders and employees are faced with these scenarios, such as the military, law enforcement, or firefighting. Leaders in these types of organizations must make risk-informed decisions on a regular basis where safety is sometimes placed below the accomplishment of the mission (defeating enemy combatants, protecting the public, and rescuing victims from burning buildings). The protection of employees should be among the highest priorities, and even if these are extreme examples, it is likely that loss–gain situations impact your organization at some level, and Table 8.1 illustrates the types of factors faced by leaders as they attempt to work through the difficult decision-making process.

Some may refer to this process as calculated risk-taking and this isn't necessarily a bad way to look at it. All organizations must take risks in order to push the boundaries of what is possible in the quest to create increasingly better products and services, and to tap unexplored markets. That is part of the creativity and innovation process that can make the world so amazing, and can help to build organizational resilience. However, it is not fair to keep the risk decision criteria hidden from employees and expect them to simply comply with excessively high-risk operations. Acceptable risk may be described as the level of risk for a given situation, which can only be lowered through a disproportionate level of resource investment compared to the amount of decreased risk. (American Society of Safety Engineers 12). Risks should only be accepted when the benefits outweigh the costs (or the potential gains outweigh the potential losses), but explaining the cost and benefit calculations and the rationale for risk-informed decisions is a responsibility of leadership. As a team leader, you may be more likely to earn the respect of your teams if you can talk to them in a candid manner and explain how risk-informed decisions are made than if you keep them ostracized from the decision-making process, or if you fail to explain the rationale behind your decisions. Organizations should make the effort to elucidate the cost–benefit assessment process and provide leaders at all levels with methods for determining what level of risk is acceptable and at what level certain high-risk decisions can be made. Even in extremely high-risk industries, leaders should make robust attempts at risk mitigation efforts to reduce risk to a level as low as reasonably practicable, and acceptable risk policies should be made explicitly clear to all employees throughout the organization.

US Marine Corps and Navy aviation provide some great examples to help illustrate these points. In primary aviation training students with very little experience are trained to operate their aircraft in high-hazard environments and there are many factors affecting risk that must be evaluated every day. Additionally, the aviation training squadrons have production quotas (in the form of trained students) to meet on a regular basis. However, the students have such limited experience and the process of training them can be so hazardous, that in some cases the risk of loss outweighs the potential gain, and the potential risk of loss as a result of not performing an operation is outweighed by the potential risk of loss if the operation is performed. Table 8.2 expounds upon this concept with a hypothetical example. Suppose in this case the flight crew and operations department are faced with the decision to conduct a training mission with thunderstorms near (but not necessarily in) the training area. In this case if they perform the flight there is a potential to achieve their training goals and meet production quotas, yet there is a potential to lose the entire aircraft and aircrew if they inadvertently fly into a thunderstorm. On the other hand if they don't perform the flight they will miss the production quota by one day, yet they will not lose the aircraft or aircrew. In this case, since the potential cost of fatalities and total loss of aircraft outweighs the potential gain in terms of production quota, the benefits do not outweigh the costs and the flight training mission would likely be canceled. Fortunately many military flight operating instructions and organizational policies provide explicit rules in these situations making the decision-making process easier.

Table 8.2   Loss–gain analysis in naval aviation training (notional)

Perform Training Mission	Don't Perform Training Mission
Cost: Total loss of aircraft and aircrew after inadvertent flight into thunderstorm	Cost: Lost training day resulting in sliding production quota by one day
Payoff: Achieve production quota on schedule	Payoff: Preservation of the safety of aircraft and aircrew

The level of certainty associated with potential loss and gain may vary with each decision scenario as well. In many cases, the higher the level of uncertainty the harder it is to make a decision. Therefore, as part of the decision-making process, as leaders gain clarity on uncertain information they should interject this new information into the risk-informed decision-making process.

Consider the additional hypothetical loss–gain scenario related to combat aviation operations in Table 8.3. In this hypothetical scenario an aircrew has been on duty for over 12 hours and is beginning to succumb to the effects of fatigue. However, the operations department has just been informed that friendly infantry ground troops are engaged in a firefight with enemy forces. They are desperately in need of aviation support, which could potentially save their lives. If the fatigued aircrew performs the mission, they could potentially inadvertently fly their aircraft into terrain, resulting in total loss of aircrew and aircraft, yet there is a potential gain of protecting the lives of the ground troops who are in need of aviation support as well as providing the air support the ground troops need to defeat the enemy. On the other hand, if the flight mission is not performed there is a potential loss of numerous infantry troops and a larger loss in the form of ground combat mission failure and the inability to defeat enemy forces, yet there is a potential gain in the form of aircrew and aircraft preservation. This may be a tough call, and may be a decision that needs to be made at higher levels by those who can make decisions regarding acceptable risk levels with so much at stake. In either case there is a potential loss of life. However, the determination must be made regarding which cost is higher and which benefit is higher. While there may be certain ways the squadron can mitigate the risk, such as swapping to a fresh aircrew (which would reduce the loss as a result of fatigue), in some cases the risks have been mitigated as much as is feasible. If that is the case, then the remaining risk must either be accepted, or, if the risk of performing the flight is deemed too high, other methods may need to be considered, such as finding another unit to perform the mission.

Table 8.3   Loss–gain analysis in combat aviation operations (notional)

Perform Combat Mission	Don't Perform Combat Mission
Cost: Total loss of aircraft and aircrew after Controlled Flight Into Terrain due to excessive fatigue	Cost: Loss of lives of infantry troops who will not receive needed aviation support, and infantry mission failure (inability to defeat enemy forces)
Payoff: Provide support to infantry in ground combat operations, and potentially save lives and enable infantry mission accomplishment and defeat of enemy forces	Payoff: Preservation of the safety of aircraft and aircrew, who will not fly into terrain

Another consideration regarding loss–gain comparisons is the ability to reduce risk so that the potential loss is decreased either through reducing the likelihood of loss occurrence or by minimizing the potential consequences of loss, and in some cases decision makers may consider a defense-in-depth approach. As a decision maker, though, you should make a comprehensive assessment of the impacts associated with the risk-reduction strategies. What may indeed reduce potential losses, may in fact inhibit the potential performance gains by preventing teams from accomplishing their work. Safety measures should both protect employees and enhance the operational functions of the team, and the operational processes teams use to perform their work should be used safely, but at the point where safety measures prevent job accomplishment, the return on investment may be negative in some respects.

Conclusions

Making sound decisions requires expert judgment and a repeatable process, and can be enhanced by building diverse collaborative teams. Yet, in some cases, there will be high pressure placed on the team leader to make decisions in time-compressed situations, and by using these guidelines leaders should be able to rapidly work through the process to select an appropriate COA. By focusing on the objectives and understanding resources and constraints leaders should become more and more skilled at the decision-making process. Safety should always be included as part of the process, and leaders should also consider using what-if scenarios and backup plans to recover from failures if the COAs turn out to be ineffective.

Decision making and leadership can be some of the most challenging, yet rewarding aspects of job performance. The satisfaction that comes from working through the decision-making process, including assessing the situation and determining the impacts of system elements, selecting an appropriate COA, and reaping the benefits can be unparalleled, and the process itself can be part of the leadership development journey. Additionally, every time a decision is made, particularly when it concerns high-hazard situations and the potential for remarkable gains, organizational learning should occur, so the process can be repeated in the future.

Chapter 9
Mutual Support and Backup

Even with the most advanced safety engineering hazard controls, safety management systems, and standardized operations programs, production and safety performance must rely on critical employee behavior to ensure effective system functioning over the course of time. Without sound and consistent leadership and management efforts to keep these programs and systems functioning, serious errors and breakdown can occur. Despite the efforts of the most effective leaders and managers running these programs, they cannot be completely error-free, and consistent supporting efforts by employees and operational team members are required to detect the gaps and errors when they occur. Of particular importance is the need for supporting efforts between operational team members on a peer-to-peer level, as well as a subordinate to senior level and vice-versa. By providing support to one another (which includes the verification of work performance, correcting each other when work is performed incorrectly, speaking up to halt an unsafe activity or event, and challenging assumptions and poor decisions), team members at all levels can help keep safety and operations management systems functioning effectively and may serve as key agents to catch errors and gaps in safety coverage before they escalate. In many cases this requires employees to shift their attitudes and behaviors, including learning how to assert their opinions when they see something wrong. While this process may take some adjustment, particularly in organizations with rigid hierarchical structures that rely on obedience to orders, if used appropriately mutual support and backup can play an important role in error detection and mishap avoidance. In some cases, if executed properly this concept may mean the difference between a near-miss and an accident.

Mutual Support and Backup—A Philosophy for Improved Team Performance

Imagine that for every decision you made, every task you completed, and every hazard you were exposed to you had a set of safety checks and balances that would follow alongside you as you performed your work. What would your work look like if you had a tool that could assess your performance, and perhaps even help you anticipate what would happen in the immediate future, and either confirm your actions or advise you regarding what you should correct if something was about to go wrong? Some might think this would be an annoyance, and perhaps in low-hazard environments it might be (for example, perhaps spell-checking in real-time through the underlining of words is an aggravation to some employees). However, in high-hazard environments, where every move counts toward success or failure and missteps or mis-cues can result in serious negative consequences, this type of feature could be extremely useful. If easy-to-use tools could help prevent or reduce the consequences of errors and hazard occurrence they would probably be worth the return on a nominal investment. What if these tools already exist and just need to be properly implemented? Have you ever received a holiday gift, but due to the hustle and bustle of the holiday rush, placed it away in a closet, and forgotten about it until months later? The potentially useful gift is there, waiting to be opened, and all you need to do is open it. This may also be the case with mutual support and backup strategies in your organization. As a tool to help you detect and correct error, and potentially prevent or reduce operational losses, mutual support and backup may be the low-hanging fruit that could tip the operations and safety performance scale in favor of organizational success and employee well-being.

The notion of support may be common in team-oriented environments, where team members are used to helping each other, but mutual support and backup as an Essential Component of team leadership and performance may require a shift in perspective. When used in this context it takes support to a new level, asking employees to learn to balance obedience and task completion with assertiveness and challenging orders when those orders could result in unsafe situations. Mutual support and backup may be thought of as an individual and team-based skill requiring team members to work together, and brace each other to avoid failure, while maintaining a reserve or substitute capacity for action, particularly in the face of stress, change, or hazardous conditions. So, rather than simply helping each other during job tasks, this skillset actually requires teams to use coordinated actions for avoiding failure, and includes maintaining the ability to take action in favor of safety and the preservation of health and life in high-hazard operations.

A very important part of this ability includes taking action when hazardous situations are detected and speaking up to challenge the current COA, despite organizational or team barriers, such as overbearing peers or leaders. In Marine Corps aviation CRM terms, this skill is referred to as assertiveness. From a very basic perspective assertiveness may be viewed as employees stating their opinions, even when challenged and pressured by others to comply with orders. From a crew or team performance perspective, particularly in high-hazard environments, assertiveness may be defined as "an individual's willingness to actively participate, state, and maintain a position, until convinced by the facts that other options are better. Assertiveness is respectful and professional, used to resolve problems appropriately, and to improve mission effectiveness and safety" (*NATOPS General Flight and Operating Instructions* 3–17). This definition gets more to the heart of assertiveness as it applies to mutual support and backup in high-hazard environments because it is not simply a one-time expression of opinion, but includes an element of "standing one's ground" until convinced otherwise by factual information. In the face of unsafe situations this can be of particular importance because a one-time statement may not be enough to help avert catastrophe, so training employees to understand the concept of assertiveness and how to develop and exercise this as an essential job skill can potentially be a determining factor in the effectiveness of mutual support and backup strategies.

Assertiveness versus Disobedience

While this concept may be quite common in some organizations, especially those that have established effective SWA policies, in other organizations this concept may be extremely foreign and may be seen as a sign of disobedience or insubordination. Additionally, even if an organization has an established SWA policy, this may only apply to specific unsafe situations, and may not necessarily capture the true nature of assertiveness as a form of team backup, such as when employees detect errors and challenge team members to correct them. Also, in some organizations with a very rigid organizational culture, a SWA could exist in name only, without the required supporting leadership and management attitudes and behavior. In these cases, oftentimes when employees try to exercise the SWA they may be chastised or reprimanded. This may be because the organizational leadership views assertiveness as a way to negatively challenge the existing leadership authority, and on a personal level could be because leaders and managers feel threatened by this behavior. If this is the case, the organization may have to adopt a mutual support and backup strategy slowly and cautiously and try to win over those leaders by explaining the benefits of the strategies.

One way to help smooth the transition is to assure employees at all levels (including senior managers and leaders) that assertiveness is a component of mutual support and backup, which is designed to help the organization and protect employees, not to remove anyone's authority. Simply because an employee is expressing her opinion does not mean she is being disobedient or insubordinate when given job instructions. In fact, by explaining one's position in a professional and respectful manner an assertive employee may actually help the employee being challenged understand that no harm or disrespect is intended. Assertiveness should be used as a mission-enabler to help improve processes and outcomes, as opposed to blatant disobedience and insubordination to appropriate job instructions, which can pull teams apart and destroy team cohesiveness. Assertiveness is not an excuse to usurp authority from leaders and managers, but is used to provide support to the team and mission. As an operational team leader one of your responsibilities will likely include managing this delicate balance.

Designing Mutual Support and Backup Strategies into Your Organization

It is easy to talk about assertiveness and how it can be used to support team performance, but implementing these types of strategies is another challenge altogether. If assertiveness is simply talked about by leaders without designing formal policies for using assertiveness as an on-the-job skill, some employees may naturally become more assertive in the face of hazards while others, who are less comfortable with confrontation, remain quiet. Without formal policies that encourage (and perhaps require) assertiveness in hazardous situations, some employees may be afraid to speak up. Formal policies are the backing employees need to justify their assertive actions, so organizations should design mutual support and backup policies that encourage employees to speak up when injury or harm could occur and to challenge incorrect information when it could impact successful job accomplishment.

While assertiveness is an important component of mutual support and backup, it is not the only factor that helps to shape operations and safety outcomes in the face of hazards. For these concepts to be a truly effective strategy, organizations must surround assertive behavior with policies and support structures that incorporate opportunities for employees to check each other's work, to participate in decision-making processes, and to interject their opinions if they feel there is a need to select a different COA. As part of an organization's responsibility, leadership and management staff can design policies for team-based environments where employees double-check each other's work to validate correct performance. This requirement can be part of

SOPs or operational checklists. For example, in some military aviation units that operate crew-served aircraft, two pilots may be required to check the data entry into mission computers and flight management systems. If errors are detected they are trained to challenge the error and double-check the information. Additionally, these crews are normally trained to offer different solutions when they detect errors, not simply call out the error and wait for someone else to fix it. In this manner, mutual support and backup is not only a reactive component of team leadership and performance, but it is also proactive, empowering employees to devise strategies for fixing problems rather than simply calling out errors.

These concepts may not be easily implemented in organizations with low trust environments or those with rigid hierarchical structures. In those types of organizations it may be wise to start with a top-down approach. Top-level leaders must model the behavior they wish to see in their subordinate leaders and employees. Leaders must not only develop mutual support and backup policies, but must also defend employees who use them. Leaders should also avoid succumbing to high-level production pressure and giving mixed signals to team members. Caving into excessive production pressure without assessing safety impacts, yet expecting team members to exercise mutual support and backup policies, is an easy way to lose the respect of employees. For example, as an operational team leader consider how your team would feel if you tell them, "Today's job is very important. You should be assertive if you see something unsafe or spot errors that will jeopardize quality or production goals, but make sure you keep the production line moving as long as possible because we must meet quotas today." These conflicting statements place employees in a position to either choose safety and quality or production speed. Instead, leaders should set the example by encouraging teamwork (including support and backup, assertiveness, verifying work performance, and challenging each other when it appears that an incorrect decision or errors have been made) and understand that this type of approach will facilitate a more comprehensive strategy for meeting production quotas.

Another way leaders can derail the effectiveness of mutual support and backup strategies is to react in anger when challenged by subordinates, thereby displaying the opposite type of behavior they wish to see in others. Rather, they should publicly accept feedback when offered by subordinate employees. This does not always mean they will agree with other employees, nor does it require leaders to be excessively nice or pushovers. Ultimately leaders must make the decision, even if it means acknowledging and considering this feedback from employees, but rejecting the recommendations in a professional manner.

It may also be helpful to publicly acknowledge the positive efforts of employees displaying assertiveness and mutual support and backup behavior, even if the decision-maker ultimately does not accept their recommendations.

An additional skill which operational team leaders should attempt to develop within themselves is empathy. The ability to share and understand the feelings of subordinate employees is an extremely important aspect of operational team leadership, but in some organizations this need may rarely be discussed. In some cases subordinate employees may lack the courage to provide immediate feedback, especially if it involves challenging more experienced leaders. It can also be very difficult for many team members to challenge their peers. In high-stress/high-hazard environments these difficulties may be magnified. Employees may fear becoming disliked or unpopular, being publicly reprimanded, or being terminated. As a team leader, try to imagine yourself in your employees' positions. One of your responsibilities should be to create an atmosphere where employees feel good about themselves when they demonstrate mutual support and backup behaviors, including assertiveness when necessary. Trust is a key component required for this strategy to work and when the trust is broken employees may stop speaking up about errors and may stop being assertive in the face of unsafe situations. Additionally, when employees feel shut down by team leaders whenever they assert their position, this can result in a cessation of support and backup. This can be a lonely position for team leaders and when you need your team members the most, you want them to be there for you. So, try to encourage and reward their behavior (even in simple ways). Sometimes a little "pat on the back" can go a long way in building morale and trust.

Mutual Support and Backup Guidelines

The following list provides some basic guidelines that can help organizations more effectively implement these types of policies.

- Design clear and unambiguous policies, procedures, and rules: Knowing the rules and policies is essential. How can employees challenge each other or their team leaders, and how can team leaders challenge their team members when they do not even know the requirements? For example, if a procedure is about to be performed and a fellow team member feels that it violates a policy (yet that policy is extremely vague), when he attempts to support the team's safety and performance goals by asserting his point of view, he has little to justify his position. This type of situation can lead to arguing, bickering, and ineffective teamwork, with no clear end in sight, and which might put the team leader in the position of tie-breaker. This can be uncomfortable, but there are worse implications if this situation occurs when an accident needs to be prevented. Arguing over who is right or wrong is unlikely to stop imminent danger. Clear policies and rules (even if some rules are used with upper and lower boundaries as opposed to prescriptive absolutes) provide teams with justification if they detect an impending violation. Here's an additional tip: as a team leader you should know these policies and make sure the team members know them as well, and if feasible, keep a copy of the SOP or other policy manuals on hand to serve as quick-reference guides.

- Develop standardization policies or rules with upper and lower boundaries to provide a safe space for action and a clear understanding of when a violation occurs: Similarly to the creation of clear policies, providing upper and lower limits to rules allows a degree of freedom of action on the part of team members before crossing a safety threshold into a policy violation. Consider a hypothetical example of complex construction equipment that must be operated within a specific temperature range. The temperature gauge has a lower limit (minimum cold temperature) and an upper limit (maximum high temperature) and as long as the operator stays within the limits, no safety violations related to temperature have occurred. This way the equipment operator may use approved techniques as long as the temperature limits are not violated. If the limits are exceeded (and preferably before they are exceeded) other team members should speak up to correct the actions to avoid equipment damage or other hazardous situations. If there are other ways to use rules with a boundary range, this may provide employees with a space for effective and efficient action while also providing clear knowledge of when a safety violation could occur.

- Clearly explain which rules are absolutes and which ones are variable (and where the boundaries of variation stop): If rules are going to be designed using boundaries, employees must understand where the limits lie. If rules are absolutes they must be clearly explained as such. Additionally, organizations should work to clearly and explicitly identify which rules are inviolable absolutes where violation results in no-questions-asked disciplinary action (sometimes referred to as red rules) and which rules may include some latitude (and potential management review before disciplinary action is taken).

• Design explicit policies for holding team members accountable for correct execution of procedures and staying within rule boundaries: Even if policies are well-understood and if rules are designed as either absolutes with exact requirements, or as boundaries with upper and lower limits, without a clear policy explaining what team members should do or how they should be assertive and provide mutual support and backup when a violation occurs, corrective behaviors may be highly variable. Organizations may be able to provide either prescriptive language or general guidelines to help employees assert their position when a rule has been violated or a procedure has been executed incorrectly. Like checklists, these could possibly include challenge and reply statements, where the team members call out the incorrect actions or rule violations. Given the previous example of a temperature range on a piece of equipment, if one team member notices the temperature is about to exceed an upper boundary he or she may be provided with prescriptive language to challenge the team member operating the equipment. This mutual support and backup language could be listed as a warning or caution statement in part of the operational checklists or SOPs:

WARNING: DO NOT OPERATE THIS EQUIPMENT
OUTSIDE THE TEMPERATURE LIMITS OR
DAMAGE MAY OCCUR. IF YOU WITNESS AN
OPERATOR USING THIS EQUIPMENT OUTSIDE THE
TEMPERATURE RANGE STATE, "TEMPERATURE OUT
OF LIMITS, INITIATE SHUTDOWN PROCEDURES!"

With this type of language integrated into operating procedures it provides team members with a source of justification as they attempt to apply mutual support and backup actions. As with other elements of work system design, these types of approaches should be examined using a system approach to ensure no violation of regulations, or manufacturer operating policies or procedures exist or that other consequences do not adversely impact team operations.

- Institute programs and policies that encourage employees to stay within safety boundaries and follow rules, yet to speak up when the rules aren't working anymore: This is a delicate balance. On the one hand you want employees to follow the rules and work safely, but on the other hand you don't want them to blindly follow rules that don't work, make work methods less safe, or seriously degrade production capacity. However, if team members understand the intent behind these policies and see the benefits of both sides of the rule-following/rule-modifying tightrope, continuous improvement and adaptation may be achievable while maintaining appropriate levels of safety. Employees should be encouraged to provide feedback to the work system design process, including direct participation during work system design studies and innovation experiments to help improve the way work is both designed and performed, and to help improve multiple goals, such as safety, production efficiency and effectiveness, quality, and reliability.

Ultimately, organizations should seek to develop a culture where employees are willing to correct each other regardless of rank or job title, employee position, or experience. All employees should understand that this correction is a method for providing support to each other and the organization, rather than as a personal affront. By empowering employees to speak up and challenge their coworkers and leaders, and to offer alternative suggestions, these mutual support and backup strategies may be viewed as a way to trap errors and stop mishaps from occurring, to develop effective solutions, and to help the overall team, rather than simply as a way to identify problems.

This may sound great in principle, but in practice it requires deep commitment at all levels and continuous reinforcement. Classroom discussions, tailgate talks, and safety stand-downs offer opportunities to discuss the concept and leaders' expectations for mutual support and backup. Prior to conducting training or discussions, establishing some basic ground rules for employees will help. Here are some general guidelines to help employees understand what mutual support and backup (including assertiveness) means:

- Team members should state their position to each other and team leaders.

- Team members should clearly explain what appears to be wrong and maintain their position until convinced by facts that their position is incorrect.

- Rather than simply stating an objection or calling out a problem, team members should try to offer a helpful solution, if able.

As part of training strategies, operational teams can use case studies, role-playing scenarios, and simulation, where team members take turns playing different roles. As an example, one role could be an overbearing supervisor who violates rules and another role could be an assistant or technician who must speak up during an uncomfortable situation to stop the supervisor from performing an unsafe act. Other team members would be able to watch the scenario unfold and provide constructive feedback to both actors. This process should be conducted by a facilitator who can manage the scenario and help engage the audience in the discussion by asking guiding questions. In some cases, this facilitator may be the team leader, but it may be effective to bring in a neutral third party. If conducted effectively, this role-playing and simulation process may help the entire team to learn ways to provide mutual support and backup, and it also demonstrates the organization's commitment to these strategies.

Another method for inculcating mutual support into operational teams is to specifically address the subject during the team briefing and debriefing processes. During the pre-job brief, the team leader can state his or her expectations about the use of mutual support and backup strategies during the job. During the debrief, the team can discuss how mutual support and backup was used effectively or how it could be improved. From a peer-to-peer standpoint, sharing personal lessons-learned with each other may help to build camaraderie and morale, and when senior, more experienced employees share lessons-learned about assertiveness and mutual support with junior employees it may help those less-experienced personnel to develop the courage and confidence needed during potentially tense situations.

Conclusions

Mutual support and backup may seem like a simple concept, but in some organizations policies must be made explicit so teams know how to handle unsafe situations. Without mutual support and backup strategies, team members may grow numb to errors and violations of rules, and over time they may simply accept hazardous activities as a normal part of operations. This type of operating environment can put teams in very precarious positions because eventually errors will occur and safety may be compromised, and mutual support and backup could potentially be the last line of defense to prevent an error from escalating into a catastrophic mishap.

So, does this mean that designing these programs is easy and that every time assertiveness is exercised it will be well-received? Probably not. Mutual support and backup is a way for improving team performance in the organization, not simply a license for disobedience in the workplace. Additionally, in many cases, conflict may emerge when team members challenge each other. That is understandable, but the conflict must be managed as the team works to find the correct answer when one team member asserts his position. Standardization and clear rules can help build a support structure for mutual support and backup techniques, which can help assertive employees defend their positions. Additionally, if leaders set the proper tone and lead by example, demonstrating the appropriate behavior when challenged by an assertive subordinate employee, other team members may choose to model that behavior. This may help deescalate confrontational situations by creating a culture that views mutual support and backup as a professional way of conducting work.

While this has been the shortest chapter in this book, the subject of asserting one's position for the sake of safety and to help ensure proper operational performance is an extremely important subject, and one that should not be taken lightly. Just like designing a defense-in-depth approach with multiple redundant safety systems and hazard controls, mutual support and backup should be viewed as an additional approach to help make operations safer and more effective. Mutual support and backup as a strategy may not be a hazard control itself, and although these approaches may not catch every error or stop every unsafe situation, when combined with a well-designed hazard control system, mutual support and backup can serve to make operations safer. Particularly when every team member is trained in these concepts and is willing to speak up, a new level of safety may be attainable.

Chapter 10
Time-Sensitive Risk Management

Risk management is a process that is often discussed at all levels within an organization. Risks can emerge in many forms, including risks to finances, schedules, and quality. In this chapter the impact of risk will be described in numerous ways, but the predominant focus will be on risks to the safety of personnel, equipment, and the environment, and risks to operations continuity. Since risk occurs in so many facets of business, many employees are well-versed at some aspects of managing risks. However, time-sensitive risk management during operational execution can include several factors that affect the decision-making methods and which set it apart from other forms of risk management. Due to the dangers of high-hazard operational environments, and the time-compression associated with the rapid risk-reduction requirements necessary for injury avoidance, the risks and decision processes faced by operational team leaders are often quite different from those in low-hazard environments.

This chapter is not intended to be a comprehensive risk management tutorial. There are many other books that include in-depth training in risk management, from basic to advanced levels. It is also not intended to make you an expert at risk management. However, this chapter will begin by providing a broad overview of risk management in order to facilitate the follow-on explanations of the time-sensitive risk management process used during operational execution. Ultimately, it is hoped that operational team leaders, safety professionals, and front line team members will understand how to work through the required risk management steps in a timely manner to mitigate losses during operational execution. By understanding the basic definitions about hazards and risks, elements of risk-informed decision making, and strategies for controlling risks during time-sensitive situations, front line operators may be better equipped to deal with hazards they contend with during routine operations. They will also have a decision-making framework to employ when faced with unique and untested risk scenarios that may be encountered during non-routine operations or that could be faced when routine operations go awry.

Risk Management Overview

Time-sensitive risk management is the process for dealing with risks in time-compressed situations where there is limited time to work through a formal risk identification, assessment, and management process. It incorporates some elements of other hazard analysis and risk assessment activities, but in a more rapid fashion. The major differentiating factor between time-sensitive risk management and other types of risk management is the time required to make a decision (which also affects mitigation strategies and the controls that may be implemented). This type of risk management is often needed after operations have commenced and employees are actively engaged in their work tasks. Unlike more long-term forms of risk management that may be planned into system design, this type assists employees in real-time when faced with immediate threats to their well-being or to operational processes. However, there are some common threads between the multiple forms of risk management, and explaining those commonalities through a lexicon will help provide a risk management primer before discussing the specific aspects of time-sensitive risk management.

- Hazard: While different forms of risk management may have various terms to describe things that can go wrong, a hazard can be thought of as an object, condition, or event that could result in some form of harm or damage if it occurs in the presence of people, equipment, or the environment (*Department of Defense Standard Practice for System Safety* 5). For example, a sharp edge on the corner of a metal structure could be a hazard and injury could occur if team members walk into it. Excessive oil temperature in a piece of industrial machinery is a hazard that could cause equipment damage if the machine is allowed to continue operating. Excessive pressure in a pressure vessel or pipeline containing hazardous liquids could be an environmental hazard because pipe rupture could lead to ground contamination. Hazards can lead to harm in other areas as well, including operational processes (such as degraded production capacity) and organizational reputation (such as a loss of customer confidence and trust after a hazard occurs and leads to other forms of damage).

- Risk: The term hazard and risk are often used interchangeably, but they are actually quite different. Risk may be thought of as an expression or assessment of a hazard in terms of probability (or likelihood) of occurrence, and severity of impact (or consequence).

A key area of inquiry is identifying how likely it is that a hazard will occur and if it does occur, the potential level of injury or damage it may cause. The result is a risk rating, typically expressed in qualitative terms (such as high, medium, low, or critical, serious, moderate, and so on) or quantitative terms (such as 1, 2, 3, and so on) (*Operational Risk Management* 7). When conducting time-sensitive risk management it may be tempting to simply focus on the hazard itself (such as an object) and immediately take steps to protect employees with PPE, which is understandable in some cases, but time permitting, leaders and employees should consider both the likelihood of injury or damage occurrence and the potential severity when developing risk control strategies. Additionally, PPE is often considered the least effective method for controlling risk, yet it is often the first "go-to" strategy chosen by many.

- Risk Management: Hazard identification and risk assessment are large components of risk management programs, but risk management includes a spectrum of activities. As previously mentioned, part of risk management includes identifying and assessing hazards in terms of probability and severity. When evaluating probability, assessors will often use qualitative or quantitative methods. Other methods exist, such as semi-quantitative approaches, but are beyond the scope of this book. While quantitative approaches can offer quite a bit of data to help risk managers, in an operational context they can sometimes be difficult for team members to interpret. For example, asking an operational team leader or her employees to understand how to approach risk mitigation for a hazard with a 10^{-5} probability of occurrence may be asking too much, particularly when they are trying to focus on getting the job done as safely and as efficiently as they can. It may be easier or simpler for operational teams if risk probabilities are explained in qualitative terms, particularly when time-sensitive risk-informed decision making is required. A qualitative assessment of probability could include descriptive language, such as the potential that an accident is likely to occur, probably will occur, may occur, or is unlikely to occur and include a certain time period, such as within the next several days (*Operational Risk Management* 5–6). In many cases team leaders and team members alike may have a difficult time making predictions on probability, because this is not necessarily a core job skill in many industries and employment positions. Additionally, while many people may often feel like they are good estimators of probability, in reality, making accurate predictions can be a very difficult endeavor. On the other hand, employees are often well-versed at understanding severity levels, which is the other component of hazard assessment to determine risk ratings. Severity may be expressed in terms of harm (including bodily injury and/or monetary loss) or production losses (such as a certain number of equipment downtime days). Other risk impacts may be harder to capture, such as loss of reputation and may seem like more downstream or ancillary effects. Nonetheless, they can still have significant impacts on the organization as a whole. Risk management also includes the design of controls to either reduce the probability of hazard occurrence, the severity of impact or consequence, or a combination of both approaches. In addition to hazard analysis, risk assessment, and control development and implementation, risk management also includes determining what level of risk is acceptable or unacceptable to the organization, which typically involves top-level leadership involvement. Employees and operational team leaders should not be forced to make risk decisions that exceed their capabilities, so in many cases department heads and executive-level leadership should be involved with risk management processes, including making the final decisions when required (*Operational Risk Management* 4). Additionally, the risk management process includes communicating risks throughout the organization, so employees and operational team leaders understand what is acceptable and what is not, and to external stakeholders, whose support may be vital for business continuity (particularly if failures occur).

Risk Management Process

Risk assessment is a large component of the risk management process and therefore deserves some specific attention. Operational team leaders may be at least somewhat familiar with this process, as it often follows a rather intuitive progression. Understanding and properly executing the risk assessment process is a central requirement and should be considered a critical job skill for operational team leaders who work in high-hazard environments. The process is as follows:

- Hazard identification: As part of the operational planning process team leaders, team members, and safety professionals should work together to identify the potential and actual hazards that could cause harm to the team during all phases of work, including travel, preparation, setup, execution, tear-down/dismantling of equipment, and return travel. Each phase should be examined and a methodical process used for determining the hazards that may exist during the phases. One method includes the use of hazard checklists, which can include general and specific categories. Additionally, tapping into user experience and lessons-learned can also be a source of data for hazard identification. Brainstorming with team members can also be a helpful source for hazard identification because employees may have a wealth of knowledge and may have even experienced certain hazards that may not be obvious to some planners. It may also be possible to obtain failure data from equipment manufacturers to determine the likelihood of equipment failure, which could become a hazard.

- Hazard assessment: After each of the hazards has been identified they should be assessed in terms of probability and severity. As stated earlier, either a quantitative, qualitative, or semi-quantitative approach may be used, but the qualitative approach may be well-suited for many operational tasks, particularly when time is of the essence. During the hazard assessment process it is often helpful to identify the potential causes of the hazards or the ways failures can occur. Time permitting, identifying the immediate cause as well as the root cause or causal factors may be helpful. The immediate cause is often the event that immediately precedes a hazard while the root cause is often a deeper cause that may exist further back in the mishap sequence.

- Risk ranking: After hazards have been assessed in terms of probability and severity, the result is a set of risks. Risks may be categorized by using a risk assessment matrix, such as that listed in Table 10.1, which has been adapted from Marine Corps Order 3500.27B, *Operational Risk Management*. Using such a matrix can help with grouping risks into specific categories, which then helps risk decision makers determine if risk levels are acceptable or unacceptable. When risks are examined prior to the introduction of controls, they may be thought of as Initial Risk Codes, or IRCs. These IRCs may then be ranked in order (highest IRC to lowest IRC) so decision makers can focus their risk control efforts.

Table 10.1   Risk Assessment Matrix, adapted from Marine Corps Order 3500.27B, *Operational Risk Management*

		Probability			
1 = Critical Risk 2 = Serious Risk 3 = Moderate Risk 4 = Minor Risk 5 = Negligible Risk		A	B	C	D
Severity	I	1	1	2	3
	II	1	2	3	4
	III	2	3	4	5
	IV	3	4	5	5

Probability Codes:	Category A: Likely to occur immediately or within a short period of time. Expected to occur frequently to an individual item or person or continuously to a fleet, inventory, or group.
	Category B: Probably will occur in time. Expected to occur several times to an individual item or person or frequently to a fleet, inventory, or group.
	Category C: May occur in time. Can reasonably be expected to occur some time to an individual item or person or several times to a fleet, inventory, or group.
	Category D: Unlikely to occur.
Severity Codes:	Category I: Death, loss of facility/asset, or result in grave damage to national interests.
	Category II: Severe injury, illness, property damage, damage to national or service interests, or degradation to efficient use of assets.
	Category III: Minor injury, illness, property damage, damage to national, service, or command interests, or degradation to efficient use of assets.
	Category IV: Minimal threat to personnel safety or health, property, national, service, or command interests, or efficient use of assets.

- Risk control design, selection, and implementation: At this point leaders must make a decision about which risks require controlling and at what level. There are various strategies for controlling risk, including finding ways to eliminate risks altogether, substitute less hazardous materials or work methods, installing engineering controls to either protect employees or interrupt a potential mishap sequence, developing warnings and cautions to help raise awareness of hazards, administrative controls, such as procedures, work processes, or team coordination actions, and PPE (American

Industrial Hygiene Association 53). The level of control should be commensurate with the IRC, meaning that generally, the higher the risk the more effort should be placed on higher-order controls and/or using a combination of control methods.

• Reassess risk: Once risk controls have been designed, leaders should reexamine the IRC and consider the potential hazard probability and severity after the controls have been identified to obtain a Final Risk Code, or FRC. While this is not a foolproof process, it is necessary to reassess the risks as if the controls were in place to estimate how much the probability and/or severity was reduced. At this point decision makers can either choose to accept the FRC or if the risk is deemed unacceptable, they should work through the process again to determine if there are ways to lower the risk further. Particular attention should be paid to low-probability/high-consequence scenarios because, although they may not happen often, if they do happen they could have devastating consequences to personnel, the environment, and the organization. Additionally, since probability can be difficult to estimate in some cases, adding a degree of focus to the high-consequence hazards may help teams develop controls to avoid the most severe types of injuries or mishaps, even if they are unsure of the likelihood of occurrence.

• Monitor control effectiveness: After the controls have been implemented and operations commence, the risk assessment process is not over. This process requires continuous monitoring and feedback to determine if the controls work as intended/designed and if there are any unintended consequences or additional hazards that have been introduced. As a general rule, if a risk control reduces risk in one area, but increases it to a higher level in another area, or if the control prevents the teams from performing their work (which could also lead to additional hazards if they develop workarounds), then the control lacks appropriate levels of effectiveness and should be reexamined. Risks and controls should be monitored throughout the operational phases and as new information is obtained during operational execution, risk ratings should be continuously revised until the work is complete. In some cases, such as high-tempo operations, this may simply be a mental or oral reassessment of the risk conditions and controls, and in other cases, the formal process may need to be repeated. Then debriefing and lessons-learned activities should capture information about the risk management process.

Of course, risk management includes other aspects as well; including communicating the information to those who may be impacted by risks or the risk-informed decision-making process, but this six-step process includes most of the activities operational team leaders will deal with on a regular basis. It should also be noted that there are numerous risk assessment matrices available, and organizations must choose the type of matrix that suits their needs. Additionally, leaders should be aware that a risk matrix is not necessarily the solution for all safety challenges, but some type of risk assessment or risk modeling tool is a foundational element of any safety program. Risk matrix or other risk assessment tool usage should not be considered a once-and-for-all activity. Just because risk is assessed and controlled one time does not mean it will not change. In complex organizations risk can be like a living organism that can change as workers, teams, and organizations adapt. Therefore, risk should be continually assessed. Additionally, other areas that leaders must consider are the organizational culture, risk perspective, the social influences on risk assessment, and the risk-taking behavior of employees in their organizations. These areas may be considered during the risk-informed decision-making process.

Risk-Informed Decision Making

One of the most challenging aspects of risk management is making sense of the information and actually using the knowledge you have gained about risks to make a decision or set of decisions. Most decisions include multiple attributes, and oftentimes some of these attributes fall outside the area of safety. For example, decisions about risk mitigation must often be balanced with operational performance requirements and the resources and constraints associated with risk controls. So, operational team leaders and other decision makers often have their work cut out for them. As an operational team leader, your primary focus is most likely protecting your team and accomplishing the mission. Explained in other terms, this may be referred to as safe mission accomplishment. But what does safe mission accomplishment really mean? It sounds nice, and leaders who use this phrase may have great intentions, but without details to support it, these may be just empty words.

When leaders in high-hazard environments are required to make decisions surrounding operational performance and the protection of employees, it is necessary to use a multitude of information as part of the risk-informed decision-making process to choose COAs regarding activities, organizational goals, and desired work outcomes. As part of this process leaders must determine how estimated risk levels compare with the level of risk the organization is willing to accept and make decisions about risk acceptance. These can be uncomfortable decisions to make, and without a clear understanding of what is and what is not an acceptable level of risk, operational team leaders, sub-team leaders, and employees may have no idea whether or not they may perform an operation. Clear acceptable risk limits may help teams avoid confusion when making decisions about operational tasks and hazardous conditions, and may help them understand if conditions are safe enough without controls, whether they need to implement initial risk controls, and if they need to revise risk assessments based on new information and implement new or additional controls to reduce risks even further.

Acceptable risk levels will probably vary between industries and between organizations and, generally speaking, in low-hazard environments acceptable risk levels will have lower FRCs than in high-hazard environments. For example, the risks firefighters, offshore oil rig workers, and underground miners may be willing to accept are likely higher than those risks that sales and administrative professionals in an office environment are willing to accept in the performance of their jobs. In many cases the risk-reward ratio must be continuously calculated and revised and risks should only be accepted when the benefits outweigh the costs. Additionally, it is extremely helpful to provide explicit policy guidance to help operational decision makers determine which employee level can make decisions on risk acceptance. For example, using risk ratings from Table 10.1, perhaps a line operational employee (not a DL) may only be allowed to accept risk with a FRC of 5—Negligible and supervisors or sub-team leaders may be allowed to accept risks with an FRC of 4—Minor. Using this pattern, as the level of FRC increases, the organizational decision maker level increases as well. Typically, any decisions surrounding the highest level of risks would only be made by those at the highest levels in the organization, and in some cases, organizations may actually provide explicit guidance that a certain level of risk will never be accepted, regardless of the potential benefit or payoff. These decisions may be unique to the specific organization and industry, so there is no clear-cut, one-size-fits-all answer.

Hopefully it is evident by now that risk management should be a deliberate part of every organization's planning processes. Once acceptable risk levels are identified, leaders and decision makers can then evaluate operational risks during the planning phase, before work commences, and identify the required resources and expenditures necessary to implement controls that will reduce risks to acceptable levels. If, during the assessment process, employees and team leaders realize the risk is beyond their level of decision making (based on their employment level or position in the organization), they should elevate the risk situation to the appropriate level decision maker(s) within the organization based on the pre-defined criteria. Employees should never be placed in a position to make a decision on risk acceptance that is beyond their capability. It is understandable that in some emergency/time-critical situations decisions must be made by those on the scene, particularly if a failure to decide and take action might result in greater harm than waiting. However, as a general rule, employees should be insulated from risk decisions that are above their level. If a team leader evaluates risks and the risk level is beyond acceptable limits for his decision-making position, then additional risk mitigation strategies should be considered. If, after implementing the controls that are available to the operational team leader, the risk is still too high, then the risk should be elevated. At that point, the risk decision maker(s) should identify additional methods to lower the risk, which may include additional planning and resources. Organizations may also choose to identify absolute maximum levels of acceptable risk. By making and communicating this explicit risk decision to employees, it helps hold the organizational leadership accountable when risk–reward deliberations are being conducted. Using this type of maximum acceptable risk policy, decision makers have a tool they can rely on to help them make the decision to either exhaust more resources to lower the risk or to not perform the operation. Without an absolute policy, acceptable risk could potentially become a continuum, swaying back and forth, where the maximum risk the organization is willing to accept is based on the opinion of the leader in charge, or is driven by economic forces.

It may be easier to create absolute maximum acceptable risk policies in some organizations and industries than others. A large part of this decision must take into consideration the potential organizational losses if risks are not taken and comparing these potential losses to the level of risk the organization, employees, and stakeholders are willing to tolerate. A key question to ask is whether performing the operation to obtain the potential benefit is worth the potential human, material, environmental, or reputational losses. If the potential benefit is high and the potential loss is low, the decision may be easy. However, if the potential benefits and losses are both high the decision becomes much more difficult. Maximum acceptable risk policies may make this decision more clear-cut.

Strategies for Risk Mitigation

Before discussing the unique aspects of time-sensitive risk management, it will be helpful to describe some of the strategies for risk mitigation, because, even in time-compressed situations team leaders and employees may need multiple options when considering how to control risks. In some cases, controls that are aimed at reducing severity levels (such as PPE) may be ineffective due to the energy levels associated with certain hazard sources (Ericson 28). Alternatively, in certain high-hazard operational environments some hazards may be so likely to occur that the only credible means of reducing risk is to limit the potential damage through barriers, or PPE. Personnel should be trained to identify hazards, including the hazard itself (the object or condition that can cause harm), the cause(s), and the effects. Equipping operational teams with the knowledge to identify hazards and to implement a range of control resources should be part of the risk management training process, and organizations should endeavor to ensure employees understand these skills. Several strategies may be utilized to control hazards, thereby reducing risk levels as part of the risk management process:

- Controls designed to reduce probability of hazard occurrence: When assessing hazards it is helpful to identify not only the hazardous object or condition, but also the aspects of the hazard that actually result in harm to people, equipment, or the environment. Identifying the cause (or multiple causes) can help leaders understand how the hazard may lead to harm so that controls may be developed to reduce the likelihood of that cause actually occurring. When examining causes it may be helpful to examine the immediate cause that precedes a hazard occurrence as well as the root cause or causal factors that may reside somewhere deeper and further back in a potential hazard chain of events that sets a hazard sequence in motion. These root causes can exist deeper within the organization. Oftentimes decision makers simply try to control the immediate cause, but in many cases eliminating the root cause or causal factors could potentially stop the hazard occurrence. There may be certain high-consequence hazards where the only effective method for reducing risk levels is through reducing the likelihood of occurrence, often by addressing one or more causes and causal factors (Ericson 28). For example, in situations with high amounts of uncontrolled energy release it may not be feasible to truly reduce the consequence to acceptable levels, so organizations may opt to design-in multiple controls to reduce the probability of the energy release occurring in the first place.

- Controls designed to reduce the effect or severity if the hazard does occur: The other part of risk concerns hazard effects, or the impacts on people, equipment, or the environment. When assessing risk, leaders should consider what could possibly happen to employees, equipment, or the environment if the hazardous condition were to actually occur. By identifying the potential level of damage leaders can then identify ways to protect employees (and possibly equipment and the environment) from the effects, such as through barriers and/or PPE. For certain types of risks, these controls aimed at limiting damage may be effective.

• Defense-in-depth approach: In some cases reducing either the probability of occurrence or the severity of the effects may not be enough to reduce risks to acceptable levels. In those cases a defense-in-depth approach may be required, where a combination of risk controls are implemented to reduce both the probability of occurrence and the severity of impact if the hazard actually does occur. In other cases strategies could involve multiple forms of redundant controls for both the probability and severity. As a hypothetical example, suppose an operational team is pumping high-pressure liquid through a transfer pipe. If the pipe were to burst, it could potentially result in death or severe injury. Using a combination of controls and a defense-in-depth approach, the probability of pipe rupture could potentially be reduced by installing pressure regulators and pressure relief valves, while the potential severity (effect or consequence) could potentially be reduced by designing standoff distances (requiring employees to stay a certain distance away from the pipes), approach boundaries to limit exposure, physical protective barriers, and PPE. Using this approach there is a potential to reduce both the probability and severity. Leaders should be aware, though, that in some cases adding layers of controls may not actually reduce risks to lower levels, and in those cases leaders should be keenly mindful of the potential negative impacts those additional controls may have on operations.

Long-Term Risk Management versus Time-Sensitive Risk Management

Now that we have worked through the primer on hazard description and risk management strategies, we can cover the important challenges associated with time-sensitive risk management. While the general concepts associated with risk management (including hazard identification and assessment, determination of IRCs, risk ranking, the development and selection of controls, determination of FRCs, implementation of controls, and control monitoring) are largely the same with both long-term and time-sensitive risk management, there are some unique aspects associated with time-sensitive risk management that place operational team leaders and employees in difficult situations.

Table 10.2 describes some of the differences associated with long-term versus time-sensitive risk management.

Table 10.2   Long-term versus time-sensitive risk management

Long-Term Risk Management	Time-Sensitive Risk Management
• Long lead-time for planning and identifying hazards	• Short lead time for planning (sometimes minutes) due to unexpected hazard occurrences
• Time to integrate multiple subject matter experts on team and gain input on risks	• Little time to gain input from subject matter experts
• Time to define goals and acceptable risk levels	• Goals may be ill defined due to time compression; main focus on survival/minimizing damage
• Conducted well in advance of jobs, projects, or operations	• Conducted just prior to commencing operations or during operations
• Ability to delay job, project, or operation until risks are mitigated to acceptable levels	• Inability to totally halt job in many cases

Time-Sensitive Risk Management Approaches

The basic steps used with time-sensitive risk management are generally the same as other forms of risk management, but the time-sensitive nature of hazard identification, risk assessment, and decision making regarding controls imparts unique challenges, and time-compression often requires operational team leaders and team members to rapidly work through the risk management process. Oftentimes the rapid decision-making requirements necessitate the use of a qualitative over quantitative risk assessment approaches. Qualitative risk assessment techniques are often easier to execute than quantitative risk assessment methods, which may require a deeper and lengthier data research process. When time is of the essence, operational teams may not be able to wait on manufacturers' equipment failure probability data or other time-consuming research processes to determine the historical percentages of accident occurrence. In many circumstances personnel must make rapid decisions to protect employees and the time-critical mitigation requirements associated with high-hazard operational environments can limit the risk control options available to team leaders and employees.

Understanding the risk management process and associated steps is critical for managing risks in time-sensitive situations. The process involves a rapid execution of the six-step risk management process, including hazard identification, hazard assessment (in terms of probability and severity), identification of IRCs and risk ranking, risk control design, selection, and implementation, risk reassessment and determination of FRCs, and monitoring control effectiveness. However, in time-sensitive risk management situations, hazards will often occur in unexpected ways or perhaps unique hazards will emerge that were completely unexpected and that were potentially beyond the comprehension of operational planners. In high-hazard environments these surprises could include potentially life-threatening situations or unexpected equipment failures that might result in serious injury, or significant equipment, process, or environmental damage.

In these circumstances operational team leaders must work through the risk management steps as quickly as feasible. It may be helpful to provide teams with ruggedized, water-resistant field manuals that include written procedures, hazard probability and severity codes, risk matrices, or other decision-making tools to be used when there is time to make notes or at least work through a mental or verbal decision-making process. In these situations the manuals may function as a guiding tool to help the team move through the risk management steps. If time permits, the team leader should discuss the risks with the team and obtain as much information as feasible about the risks and controls, in the time available. In these cases, obtaining feedback from experienced workers who have a vast knowledge of systems, equipment, and machinery could be vital for providing mitigation methods. Additionally, younger employees may be a source of fresh information and new ideas. In both cases, utilizing FLs to help the decision-making process can be extremely helpful. While it may not be feasible in all cases, if lessons-learned systems (such as online databases) may be rapidly queried, the teams may gain more clarity about the risks and mitigation approaches. If the operational team cannot attain enough information at the local level, and if time permits, obtaining more information from other members in the organization may help team leaders gather the required information to make risk-informed decisions.

In some cases there may not be enough time to write any information down or gain more information beyond the local team level. In those cases the process may need to be conducted verbally or mentally. Communicating the hazard situation with immediate team members and determining risk levels are extremely important. The team can be a great resource for helping team leaders determine how to mitigate the risks, including probability reduction, severity reduction, or both. In some cases the team will simply have to select from the controls immediately available or may have to change the way work is performed. They must rapidly work through the risk management process until risks are within acceptable limits. However, in some cases the available controls may not lower risk to acceptable levels and the risks may exceed the decision-making capacity for the operational team leader. Having appropriate communication tools on hand may help the team leader elevate the risk decision to the appropriate level. In some situations it may turn out that the only logical option is to shut down the operation, move teams to safety, and request emergency support, but in other cases shutting down the operation and even moving teams away to safety may not be as easy as it sounds.

The unique aspects of time-sensitive risk management require teams to be able to work through the process and make rapid decisions. Therefore, structured strategies that help to simplify the risk management process can help teams balance the need for rapid decisions with the requirement for thorough assessment. Some general guidelines can help operational team leaders:

- Risk triage: In some operational situations perhaps only one hazard occurs at a time. In other circumstances, multiple hazards could occur simultaneously, including cascading failures. For example, during the hypothetical transfer of high-pressure flammable liquid through a pipe system, if a pressure regulator fails, it could potentially result in pipe rupture, and if an ignition source is present it could potentially further result in a fire or explosion. In this case, after the pressure regulator fails, the team must deal with the possible pipe rupture and potential fire, and if the pipe rupture actually occurs the team may have to deal with the leak (or perhaps multiple leaks) and potential fire or explosion. Prioritizing and handling risks in time-compressed, stressful situations can be difficult. The concept of risk triage may help, and could be compared to the process of patient triage in hospitals. Determining the most severe risks and working from high to low using a written or verbal process may help teams understand which risks must be dealt with and in what order. They should then focus their mitigation efforts on the risks that have the highest potential consequences, particularly those that could result in employee fatalities or serious injuries. While severity codes may become intuitive over time, it may be difficult for employees to rank risks other than the most severe (such as potential fatalities). This is why a field manual to help teams understand and remember severity codes can be helpful.

- Resource determination and pre-defined actions: It is prudent to identify and mitigate as many risks as possible prior to commencing operations so that teams do not need to rely solely on time-sensitive risk management. However, even the best plans will not account for every potential risk scenario and situation. Therefore, part of the planning process should include identifying a hierarchy of controls in advance of operations to determine what controls will be available if (or when) a pre-identified or unexpected hazard occurs. Resource identification in advance can help team leaders rapidly understand available options during time-sensitive situations. Additionally, as an operational team leader, you should help your team identify potential risk scenarios and pre-defined emergency response procedures. When procedures are pre-defined and the teams conduct rehearsals and drills in advance of operations, they may be easier to execute when hazards occur during operational execution. While this method is not flawless, it may help to speed up decision making. By identifying categories of risks and aligning pre-defined actions, including control implementation, with those risks teams may be able to work through the risk management process much more rapidly. If it turns out that the hazards do not fit the pre-defined categories and associated emergency mitigation actions, it may be feasible to modify the pre-identified actions rather than create completely new strategies. This method of rapid risk assessment and control may help speed up the process. Other pre-defined strategies or controls could include stopping work in the most severe cases, using the PTA activities mentioned in Chapter 5, redirecting tasks or conducting work in a different manner to remove employees from hazard exposure, keeping barriers or other engineering controls in standby modes (to be used when required), various administrative controls, such as team/employee positioning to increase their distance from the hazard, warnings, PPE to be worn during operations, and contingency PPE to be donned when needed if a hazard occurs or escalates. A sometimes-overlooked risk control strategy is the use of checklists. Checklists can provide a source for error-checking and to help team members verify the work was performed according to operational plans, which may help prevent an error from escalating into a hazard that has the potential to cause harm.

- Time-compression and COA selection: In time-compressed situations operational team leaders and team members are often faced with a great deal of information to process, the requirement to rapidly make sense of the situation, and a myriad of choices to make. As an operational team leader working in high-hazard environments you may frequently face time-critical situations where there may not be time to deliberate over multiple decision options. By rapidly working through the COA analysis process you may be able to balance speed and thoroughness. After the hazard(s) have been identified, as a general rule you can do this by narrowing the focus of available options. This is a necessity because too many options can result in an inability to choose a COA (sometimes referred to as "paralysis through analysis"). On the other hand, too few options may limit control effectiveness. A heuristic that may generally be applied is; the less time available to make a decision, the fewer the options should be on the table to choose from, particularly when the consequences that result from a failure to act could be catastrophic. Once the number of choices is narrowed to a few options (3, for example), the least favorable option can be discarded, and the team leader chooses between the remaining two, selecting the COA that most effectively reduces risk while minimizing the negative consequences associated with risk control implementation.

Rapid Recall of Time-Sensitive Risk Management Method with Mnemonics

In high-hazard operational environments risks may often surround employees and, for one reason or another, employees may become comfortable working around these hazards over time. Perhaps this is because most risks have been identified and mitigated, team members may not have seen the hazards result in actual harm in the past, or because their intense focus on performing job tasks lowers their awareness of the hazards surrounding them. Regardless of the reason, when an employee's guard is lowered and hazards occur it can result in shock and surprise. Oftentimes in these high-stress operational environments, when hazards begin to actualize the mishap sequence can happen rapidly, so prompt thinking and decision making may be required to control the hazard and protect employees. In these types of demanding scenarios it can be challenging to remember the complete time-sensitive risk management process. One method used to help crews in US Marine Corps aviation deal with time-compressed challenges and decision making is the use of mnemonics. Mnemonics are a form of memory aid that may help team leaders and employees rapidly recall the steps of a procedure. For time-sensitive risk management, consider the mnemonic "IAC-Check," which stands for Identify, Assess, Control, and Check. This mnemonic may help simplify the risk management process by breaking it into manageable chunks of information. Each letter stands for a step in the risk management process, and some steps are combined. When the mnemonic is put together it covers the six-step time-sensitive risk management process:

I   Identify hazards: Oftentimes, during high-hazard operations, hazards that were either identified as potential hazards during the planning process or new, previously unrecognized hazards will emerge. In some cases they will be obvious to the team leader and employees when they occur during operational execution, and in other cases they may be subtler, giving only small signals of their existence. Team leaders and personnel should be adept at recognizing typical hazards that routinely occur on the job and non-obvious hazards that sometimes give off weak signals. Using hazard checklists, user experience, and real-time brainstorming may facilitate the process of hazard identification.

A   Assess hazards according to probability of occurrence (likelihood) and severity of impact (consequences): This step helps teams determine the probability of a hazard causing harm and the level of harm it could potentially cause. It also includes the determination of IRCs and the rapid ranking of risks (including risk triage).

C   Control hazards through the implementation of selected mitigation controls: This step includes the determination of controls and reassessment of risk after the controls have been selected to evaluate FRCs. After the controls have been identified and the FRCs have been estimated, the controls can be implemented if the risks are within acceptable limits (and if not, the IAC steps should be repeated or the risks should be elevated to someone who can make the decision regarding risk control and acceptance).

Check   Check the effectiveness of controls: Controls must be monitored to verify proper functioning, effectiveness at controlling hazards and reducing risks to the desired/forecasted level, and that either no unintended consequences have resulted through control implementation, or that the negative effects have been minimized. The check step should be a leadership and supervisory task. As an operational team leader you should exercise your leader–manager skills to determine if new hazards have emerged or if the hazard controls dramatically impede the team's ability to conduct their work (which could also result in additional hazards through workarounds). Any new or additional hazards should not have a FRC higher than the original hazards, otherwise the control may have mitigated one hazard yet increased risk in other areas. You should also be adept at examining if the hazard controls significantly impede mission accomplishment, and if so, you may need to search out alternative methods for mitigating the risks.

Judgment, Leadership, and Adaptive Decision Making

While this chapter has provided a framework and guidelines to help with the time-sensitive risk management process, this job responsibility is far from easy, and although some tools have been provided to help simplify the process, this responsibility should not be viewed as simplistic. There may be times when no clear-cut answer exists and the decision-making process will test your fortitude. As an operational team leader you may be required to apply expert judgment and use your team to help make decisions in situations when there does not seem to be an ideal set of risk controls. Additionally, you may need to adapt previous decisions as new information is gained. There may not be a perfect set of rules, but system and team knowledge, self-awareness and self-knowledge, feedback from peers and subordinate employees, leadership skills, FL usage, judgment, and decisiveness may help, and your teams may be counting on you to be the leader they need in demanding situations where mission success and safety are on the line.

Conclusions

Although time-sensitive risk management follows the same process as other risk management techniques, the factors affecting operational teams and team leaders in time-compressed situations can make the process more difficult. During high-hazard work, operational teams do not always possess the same degree of mitigation options available to those working with low-hazard operations or in well-controlled static environments, and when pressured to make decisions in order to avoid failure or injury, stress levels can mount. So, proficiency at rapidly assessing risk, choosing and implementing controls, and verifying control effectiveness is an important skill for operational team leaders.

However, time-sensitive risk management should not simply be left up to the team leaders. What would your organization look like if every employee understood how to identify and assess hazards, make risk-informed decisions if appropriate for their level, and elevate higher risks to key decision makers in the organization? Wouldn't it help if team members could assist you in the risk-informed decision-making process? If you are an operational team leader wouldn't your job be easier if your team members were proficient at the risk management process? If organizations seek to train employees at all levels with these skills (and particularly those who are frequently exposed to hazards) the team leader's job may be made easier and the organization may gain the benefit of improved levels of safety, production, quality, and reliability.

Conclusion:
Integrating Team Leadership and Performance into Daily Operations

This book has covered numerous concepts designed to help your organization improve operational effectiveness in the areas of team leadership, productivity, safety, quality, and reliability. Each chapter included strategies for improving team performance areas and some chapters even included examples that could be used to model team leadership, performance, and safety approaches, but integrating this information into the fabric of your organization may really be the hardest part of the change process. In some ways your journey is only beginning, and reading this book may just be the start of the journey. Operationalizing this information so that it becomes a normal part of your organization's daily work is required if organizations are to realize the potential gains from these team leadership concepts and approaches to operational safety and performance.

Each chapter of this book included strategies that may be used to integrate the concepts into daily operations, but to start the process it may be helpful to use some overall methods for introducing the approaches to your organization. If you are an employee who is not in a leadership position you may need to gain the support of your immediate leaders, which may take some time as you explain this material and encourage implementation. If you are an operational team leader you may need to explain these strategies to your senior leaders and subordinate employees. If you are a top-tier leader, working in the executive suite in your organization, or a key department head or division leader you may need to explain these concepts to your peers or subordinate leaders. Regardless of your employment level within the organization, buy-in from employees at all levels will be required if these concepts and strategies are to be successfully implemented.

Gaining this support may be easier if an overarching strategy is used before implementing some of the more technical aspects. It may be helpful to map the elements of effective teamwork and some of the general characteristics associated with the nine Essential Components of team leadership and performance from Chapters 2 through 10 in this book to your operational teams. This can be done through a gap analysis. By creating a list of the elements associated with effective teamwork from Chapter 1, and the nine Essential Components, and then creating a corresponding list describing how your operational teams either possess or lack those attributes, you may begin to understand what work needs to be done and where to start. The gap analysis results will help you to focus on critical areas and then to build key concepts into your team performance training programs. These training programs then become the "bricks" that will help build the foundation for improved team performance. Without some type of training designed to explain these concepts and show employees how to use them, your improvement efforts may be short-lived and a sound approach to training may help to bridge the gap between short-term and long-term leadership and team performance goals. Additionally, other concepts may also be employed to help your organization build support for leadership, performance, safety, and risk management improvement programs in your organization. While the following list is not all-inclusive, it provides some information that may help you to develop the support and momentum required to affect change in your organization.

- **Training Strategies:** Any training programs designed to improve team performance should include all team members, regardless of rank, experience, or levels of expertise. By allowing all members to participate it helps to create shared expectations between team members. Excluding team members may degrade the effectiveness of this training because it will create a knowledge and awareness gap between these employees, ultimately causing confusion during planning and execution. When training strategies are developed, a diverse team of experts should be consulted and should collaborate to design a training system to integrate the aspects of leadership and team performance described in this book. This cross-functional team could include (but not necessarily be limited to) Human Resource Managers, Training Managers, Safety Managers, Operations Managers, and other key leadership staff, and should also include representatives and leadership from the actual teams who will undergo the training and actually apply the training to their operational activities. Work with your teams to create collaborative approaches towards improving each area of team performance that may be lacking. Training should be an opportunity to help explain the Essential Components of team leadership and performance, and is a precursor to the actual design and integration of programs, policies, and procedures into work systems, such as specific communication and feedback procedures or pre-job planning tools. The training is taken to the next level by actually integrating the information from your training programs into work systems. Training should consist of both initial courses and refresher courses. Initial Training is when all employees will receive their first exposure to these team-training concepts and Refresher Training (also called Recurrent Training) should occur at pre-defined intervals. It is up to organizational leadership to determine the frequency of recurrent training. A suggested schedule is to conduct Initial Training, followed by Refresher Training every six months or annually thereafter, but this is not a prescriptive requirement. After examining training requirements and levels of effectiveness, leaders may determine that shorter intervals between Recurrent Training are required. Periods longer than one year between training are not recommended.

- **Integrating Essential Components into Scenario-Based Training:** After Initial Training and Recurrent Training is complete, it can be easy to let team performance concepts, including the Essential Components of team leadership and performance slip away. Designing job-specific training that deliberately includes these aspects of team performance will be a way to periodically review the concepts even outside of Initial Training or Recurrent Training. For example, when conducting training or rehearsals for a high-hazard operation, the training could include situations where employees must implement several or all of the nine Essential Components into their work functions. This approach should be balanced with the need to adhere to operations/safety-specific procedures and training designers should ensure that the ways the Essential Components are integrated into work functions do not take employees out of compliance with other required procedures or rules.

- **Operational Evaluation:** After training strategies and techniques have been designed and integrated into overall training plans, the staff that developed the training should work with operational team leaders to design methods for actual operational evaluation of team leader and team member performance after they undergo training.

This operational evaluation is a way to demonstrate that the training is actually being used under real-world conditions. For example, operational evaluations that seek to determine usage of the nine Essential Components of team leadership and performance could include evaluation forms which allow evaluators to observe job performance and to determine team leader and employee usage of techniques associated with the evaluated areas. One specific evaluation strategy could be to observe an operation from start to finish, including planning, briefing, execution, and debriefing, and evaluate the various team performance elements. For example, communications techniques used in the pre-operations briefing and during execution, the use of checklists, and how team members are empowered to serve as FLs during various operations phases could be examined. There are multiple ways to conduct these types of field evaluations, and any evaluation strategies should be aligned with the training material, and the actual policies, guidelines, SOPs, and other organizational documents. After all, it isn't fair to evaluate team leaders and employees on areas that have not been well-integrated into operational or safety procedures. Additionally, approaching these evaluations from a coaching standpoint, using experienced mentors who understand the work done by the employees under evaluation may be helpful. A coaching mindset, as opposed to a "check-the-box" mentality or an approach that simply seeks to identify and document deficiencies can go a long way. One of the main goals should be to train and mentor employees so they understand these concepts and can actually apply them on the job, and so teams can work more effectively, efficiently, and safely. An evaluation should be followed by a constructive debrief by the evaluator, including methods for improvement where applicable. This debrief should also be a time when the individual or team under evaluation is afforded the opportunity to provide constructive feedback to the evaluator as well, regarding what works well, or what may be improved. One strategy for aligning these evaluations with training is to conduct them shortly after the Initial Training and Refresher Training, so that they are conducted initially and then on a recurrent basis. This may help provide continuity between the classroom training and actual usage. Ultimately, training concepts should be integrated into the fabric of the organization to the point where employees view the techniques and procedures for team leadership and performance as "the way we do things around here." In other words, when the Essential

Components of team leadership and performance have been integrated into training, and designed into policy, procedure, and guideline documents, when checklists and other job tools have been created to help employees plan and execute operations, and when communications strategies and techniques have been integrated into work systems, these should become the normal, professional, and disciplined manner of executing work. Once the organization views these as key elements of production, safety, quality, and reliability, and these become a normal way of conducting work, and when employees and team leaders not only see improvements in KPIs, but also buy into these methods of conducting operations, the organization may be on the road to a cultural transformation. The transformation may be recognizable when these team leadership and performance methods are united with other key parts of the organization to form a cohesive process for professional and disciplined work planning and execution. When employees can no longer imagine the thought of doing work "the old way," then perhaps a true cultural transformation will be on the way.

- **Internal Leadership Development Programs:** In addition to training programs, designing hands-on internal leadership development programs will be a valuable part of any team performance improvement strategy. Some employees may have more natural leadership ability, and while many people will argue that leaders are born, not developed or "made," experience in the military has shown that regardless of background or individual personality attributes, personnel from many walks of life can be trained as leaders. Leadership development is an adaptive and evolutionary process, where personnel tend to get better over time as they learn more, experience different work situations requiring leadership and decision making, and obtain feedback on their performance. Leadership development programs may facilitate the acceleration of these skills by immersing personnel in leadership and decision-making environments. Leaders should understand that employees need time to grow and that mistakes are part of the process. Leadership development programs should allow opportunities for failure in a controlled environment, so the impacts of failures or improper decisions have minimal impact on the organization. One technique is to create role-playing situations where work scenarios are developed that mimic the actual work that would be done in the operating environment. Team members could be given opportunities to lead employees in a lab-type setting, where their behavior and actions are observed, feedback on performance is obtained, and recommendations for improvement are provided.

- **Mentoring:** The leadership training described above should include a structured approach and coaching by a mentor. Mentoring plays a strong role in individual performance and leadership. By assigning experienced, technically competent, and respected senior personnel as mentors to junior personnel, the leadership process may be enhanced. Mentors can provide guidance during the leadership development process and can also provide valuable feedback during coaching and debriefing sessions.

- **Feedback:** After implementing improvement tools or work system design improvements, leaders should develop a periodic feedback system. This system should include team member surveys, audits, and/or assessments to obtain credible information about the effectiveness of team leadership, performance, and Essential Component training and integration. Surveys and feedback can potentially be balanced against KPIs to determine if safety and performance levels are increasing. This process should be iterated and refined until your teams perform at optimal levels. In reality this process should not stop. Organizations should continue this process indefinitely because learning should be continuous. If teams feel they have reached the pinnacle of performance and safety they should reassess this process and find new ways to improve. Even if it appears that cultural transformation has taken place and operational teams have integrated these strategies into routine and non-routine work, feedback is critical to maintaining an effective team leadership and performance program and for making continuous improvement.

Conclusions: Looking to the Future

At the highest levels of performance, organizations seek to achieve continuous learning and improvement, and safety is actively created and adapted as teams learn from the past and make decisions about the future. High-performing organizations consist of high-performing teams, which in turn, are comprised of high-performing individuals. These organizations understand that learning is critical to continued success and that sharing both the good and the bad information helps to build collective awareness about what has worked, what has failed, and ways to improve. Sharing information within the organization and among team members should be viewed a sign of strength, not a sign of weakness, even if the information explains failures. Teams can learn a great deal from both successful events and from events where goals were not achieved. Learning programs should be nurtured by organizational leadership because, if conducted effectively, this type of organizational learning may help lead to long-term culture change where learning becomes a normal part of operations, which may in turn lead to improved productivity, safety, quality, reliability, resilience, adaptability, and increased adaptive capacity.

Now that you have finished reading this book, perhaps the easy part is over and the hard part is just beginning. This book offers multiple suggestions for ways to improve your organization, particularly through operational team leadership and performance. As you work to design your own training and work systems, refer back to this book as often as you need to, and use it as a resource to develop your operational leadership, safety, and performance programs. It is important to remember that this process will take time and that by having the courage to persevere and work through the challenges along the way as teams grow, you can help guide your organizations to new levels of success. Along the way, don't forget to express your appreciation for your teams and to enjoy the journey because the camaraderie you build may be something to cherish for years to come and that in itself is a worthy achievement!

Bibliography

American Industrial Hygiene Association *American National Standard for Occupational Health and Safety Management Systems ANSI Z10-2012*. Fairfax: American Industrial Hygiene Association, 2012.

American Society of Safety Engineers. *Prevention through Design: Guidelines for Addressing Occupational Hazards and Risks in Design and Redesign Processes, ANSI/ASSE Z590.3-2011*. Des Plaines: American Society of Safety Engineers.

Chapanis, Alphonse. "The Error-Provocative Situation." In *The Measurement of Safety Performance*, Edited by William E. Tarrants. New York: Garland Publishing, 1980.

Columbia Accident Investigation Board. *Report of Columbia Accident Investigation Board*. Washington DC: Columbia Accident Investigation Board, National Aeronautics and Space Administration, and Government Printing Office, 2003.

Conklin, Todd. *Pre-Accident Investigations: An Introduction to Organizational Safety*. Burlington: Ashgate Publishing Company, 2012.

Dekker, Sidney. *Drift into Failure: From Hunting Broken Components to Understanding Complex Systems*. Burlington: Ashgate Publishing Company, 2011.

Dekker, Sidney. *The Field Guide to Understanding Human Error*. Burlington: Ashgate Publishing Company, 2006.

Endsley, Mica. "Situation Awareness in Aviation Systems." Trans. Array *Handbook of Aviation Human Factors*. Garland, Daniel J., Wise, John A. and Hopkin, V. David. Mahwah: Lawrence Erlbaum Associates, 1999.

Ericson II, Clifton A. *Hazard Analysis Techniques for System Safety*. Hoboken: John Wiley and Sons, Inc., 2005.

Fenton, Norman, and Martin Neil. *Risk Assessment and Decision Analysis with Bayesian Networks*. Boca Raton: CRC Press/Taylor and Francis Group, LLC, 2013.

Frank, Michael V. *Choosing Safety: A Guide to Using Risk Assessment and Decision Analysis in Complex, High-Consequence Systems*. Washington DC: Resources for the Future, 2008.

Gawande, Atul. *The Checklist Manifesto, How To Get Things Right*. New York: Henry Holt and Company, LLC, 2009.

Harford, Tim. *Adapt: Why Success Always Starts with Failure*. New York: Farrar, Straus and Giroux, 2011.

Hollnagel, Erik, David Woods, and Nancy Leveson. *Resilience Engineering: Concepts and Precepts*. Burlington: Ashgate Publishing Company, 2006.

Hoover, Cris. "The Strategic Communication Plan." *Federal Bureau of Investigations*. Federal Bureau of Investigation, n.d. Accessed 6 Jan 2014.

IEC/ISO 31010. *Risk Management Risk Assessment Techniques*. Geneva: International Electrotechnical Commission, 2009.

Katz, Daniel, and Robert L. Kahn. *The Psychology of Organizations*. 2nd. Hoboken: John Wiley and Sons, Inc., 1978.

Keeping Patients Safe: Transforming the Working Environment of Nurses. Committee on the Work Environment for Nurses and Patient Safety, Board of Health Care Services. Washington, DC: The National Academies Press, 2004.

Kotter, John P. "Accelerate!" *Harvard Business Review*, Vol. 90, No. 11, November 2012, pp. 45–8.

Kotter, John P. *Leading Change*. Boston: Harvard Business Press, 2012.

Leveson, Nancy. "A New Accident Model for Engineering Safer Systems." *Safety Science*, Vol. 42, No. 4, April 2004, pp. 237–70.

Leveson, Nancy G. *Engineering a Safer World, Systems Thinking Applied to Safety*. Cambridge: The MIT Press, 2011.

Leveson, Nancy G., and Joel Cutcher-Gershenfeld. "What System Safety Engineering Can Learn from the Columbia Accident." *Providence*, 2004, 5. Accessed 16 Jan 2014.

Manuele, Fred A. *Advanced Safety Management, Focusing on Z10 and Serious Injury Prevention*. Hoboken, New Jersey: John Wiley and Sons, Inc., 2008.

Marciniak, Steve, Master Sgt. "C-5 Accident Investigation Board Complete." *The Official Website of Dover Air Force Base*. United States Air Force, 16 Jun 2006. Accessed 28 Dec 2013.

Mulvaney, Brendan, LtCol . "Red Teams Strengthening through Challenge." *Marine Corps Gazette*. Jul 2012.

National Electrical Manufacturers Association. *American National Standard for Environmental and Facility Safety Signs ANSI Z535.2-2011*. Rosslyn: National Electrical Manufacturers Association, 2012.

National Fire Protection Association. *Standard for Electrical Safety in the Workplace NFPA 70E*, 2012.

North Atlantic Treaty Organization. *Allied Tactical Publication, ATP-56(B) Air-To-Air Refuelling Manual*, 2010.

Ries, Eric. *The Lean Startup: How Today's Entrepreneurs Use Continuous Innovation to Create Radically Successful Businesses*. New York: Crown Business, 2011.

Taleb, Nassim Nicholas. *Anti-Fragile: Things That Gain from Disorder*. New York: Random House, 2012.

Taleb, Nassim Nicholas. *Fooled by Randomness: The Hidden Role of Chance in Life and Markets*. New York: Random House, 2004.

United States. Department of Defense. *Defense Acquisition Guidebook*, 2013.

United States. Department of Defense. *Department of Defense Standard Practice for System Safety MIL-STD-882E*. Wright-Patterson Air Force Base: Department of Defense, 2012.

United States. Department of the Interior, Minerals Management Service, Gulf of Mexico Region. *Accident Investigation Report*, 2009.

United States. US Department of Labor Occupational Safety and Health Administration. *Job Hazard Analysis (OSHA 3071)*. US Department of Labor Occupational Safety and Health Administration, 2002.

United States. Department of the Navy, Headquarters United States Marine Corps. *Command and Control, MCDP 6*. Washington DC: US Marine Corps, 1996.

United States. Department of the Navy, Headquarters United States Marine Corps. *Marine Corps Warfighting Publication 3-25 Control of Aircraft and Missiles*. Washington DC: Department of the Navy, 1998.

United States. Department of the Navy, Headquarters, United States Marine Corps. *Operational Risk Management (Marine Corps Order 3500.27B)*. Washington, DC: Department of the Navy, 2004.

United States. Office of the Chief of Naval Operations. *Crew Resource Management Program OPNAVINST 1542.7D*. Washington DC: Department of the Navy, 2012.

United States. Office of the Chief of Naval Operations. *NATOPS General Flight and Operations Instruction OPNAVINST 3710.7U*. Washington DC: Department of the Navy, 2009.

Von Bertalanffy, Ludwig. *General System Theory: Foundations, Development, Applications*. New York: George Braziller, Inc., 1968.

Weick, Karl E., and Kathleen M. Sutcliffe. *Managing the Unexpected, Resilient Performance in an Age of Uncertainty*. 2nd. San Francisco, CA: Jossey-Bass Inc. Pub, 2007.

Westli, Heidi K., Bjorn H. Johnsen, Jarle Eid, Ingvil Rasten, and Guttorm Brattebo. "Teamwork Skills, Shared Mental Models, and Performance in Simulated Trauma Teams: An Independent Group Design." *Scandinavian Journal of Trauma, Resuscitation and Emergency Medicine*, Vol. 18, No. 47, 2010. Available at: http://www.ncbi.nlm.nih.gov/pmc/articles/PMC2939527/pdf/1757-7241-18-47.pdf.

Wickens, Christopher D., and Jason S. McCarley. *Applied Attention Theory*. Boca Raton: CRC Press, 2008.

Yoe, Charles. *Principles of Risk Assessment, Decision Making Under Uncertainty*. Boca Raton: CRC Press/Taylor and Francis Group, LLC, 2012.

Zolli, Andrew, and Marie Healy. *Resilience: Why Things Bounce Back*. New York: Free Press, 2012.

Index

accountable 33, 39, 48, 53, 162, 168, 226, 240
accountability 52–3
adaptability 9, 11, 14, 30–31, 43, 173–81, 187–8, 197–8, 257
adaptation 28, 111, 124, 171, 173, 178, 181, 185–9, 192, 227
adaptive capacity 9, 11, 14, 173–81, 186–7, 192, 194, 198, 257
anticipation 119–21, 124, 200
assertiveness 10, 220–24, 227–9
  versus disobedience 221
assumptions 11–12, 59, 68, 81, 202, 219
attention 8, 66, 91, 104–5, 107–11, 113–21, 125, 127–8, 132–3, 135–9, 141–4, 153, 155, 170, 203, 234
  admitting when lapsing 116
  to checklist 130
  compound emergencies and reduced levels of 131
  correcting lapses in 115
  decreased 128
  degraded 143
  divided 110, 136
  dividing 127
  drift 115
  during message delivery 83
  lapse 120, 128, 143
  to low-probability/high-consequence scenarios 237
  message receiver 93
  regaining 114
  slipping 117
  threats to 135
  to weak signals 194
authority 7, 14, 17, 33–6, 47–8, 55–7, 59, 61, 64, 66–9, 75, 80–81, 99–100, 131, 141, 156, 158, 183, 208, 221–2
  approval for job planning 38
  centralized 35–6
  challenging in the interest of safety 63
  delegation, but not delegation of ultimate responsibility 41–2
  distribute (or delegate) levels of 35, 38
  distributing to lower levels 26
  hybrid approach to decentralization 36–7
  network-based decentralized structure 38–40
  power struggle due to blurred lines of 69
  relationship to information flow 42–4
  streamlining action with Leader's Intent and adaptable rule boundaries 44–6
  of supervisor 23

backup 10, 72, 126, 196, 219–20, 226–9
  assertiveness 221, 223–4, 227
  communication 90, 94, 134, 158
    strategies for use as focus aid 112
  engineering controls in relation to administrative controls 169

plans 175, 177, 217
resources 153, 156
barriers 1, 10, 27, 53, 105, 220, 246
    communications 27, 98–102
    to effective employee action 27
    engineering controls 133
    hazard controls 95
        engineering 112
    limiting potential damage 241
    physical 188–9, 242
    protecting employees 242
    safety 4
    safety defenses and 5
    uncoupling single points of failure
        from work 196
biases 70, 210
    toward action or inaction 40
boundaries 1, 193, 214
    acceptable risk 7
    adaptable rule 44–6
    approach 242
    exceeding safe 166
    pre-defined for decision 26
    pre-defined for enabling action 44
    pre-defined for hazardous work
        scenarios 46
    safety 45, 95, 176, 179, 181, 186,
        227
    with upper and lower limits 46,
        191–2, 225–6
    upper and lower severity 209
    of variation 225
brainstorming 235, 248
briefing 105, 118, 150, 254
    changes and re-briefing 119
    changes that are un-briefed 119
    crew 103
    guide 92
        standardized guide 92
    pre-job 95, 134
    pre-mission 92

pre-operations 92, 102–3, 118, 134,
    153–4
sub-team specific functional or
    technical 154
team 105, 118, 160, 228
templates 95, 122, 154–9, 188
timelines 150

callouts 166–9
causal factors 73, 81, 121, 235, 241
cautions 90, 133, 150, 164, 206, 236
change(s)
    in authority structures 47–8
    briefing in real-time 119
    building enthusiasm and
        momentum 76
    consideration of effect on others
        in organization or team 120
    culture 257
    demands on operational teams
        179, 181
    design 4
    embracing 177
    in the environment 149, 160, 189
    internal or external 20
    to job/work conditions 110–11,
        136
    to operational plans 67, 158–9
    to parts of the organization 30
    to products, services, or processes
        and impacts on teams 30–31
    system approach 177
    to task steps 125–6, 189
    time compression 123–4
    scheduling 181
    unbriefed during work 119
    unexpected 152, 176–7, 176
    to work processes 186
checklists 9, 122
    abbreviated 160–61, 163–4, 166–7;
        see also pocket

confirmation and feedback 104
design 9, 96–7, 160
in distracting environments 130
double-checking work 223
error detection 96, 129–30
execution 160–61
expanded 160, 164–6
as focus aid 112, 114
    during task reordering 126
focus on SOP 124
hazard 235, 238
management 129–30, 160, 162–6
    discipline 169
pocket 161, 163–4, 166–7; *see also*
    abbreviated
safety 129
strategy for revising 188–90
use as a risk control strategy 246
COA 199–210, 212, 217, 220, 222, 238;
    see also course of action
time compression 247
Coaching 6, 10, 59–60, 65, 78–9, 137,
    172, 254, 256
collaboration 24–5, 43, 47
collaborative process 27, 29
Commander's Intent 25, 44–5
communication(s) 8, 14, 19, 40, 48, 69,
    72, 81
    barriers 27, 98–102
    constituent parts
        feedback 84
        message 83–4
        receiver 83
        sender 82
    cycle 82, 84–5, 105
    effective techniques
        feedback 97–8
        signal 97
        verbal 93–4
        written 94–7
    to help senior level of authority

maintain oversight 55
    strategic 51, 54
    streamlining 104
    systems 50
    tactical 51, 54
    types
        advantages and disadvantages
            92–3
        non-verbal 87–91
        verbal 85–7
competence 61–2, 65
competency 22, 125
complacency 74, 109
complexity 5, 12, 66, 119, 204
compliance 45, 72–3, 144, 147–8, 166,
    182–3, 191, 202, 253
conditions
    abnormal 27–8, 108
    changing 46, 178–9, 190, 192, 198
    error-producing 1, 110
    unsafe 45, 63
    work 11, 109, 111, 118, 136
confidence 40, 49, 52, 54, 60–62, 65,
    78, 210, 228, 232
conflict; *see also* conflicting
    between safety and production
        goals 5
    designated and functional leaders
        79–80
    emergence when team members
        challenge each other 229
    identification as a characteristic of
        functional leaders 63
    internal team 19, 64
    scheduling 151
conflicting; *see also* conflict
    goals related to standardization
        versus adaptation 187
    statements from operational team
        leaders regarding production
        and safety 223

consequence(s)
    association with poor
        performance 108, 139
    cascade 107
    catastrophic 66, 71, 74, 96, 197
    of constraints on safety
        interventions 4
    decision 200
    decision-making level of authority
        208
    effects of errors 28
    errors leading to catastrophic 3
    escalation into higher severity 42
    of excessive performance pressure
        141
    of failure 12, 14, 35, 39, 77, 143
    hazards 18, 21, 28, 74, 115, 122,
        134, 220, 237, 241
    of high-stress/high-workload 112
    of human error 1
    of improperly executed tasks 125
    of improvising and adapting
        incorrectly 178
    of ineffective or poor decisions
        199, 209
    of ineffective teamwork 17
    of kneejerk reactions 207
    leaders not absolved from 42
    lessons-learned 185
    limiting through effective use of
        communications 105
    loosely coupled processes 195
    loss–gain comparison 216
    maintaining integrity and honesty
        75
    minimizing negative during
        leadership development 77–8
    mission-critical tasks 156
    of not making a decision 209
    potential when changing
        organizational structure 48
    reduction using a defense-in-
        depth approach 242
    resulting from poor performance 6
    resulting from unwarranted
        delays or inaction 43, 247
    risk 131, 157, 194, 199, 209, 232,
        234, 237, 248
    triage 245
    safety-critical tasks 156
    safety programs not balanced
        with operations 211
    serious 66, 100, 108, 131, 197, 220
    single points of failure 196
    surprises in high-hazard
        environments 167
    system approach to mutual
        support and backup strategies
        226
    unacceptable 156
    unanticipated 124
    of unclear messages in high-
        hazard environments 86
    unintended 3, 28, 61, 103, 115, 127,
        138, 147, 203–4, 207, 209, 237,
        249
constraints
    communications 205
    decision-making 217
    equipment 194
    financial 4, 50, 122, 194, 205
    information flow 43
    material 205
    operational 105
    personnel 194, 201, 204
    resource 59, 123–4, 143
    risk control 205–6, 238
    safety 2, 5
        interventions 4
    schedule 149
    situation assessment 201–2
    solution identification 203

system safety 4
time 194, 201, 206, 209
coordinate 56
    tasks 100
    team actions 120, 167
    team activities 134
    with team members 114
coordination 172, 236
    crew 3
    effective teamwork 20
    embedding steps into SOPs 124
    shared mental model 26
    standardized callouts 166–8
    team 14, 69
        inadequate 108
    work system 19
continuous improvement 172, 227,
    256
coupled systems/processes
    loosely 195, 197–8
    tightly 195–6
coupling
    tight vs. loose 195
course of action 199–200; see also COA
credibility 23, 86, 88
    characteristic of designated leader
        61–2
    characteristic of functional leader
        65
    damage to organizational 143
Crew Resource Management 2;
        see also CRM
CRM 2–3, 220; see also Crew Resource
    Management
culture
    change 257
    debriefing 78
    mutual support and backup 229
    organizational 29, 48, 99, 149, 221,
        238
    production 75, 149

safety 48, 75, 117, 202
    where employees are willing to
        correct each other 227

debrief 78, 135, 171–2, 228; see also
    debriefing
    modeling, simulation, and
        training 136–7
    operational evaluation 254
    time and location 158
debriefing 78, 133, 150, 159, 171, 181,
    188, 190, 228, 237, 254; see also
    debrief
    culture 78
    mentoring 256
    operational evaluation 254
    tools 135
decision making 10–12, 14, 25, 27, 34,
    36–7, 47, 69, 71, 79, 100, 186,
    197, 247, 255
    adaptive 249
    avoiding knee-jerk reactions 59
    capacity of operational team
        leader 245
    distributed 26, 44, 48, 71
    functional leader input 58, 63, 67
    journal 204
    leadership relationship to 208
    moving to those doing the work 70
    organizational risk 170
    pre-defined rules 44
    process 199–200, 202–4, 206–7,
        210, 212–15, 217, 222, 238, 244,
        249–50
    risk-informed 141, 192, 210–16,
        231, 233, 238–40, 250
    safety-related 33
    situation assessment 202
    speeding up through advance
        resource identification and
        pre-defined procedures 246

streamlining 26, 38
system-oriented approach 61
time compression 248
time-sensitive 208–10, 233, 243
defense-in-depth 92, 150, 169, 194,
    216, 229, 242
dissent 70, 75
dissenting opinions 71, 208
diversity 69–70, 99, 171, 208

emergencies 28, 96, 118, 153, 166
    compound 131
emergency
    actions 153, 246
    management 151, 153
    operations 97, 166
    procedures 95, 131, 134, 137, 153,
        157, 246
    situations 45, 112, 240
    support 245
empowerment 27, 69
error detection 128–30, 137, 151, 162,
    219
error-inducing 9, 107–8, 111, 136–7,
    143–4
error trapping, correction, and
    recovery 130–31

fatigue 43, 45, 55, 74, 107–8, 110, 113–14,
    127, 142, 151, 155, 215–16
focus aids 111–15
followership 23, 64–5

habit 176, 187, 192
hazard
    analysis 12, 37–8, 43, 118, 131,
        134–6, 157, 194, 205, 208, 232, 234
    assessment 234–5, 242, 244
    checklists 235, 248
    consequence 18, 21, 28, 74, 115,
        122, 134, 220, 237, 241

elimination 1, 130, 143
high-consequence 74, 237, 241
identification 118, 134, 150, 184,
    233–5, 242–4, 248
probability 77, 119, 133–4, 150–51,
    157, 193–4, 205, 211, 232–5, 237,
    241–2, 244, 248
severity 21, 77, 134, 150–51, 157,
    193, 205, 211, 232–7, 241–2, 244,
    248
hazard tracking systems 134–5
hierarchy of controls 246
human error 73, 107–9, 143
human factors 133
human performance 1–3, 13

initiative 3, 7, 28–30, 33, 36, 39, 48, 79
innovation 29–31, 48, 171, 182, 186,
    214, 227
interpersonal skills 13, 52

JHA 37–8, 149; *see also* Job Hazard
    Analysis
Job Hazard Analysis 37, 149;
    see also JHA
job rotation 127
Job Safety Analysis 37, 149;
    see also JSA
JSA 37–8, 149; *see also* Job Safety
    Analysis
judgment 138, 180, 200, 206–7, 209,
    216, 249

KC-130 Hercules 39, 168, 197
Key Performance Indicators 150;
    see also KPI
KPI 150, 255–6; *see also*
    Key Performance Indicators

Leader's Intent 25–6, 44–6, 134, 155, 208
leadership types

designated 8, 57–8, 62, 66
functional 8, 48, 57–8, 62–3, 66, 67, 77, 80
lessons-learned 31, 78, 133, 135–6, 140, 158, 171–2, 178, 181, 184–5, 188, 190, 194, 200, 204, 209, 228, 235, 237, 244
load shedding 112–13
logistics 30, 32, 101, 134, 145, 147, 156, 158, 204
loss–gain analysis 213, 215, 216

Marine Corps, United States 2–3, 39, 44, 57, 70, 76, 125, 168, 180, 197, 214, 220, 235, 248
mentoring 37, 59, 61, 64, 256
mnemonics 115, 247–8

Navy, United States 214
near-hit 135, 185; *see also* near-miss
near-miss 63, 73, 135, 140, 185, 219; *see also* near-hit

open system 146
operational analysis 148–9
operational drift 169–71, 185, 192
operational excellence 49, 139
operational execution 8–9, 22–3, 25, 37, 50, 52, 57, 89, 112, 118, 124, 164, 231, 237, 246, 248
operations
abnormal 33, 91, 97, 153, 157, 166
daily 14, 251
emergency 33, 97, 166
non-routine 71, 152, 231
normal 6, 142, 166
routine 33, 122, 145, 152, 157, 169, 231

Pause-To-Assess 111, 114
performance variability 1–2

Personal Protective Equipment 46, 50; *see also* PPE
PPE 46, 50, 82, 95, 133, 149–51, 167, 191, 206, 233, 236, 241–2, 246; *see also* Personal Protective Equipment
process upsets 153
production pressure 82, 101, 104, 111, 137, 139, 141, 143, 223
productivity 18, 19, 33–5, 56, 125, 132, 212, 251, 257
proficiency 2, 21–2, 38, 58, 61–2, 64, 97, 108, 110–11, 128, 137, 151, 204, 250

quality 19, 21, 50, 59, 65, 79, 81, 85, 88, 102, 104, 106–7, 117, 123, 125, 138–41, 143–4, 151, 155, 173, 182–3, 202, 223, 227, 231, 250–51, 255, 257

red teams 70
reliability 102, 139, 173, 227, 250–51, 255, 257
reputation 62, 210, 212–13, 232, 234, 240
resilience 9, 11, 14, 43, 173–4, 179, 181–2, 185–8, 192, 194, 197–8, 214, 257
levels 175–7
characteristics of 177
maturity 177–8
resource(s) 3, 12, 27, 44, 51–2, 55–7, 59, 72–3, 95, 118–19, 122, 143, 194, 207–9, 217, 245, 257
acceptable risk 214
additional for lowering risk 240
allocation 24, 123, 208
availability prior to job commencement 126
backup 156
building adaptive capacity 180–81

communications 94, 152, 205
  backup 153
constraints 4, 59, 122–4, 143, 194
decisions 42
decision-making 217
equipment 194
financial 50, 122, 194, 201, 205
human 30, 32, 34, 44, 118, 146,
  149–50, 156, 159, 175, 181, 204,
  252
identification before work
  commencement 239
inputs to operational planning
  149
loose coupling 198
material 44, 50, 118, 142, 146, 149,
  156, 159, 175, 181, 205
mobilizing for improved
  situational awareness,
  attention, and focus 128
operational 105
personnel 194, 201, 204
pre-operations brief 154, 156
protecting 12
requesting for improved
  situational awareness,
  attention, and focus 117, 128
resilience levels
  planning 176, 177
  surviving 175, 177
risk
  control 205–6, 238, 241
  management 11, 246
safety 4, 9
schedule 149
situation assessment 201–2
solution identification 203
stopping error progression 131
supplemental 123
system safety 4
time 201, 206

responsibility 7, 33, 37, 44, 47–8, 57–9,
  61, 67–8, 72, 80, 83, 94, 119, 134,
  139, 145, 154, 156, 162, 183, 186,
  207, 212, 214, 222, 249
  delegate authority, but not
    complete and ultimate 41–2
  and the role of the team leader
    34–5
  of senior leaders and managers 24
  for successful and safe outcomes 39
rework 21, 24, 70
risk
  codes
    final 237
    initial 235
  communicating 234
  control 150–51, 154, 170, 187, 194,
    205, 206, 233, 235–9, 242, 244,
    246–7, 249
  controls
    administrative 133, 150, 160,
      205, 236, 246
    elimination 21, 132–3, 144, 150,
      236
    engineering 133, 150, 191, 206,
      236, 246
    Personal Protective Equipment
      46, 133, 150–51, 191, 206,
      233, 236, 241–2, 246
    substitution 150, 236
    warnings 206, 236
  management
    long-term vs. time-sensitive
      242–3
    time sensitive 10–11, 14, 131,
      157, 170, 188, 197, 231–2,
      240, 242–50
  mitigation 4, 29, 44, 65, 89, 100, 194,
    198, 201–2, 214, 233, 238, 240
  qualitative assessment techniques
    11, 209, 233, 235, 243

quantitative assessment techniques 11, 209, 233, 235, 243

semi-quantitative assessment 233, 235

triage 245, 248

unexpected 173, 192, 194, 196

unknown unknown 194

root cause 235, 241

rule(s)

absolute 45, 191, 225–6, 240

adaptable 44–6

making 192

red 226

variable 225

safety

behavior-based approaches 130

information systems 133

leadership 72–4

management 10, 72–3, 160

management systems 184, 219

technology 3, 11

shared mental model 26–7

signage 90, 96, 153

signal-to-noise 91, 97

signals 84, 85, 87, 90–94, 97, 153, 158, 192–4, 223, 246, 248

single points of failure 156, 196; see also SPF

situation assessment 201–3, 207, 209

situational awareness 8, 110, 129, 143–4

administrative and engineering controls raising 169

admitting when levels reduced 116–17

building before job commences 118

definition 109

fatigue as a source of decreased 127

focus aids to help maintain higher levels of 112, 114

modeling, simulation, and training 136–7

pre-operations brief 154

rebuilding 128

recognizing degradation in 115–16

responding to unexpected situations 110

requesting assistance from other team members to rebuild 117

safety information systems 133–5

surge operations 142

task overload 122

techniques for maintaining 115

SOP(s) 89, 91–2, 94–5, 98, 104–5, 124, 129, 188–90, 219, 223, 225–6, 254; see also Standard Operating Procedure

span of control 100, 119, 124–5

SPF 156, 196; see also single points of failure

staffing 19–20, 64

Standard Operating Procedure 89; see also SOP

standardization 27–8, 30–31, 92–3, 97, 123, 170, 182–3, 187–9, 225–9

Stop Work Authority 66, 94, 113

stress 64, 74, 83, 108, 111

high 49, 224, 247, 250

environments 93

work 55, 108, 112

inducing conditions 143

surge

in demand 181

operations 141–2

production 142

sustainable growth 133, 139, 143, 188, 198

SWA 66, 75, 94, 113, 141, 221; see also stop work authority

synchronous evolution 30

system safety 2, 4, 13

task overload 110, 122–4
task underload 110
templates
    briefing 188
    checklist 161
    job briefing 154; *see also* pre-job
        briefing
    operational team briefing 122
    planning 122
    pre-defined [for pre-operations
        briefing] 154
    pre-job briefing 95; *see also* job
        briefing
time-compression 45, 124, 199, 243,
        247
time-sync 154
training 6–8, 31–2, 37–8, 61, 64, 98–9,
        110, 214–15, 252
    assertiveness 221
    checklists 97–8, 124, 160, 164, 169
    to continuously reexamine
        operational risks 192
    decision-making strategies 208
    description 22
    hazard analysis 194, 208
    impact on team when improper 19
    initial 22, 253–4
    job planning 151
    leadership 76–8, 256
    methods for implementing
        decentralized leadership 33
    mutual support and backup 227–8
    and qualification 22
    refresher/recurrent 22, 253–4
    replacement employees 23

risk
    assessment 194
    management 231, 241
    scenario 136–7, 228, 253
    SOP 124
    standardized 27
    strategies for improving team
        performance 252–7
    versus proficiency/competency
        and qualification 22
    in ways to handle error-inducing
        conditions, distractions, and
        hazards 144
trust 36–7, 39–40, 47–8, 68–9, 71, 73,
        77, 86, 116–17, 125, 171, 189,
        191–2, 223–4, 232
turnover plan 158

uncertainty 12, 35, 45, 59, 65, 93, 130,
        152, 169, 174, 176–7, 192–9, 202,
        215
urgency 84, 87, 91

vision 25, 45, 51–4, 67, 180, 208

warnings 90, 133, 150, 164, 206, 226,
        236
waste 18, 20–21, 24, 70
work system design 4, 6, 13, 21, 28,
        31–2, 73, 124, 132–3, 145–8, 178,
        181, 184–8, 190, 192, 226–7, 256
work system designers 112, 148
working alone 153, 169
workarounds 126–7, 147, 237, 249